Russia's Other Writers

Russia's Other Writers

selected and introduced by
Michael Scammell

foreword by
Max Hayward

Longman

LONGMAN GROUP LIMITED
LONDON

Associated companies, branches and
representatives throughout the world
© Possev Verlag, 1964, 1966, 1967, 1968
© V. Gorachek KG
English translation © Longman Group Limited 1970
Introduction © Michael Scammell 1970

First published 1970
ISBN O 582 12782 3

Printed in Great Britain by
T. and A. Constable Ltd., Edinburgh

Contents

Foreword

There is nothing all that new or unusual about literary censorship, particularly in Russia. What is, however, remarkable to an outsider, as this book so well exemplifies, is the sheer scale on which Russian writers seek to defy and evade it—there is nothing remotely parallel in the history of any other modern literature.

The situation in the Soviet Union has to some extent been inherited from Tsarist times. From the eighteenth century to the present day, the rulers of Russia have always thought it their business to 'protect' their subjects from the written word, and Russian writers have traditionally had recourse to a variety of evasive techniques: the use of allegorical language, the circulation of forbidden works in manuscript and—generally as a last resort—publication abroad.

But under the Tsars, censorship was a pretty amateurish affair with modest aims—to prevent the appearance in print of obviously subversive or blasphemous sentiments. The Tsarist censor struck out occasional offending words or phrases, but he rarely banned whole works or proscribed authors for failing to give active support to the official point of view. If the history of Tsarist censorship can be told in a series of somewhat comic anecdotes, the history of Soviet censorship is the far more serious story of how a great literature was stifled and traduced. The Russian critic Arkadi Belinkov has pointed out that all the scholarly editions of the nineteenth century Russian classics produced in post-Tsarist times, with the benefit of full access to the archives, have not basically modified or enlarged our previous picture. If, on the other hand, the literary archives of the last fifty years become available, we shall have a *different* Soviet literature—its whole history will have to be completely revised. This much is already clear enough from what has seeped out since Stalin's death. Writers once boasted and acclaimed will recede into the background, if not into total oblivion, and many shadowy figures will emerge to take on the substance long denied them. Not only will there be a radical shift of perspective and emphasis in the overall picture, but the work of many individual writers will have to be reinterpreted in the light of material suppressed or fuller information about work actually rewritten under duress.

The process of redressing the balance was begun inside the Soviet Union during the fitful 'liberalisation' initiated by Khrushchev's 'secret speech' about Stalin at the Twentieth Congress in 1956. Many writers murdered or imprisoned in previous decades were 'rehabilitated', that is, formally cleared of the grotesque charges once made against them, and in some cases their work was selectively republished. But this was done grudgingly and in the teeth of increasing opposition from all those whose reputations cannot survive a revision of the old stereotypes. Under Khrushchev's successors 'liberalisation' has been halted and even—cautiously so far—put into reverse. This means that Soviet citizens are more than ever dependent on *samizdat*—the extraordinary system, described by Mr Scammell in his introduction, of circulating manuscripts in typewritten copies, if they wish to read their modern authors, both living and dead, in uncensored form.

Except for one item written abroad, the present volume is virtually an anthology of *samizdat* and its appearance at a time when Soviet writers are again under strong pressure to conform is doubly opportune. Apart from giving an excellent idea of the range and quality of the literature which is passed from hand to hand in Moscow, Leningrad and other major Soviet cities, it is an important contribution to the vast and continuing labour of correcting the distorted image of Soviet literature created by fifty years of suppression.

Max Hayward.

August 1970

Introduction

The stories gathered together in this anthology have been taken and translated from the pages of a remarkable Russian-language review called *Grani* ('Facets'), a literary magazine published by a Russian expatriate organisation in Frankfurt-am-Main. The purpose of that organisation is to form a political opposition to the Communist Party of the Soviet Union and *Grani* reflects the interests of its parent organisation in its articles and reviews. Yet at the same time—and this is of more immediate relevance to lovers of literature—*Grani* maintains an extraordinarily high standard of contributions. Moreover, it has become, in recent times, the repository of a large quantity of prose and poetry from the Soviet Union, much of it, as I hope these pages will show, of the highest quality and interest.

The question arises: how is it that some of the best of contemporary Soviet literature is to be found in the pages of a relatively obscure Russian magazine published in West Germany? And indeed, how can it be that for anyone seriously interested in the progress of recent Soviet literature, it has been essential to follow the pages of mainly two magazines—one Soviet: *Novy Mir* ('New World'), and the other émigré: *Grani*?

Behind this symbolic situation lie circumstances that are intricate and complex, and politics has much to do with it. It has to be borne in mind that a mixture of literary and political concerns is highly typical for Russian literature, both past and present, Soviet and émigré, and that any consideration of one sphere is practically inseparable from consideration of the other. This does not mean that what is valid for literature in other countries is invalid for literature in Russia, that different criteria have to be applied or that the autonomy of literature is in any fundamental way infringed. Many Russians would have it so, particularly Soviet theorists, but such a view cannot be substantiated. Nevertheless, one has to reckon with the fact that in a country where politics impinges on *everything* and claims to be the universal regulator of all human activity, where such claims stretch back in an unbroken line until they disappear into the mists of Russia's remote Byzantine past, there is a tradition of political pressure on literature that cannot be ignored. Indeed, so ubiquitous and all-pervading is that pressure that the very absence of political commitment comes to be, or to seem, an overt political act. Polarisation is thus inevitable, while didacticism is built in automatically and becomes the literary norm. If any proof be required of this assertion, consider for a moment the militant 'non-commitment' of a Russian émigré writer so removed from the everyday Russian scene as Vladimir Nabokov, the very steadfastness of whose hostility to didacticism itself becomes what it seeks to avoid.

There is no possibility, therefore, of evading the issue: it has to be met fair and square. And there are gains and losses to be recorded. For this tradition, which is as natural to Russians as it is strange, say, to Englishmen, is of centuries' long standing and adds, as it were, an extra dimension to the pursuit and study of literature. Equally there can be no doubt that the tension so generated gives rise to the frequently sterile exercise of 'taking sides', a process that generally leads to attitudes being struck, irrelevant criteria being applied and widespread suspicion as to the motives of participants in the literary debate. It must be clear, therefore, at the outset, that the stories printed in this anthology have been chosen for their literary merit. The fact that they have come, as I have indicated, from the pages of an émigré magazine and that they have not, with rare exceptions, been published in the Soviet Union is clearly relevant, for the source conforms to Russian mores. But the stories themselves have not been chosen to illustrate a thesis or to accord with some sort of counter-philosophy that acts as but a mirror-image of Soviet selection techniques. They should stand—or fall—by their own literary qualities. But before going on to discuss them in more detail, let us consider how they came to be in *Grani* and why it is but one of many ironies in the Soviet situation that the stories here, like many better known works of Soviet literature, are being introduced to the outside world before becoming accessible to most readers in their homeland.

The first thing to note is that, with regard to Russia, the setting up of presses abroad and the publication abroad of works written inside the country is no new phenomenon. The most famous instance of the past is Alexander Herzen, who set up a 'free press' in London in the 1850s and published a highly influential political review called *The Bell*. At the turn of the century Tolstoy's followers set up the Free Age Press at Christchurch in southern England, their aim being to publish those of Tolstoy's works that were forbidden by the censors. And a few years later, no less a person than Lenin arrived in London from Germany, bringing with him his clandestine magazine, *The Spark*.

The character of these presses and the motives behind their establishment was primarily political, answering to the kind of pressure that was being applied to them from within Russia. Writers of *belles lettres* as such, though needing to be on guard and heedful of the censorship's demands, did not suffer nearly as much—normally they were able to handle the pressures put upon them without compromising their creations. It might even be argued that the tension induced in literature at that time turned out to be fruitful rather than malignant. With the triumph of the Bolsheviks, however, and the dramatic reversal in the role of Lenin—from clandestine author to director of the censorship process—the situation changed, and the émigré presses that came into existence after the Revolution, although established on similar lines to those of their predecessors, frequently differed from them in character and aims.

The reasons for this must be sought in the changes that took place in Russian literature itself, and in its changed role in Russian (now Soviet) society. These changes were gradual and spasmodic at first and took place by and large between 1918 and 1932. By the end of this period, the largest emigration in the history of the Russian state had taken place, including some of the most talented Russian writers of the twentieth century. So it is not surprising that the magazines they set up, or contributed to, came to differ radically from earlier émigré publications. For the first time, major works of Russian literature were being published (and sometimes written) abroad and this richness of expatriate literary talent established both a split in the Russian literary world and a literary tradition abroad that has remained alive till the present day.

But let us look a little closer at what actually happened. The peculiar relations obtaining between the two wings of the Russian literary world at that time are difficult to describe, but there was a period when reasonably strong links were preserved between writers who had fled to western Europe and those who remained behind. Allowing for all the bitterness bred by the civil war and the harsh necessity of willy-nilly 'taking sides' at this time, it is fair to say that a certain literary solidarity survived the upheaval—and indeed it was often by the purest accident of personal circumstance that writers ended up on one or the other side of the political fence. It was also reasonably common for writers to 'change sides' at this time. As a result, when Russian magazines and presses were set up abroad, writers who remained in Russia were often able to have their works published in them, while writers abroad, although to a lesser extent, were able to publish at home. One reason for this was the sheer chaos reigning in all departments of Soviet life during and after the civil war. In all the welter of taking sides and setting up literary organisations and magazines of differing persuasions, it was often unclear who stood where. Jockeying for position became a continual process. But the main thing was that at least there was a multiplicity of organisations and points of view, and multiplicity meant a certain degree of freedom. Another factor, purely technical in origin, was that the Soviet government refused to recognise the international laws of copyright (it still does), as a result of which a special press was set up in Berlin to publish the works of Soviet authors simultaneously with their appearance in Moscow. In this way they were enabled to retain control over translation and other rights abroad. And as a consequence, Russian literary life, although split, continued its existence with some semblance of normality, with literature still able to demonstrate that it was no respecter of political divisions or of state boundaries. Artificial divisions between 'us' and 'them', i.e. between writers who remained at home and those who went abroad, though real enough in political and social relations, remained meaningless and unsustainable on the literary plane.

This confused and brittle equilibrium was brought to an end, however, in the late 'twenties, when Stalin began to turn the screw on all fields of activity in the Soviet Union. Literature was forced into the same procrustean bed as all other activities. 'Émigré' become an unspeakable term in the Soviet lexicon, while the word 'Soviet' underwent a subtle metamorphosis. Already in 1929 the *Literary Gazette* announced that the term 'Soviet writer' indicated not a geographical concept, but a social and moral one. Henceforth 'Soviet' was to become more and more a value judgement and less and less a form of description. The gap was then persistently deepened and widened, as it was indeed between the Soviet Union and the whole of the outside world, until it became an unbridgeable chasm. The emigration was left to go its own way in ever-increasing isolation from the motherland, while writers at home were cut off, gagged, suppressed and even, in certain cases, exterminated. From 1932, when the monolithic Union of Soviet Writers was founded, until the outbreak of the Second World War, an almost total silence descended on Russian literature at home, the nadir being reached during the Yezhov terror in 1937. Then, when the war came (incredible as it may seem to us) it represented a sort of breather for Soviet writers, during which the demands made on them by the state coincided, to a limited extent at least, with their own creative impulses. But this in turn was succeeded by the imposition of yet another terror and an even deeper blackout on literature that lasted until Stalin's death in 1953.

From that time on we are dealing with events that have direct bearing on the present day. The death of Stalin in 1953 brought a definite but gradual relaxation of controls over Soviet literature that has since been characterised by the title of Ehrenburg's novel of the following year, *The Thaw*. This was accelerated in 1956, after Khrushchev's famous speech on Stalin to the Twentieth Congress of the Communist Party, and there followed a period of increasing liberalisation. For the first time since the 'twenties literature came alive again in the Soviet Union. New, talented younger writers appeared on the scene (Voznesensky and Yevtushenko are perhaps the best-known names). The works of older writers who had somehow managed to survive the purges, such as Pasternak and Akhmatova, began to be published once more, and previously forbidden names were mentioned for the first time in decades, and suppressed writers were rehabilitated and reprinted. Naturally this development was kept on a firm rein. There were still plenty of works that could not pass the censor, still names that could not be permitted to be seen in print, but the direction of the trend was unmistakable and it culminated with the publication, in 1962, of Solzhenitsyn's sensational novel of prison camp life, *One Day in the Life of Ivan Denisovich*.

At the time, this looked like the harbinger of a new period of even greater liberalisation in the Soviet arts, the dawn of a new era, but it turned out in reality to be the high-water mark. The course of events set in motion by Khrushchev had succeeded, it seemed, in unleashing forces which the government had not foreseen. The authorities took fright and began to back-pedal. Controls began to be applied again and by the time of Khrushchev's dismissal in 1964, the trend towards liberalisation had been slowed and almost halted.

There had been straws in the wind, of course, for a long time before this. Side by side with the official liberalisation, the government's relaxation of control had led to other unforeseen incidents. Right at the beginning of the period, in 1957, there had been the noisy affair of Pasternak and *Doctor Zhivago*, which set a number of important precedents for similar incidents to follow: non-publication in the Soviet Union, publication abroad, persecution of the author, international scandal. In Pasternak's case his fame, together with the award of the Nobel Prize, were sufficient to protect him from the worst effects of the government's wrath. He may also have benefited from the comparatively liberal mood of the time. But then came other and more disquieting cases.

The first of these was the affair of the young poet, Iosif Brodsky, which set an even more ominous precedent: in 1964 he was put on trial and sentenced to five years' hard labour. Officially he was tried for being a 'parasite', i.e. for having no officially registered occupation, but his real crime, like that of Pasternak, was writing works opposed to the Party line on literature and to the norms laid down for socialist realism. He was released eventually, after serving only a year and a half of his sentence. Worldwide publicity again played a part in his release. But his poems continued to be suppressed and have never, with rare exceptions, been published in the Soviet Union.

Thus by now another trend had been established, a trend that was to supplant liberalisation and go on longer. It was that of repression. In 1965 two more arrests took place. Andrei Sinyavsky and Yuli Daniel were simultaneously taken into custody for having published their works abroad under the pseudonyms of Abram Tertz and Nikolai Arzhak respectively. Again there was a disparity between the official charges and the real nature of the government's grievances. The charge was anti-Soviet propaganda and subversion, but at the same time it was made plain that what really outraged the authorities was the two authors' effrontery in deliberately arranging for their works to be published abroad. Even so, it seemed for a moment as if there was some apparent substance to the charges in that Sinyavsky and Daniel, with publication abroad in mind, were able to be far more outspoken than Pasternak and Brodsky and thus seemed to be more anti-Soviet. But on closer examination this idea proved to be illusory. It was merely that Pasternak, hoping none the less for publication, had 'observed the decencies' and shrouded his message in suitably Aesopian form, while Sinyavsky and Daniel were less indirect. As a result, they received seven and five years' hard labour respectively, to be spent in Soviet labour camps.

Since 1966, when Sinyavsky and Daniel were sentenced, there have been many more arrests and trials, some of them of writers of *belles lettres*, but mostly of publicists, of ordinary citizens publicising the more outrageous violations of legality by the Soviet authorities, or of young writers for extra-literary activities. The Sinyavsky-Daniel trial, in fact, set off a chain reaction of protests, books of documents, arrests, trials, further protests, further books, further arrests, and so on, until the protest movement must have come to seem to the Soviet government like some multi-headed hydra. All this is part of the history of both the politics and the literature of our time—the chief activity of the participants, after all, and their chief crime, has been the composition and compilation of documents and books—but it is peripheral to the thread we are now tracing.

More to the point is the treatment of Alexander Solzhenitsyn.

The publication of his novel on life in Stalin's labour camps in 1962, as we have noted, marked the high point of Khrushchev's liberalisation policy. Three short stories of Solzhenitsyn's were published the following year and a further story appeared in 1966, but apart from that a complete blanket of silence has been lowered over his works. Yet Solzhenitsyn is a most prolific author and since that time has seen numerous other works of his appear—first clandestinely in the Soviet Union and then abroad in Russian and in unofficial translations. They include two lengthy novels, *Cancer Ward* and *The First Circle*, two short stories, two plays and a group of poems in prose. Of these the novels have each created a sensation, and in almost every respect the situation of Pasternak has been reproduced. Over the past few years the author has been subjected to a carefully orchestrated campaign of vilification, expelled from the Writers' Union and given hints that he should consider going abroad. It was suggested to Pasternak, too, that he go and live in the West.

The case of Solzhenitsyn illuminates with peculiar vividness the state of Soviet literature today, together with the dilemma of the writer. Solzhenitsyn's fame is in some ways a product of the period of liberalisation, that is to say, if his first novel had not made its appearance just at the right time, it might never have been officially published. As it happened, the novel was a pawn in Khrushchev's power struggle with his opponents (Khrushchev himself gave the word for its publication), just as it later became a pawn, like its author, in the manœuvrings of Khruschev's successors. Solzhenitsyn's career has thus run parallel with the climax and decline of the period of liberalisation and can be regarded in fact as a barometer of its ups and downs and gradual extinction. At the same time, it also illustrates the notable change that has taken place in the Soviet literary scene since the time of the Pasternak affair (a change which Pasternak's book was instrumental in bringing about), and the even more notable change since the time of the 'thirties and 'forties.

The truth is that the atmosphere now is vastly different from what it was thirty years ago, or even fifteen. Soviet intellectuals and artists have experienced the period of liberalisation, they have experienced that huge sense of relief and hope and freedom, however relative and temporary, that liberalisation brought with it. And even if they are now undergoing a period of renewed repression and freeze, the memory of it remains. Allied to this is the undisputed fact that, no matter how gloomy the immediate outlook, there has so far been no return to the draconian measures employed by Stalin. Again this is a relative concept. In Stalin's day dissent meant certain arrest and almost certain death in inhuman labour camps. Now it means probable arrest, exile and near-starvation in camps that are only marginally better than before. But the difference, however small, is crucial, for it is the difference between life and death.

All this means that there has been a decisive shift in the relations between artists and intellectuals on the one hand and the state on the other. In Pasternak's day this shift was only beginning to be perceived, but now it has been experienced and its lessons have been digested. And it is in the context of this development that two new elements have entered the equation of Soviet literature: the appearance of *Samizdat* publications and the 'reactivation' of the Russian press abroad.

Samizdat is an abbreviation (its form is an ironic allusion to *Gosizdat*, the standard abbreviation of the State Publishing House) standing for 'self-publishing'. It refers to the private reproduction of books, documents, letters, essays, poems, etc., by means of simply typing and retyping them for distribution by hand. As with most spontaneously generated form of activity it is not clear exactly when *Samizdat* began or when it was transformed from isolated instances of copying into a flourishing, semi-organised, underground industry. Some commentators date its beginnings from about 1955-6, and it is certain that the unprecedented avidity for copies of *Doctor Zhivago* gave *Samizdat* a tremendous boost in the years immediately following 1957. At about this time the first clandestine magazines began to appear, with names like *Syntax*, *Boomerang*, *Phoenix*, and later *The Lamp*, *Workbook* and *Russian Word*. Soon more and more books also began to find their way into *Samizdat*, until it gradually became an integral part of Soviet cultural life and indispensable to the bulk of the intelligentsia.

Its popularity is reflected in the following Soviet anecdote. A secret typist, it is said, was startled one day when an angry, middle-aged man burst into her room waving a great thick book at her. Was she, he demanded, a typist of *Samizdat* works? Frightened at first, she finally confirmed that she was. 'Good,' said the man, 'then I want you to type this out for me.' 'What is it?' she asked. 'Tolstoy's *War and Peace*.' The girl was taken aback and demanded to know why she should type it out when it was already available in print. 'Because', answered the man, 'the only thing my daughter reads is *Samizdat*. She won't look at anything that's not in typescript. So how the hell am I going to get her to read anything decent unless I get it typed first?'

The exaggeration, pardonable in an anecdote, points to two important characteristics of *Samizdat* publishing: its tremendous popularity among the young and its tendency to concentrate on certain types of works.

Popularity with the young, of course, has a lot to do with the notorious generation gap—no less real in the Soviet Union than elsewhere—and is attributable to the relative lack of fear and guilt feelings in the younger generation in comparison with its elders. This phenomenon, which is even stronger than the general sense of relief mentioned above, has encouraged the young to indulge in activities that are in any case natural to them: writing, discussing, founding magazines, distributing texts, and so on. But in the Soviet Union these comparatively innocuous activities inevitably take on a new resonance, which makes them rather difficult to evaluate. The situation has been well expressed in an article, 'What Price Censorship?' by Maurice Friedberg[1]: 'By and large underground literary periodicals in the Soviet Union are "illegal" because the Soviet authorities chose to make them illegal. Elsewhere they would be described as "ephemeral", "experimental", "amateurish", perhaps even "sophomoric"—but not as "illegal". In the U.S.S.R. they lead a clandestine existence because their appearance is not legally sanctioned by the authorities, and *not* because the bulk of their contents would—even under existing Soviet conditions—preclude their authorised publication. In fact one is often surprised by the restraint, responsibility and good taste exhibited in these "outlaw" journals: one finds in them no hysteria, no pornography and, happily, none of the vitriolic hatred towards opponents that is all too common in the state-approved literary journals.'

This calls for modification, in that the serious 'oppositionist' element in the *Samizdat* magazines seems to be growing.[2] Whether this would have developed anyway is a debatable point, but it does indicate the way in which inexorable political pressure inevitably affects every possible form of activity and attempts to transform it in accordance with its own laws. Whatever *Samizdat*'s intentions might be, it can never be allowed to 'go its own way', which contributes to it becoming an even more confused and confusing phenomenon,

[1] In *Problems of Communism*, Vol. XVII, no. 5 (Sept.-Oct. 1968). Nos. 4 and 5 of this journal are devoted to the whole problem of dissent in the Soviet Union under the joint title, 'In Quest of Freedom', and have since been published under that title as a separate volume (Pall Mall Press 1970).

[2] For a more detailed discussion of these magazines see the introduction to a companion volume in this series, *Russia's Other Poets*, translated by Keith Bosley, with Dimitry Pospielovsky and Janis Sapiets (Longman 1968).

depending for its character as much upon the negative demands of the government as on the positive desires of its agents. An excellent example of its mixed character can be seen also in the 'serious' literature appearing in *Samizdat*.

It is only natural in view of the above that many of the books should be ones that are openly critical of the Soviet Union or some of its aspects. Thus Solzhenitsyn's two great novels, *Cancer Ward* and *The First Circle*, are typical *Samizdat* productions, as also are similar works about the unjustly condemned, exiled and imprisoned, books such as *Into the Whirlwind* by Evgenia Ginzburg, *The Deserted House* by Lydia Chukovskaya, Anna Akhmatova's long poem, *Requiem*, the memoirs of Anatoly Marchenko (*My Testimony*), and the stories of Varlam Shalamov. There have also been the stories and poems of Sinyavsky, Daniel, Tarsis, Yesenin-Volpin and a host of others. Yet at the same time there have been numerous works containing no overt criticism at all of the Soviet Union, or perhaps only criticism of the mildest kind. They include, for instance, the later poetry of Pasternak, the poems of Akhmatova, Tsvetayeva, Brodsky, Gorbanevskaya and others, or Solzhenitsyn's play, *Candle in the Wind*, and his poems in prose. The deciding factor seems to be partly negative: they are works that the authorities will not allow into print; and partly positive: their authors are admired and respected for their talent.

The process is further complicated by two other factors. One is that *Samizdat* republishes many suppressed authors from the past whose works are still banned by the Soviet censorship. Some of them were even liquidated by Stalin. The works of Osip Mandelstam, for instance, have been widely circulated in recent years, as also have those of formerly forgotten writers such as Mikhail Bulgakov and Andrei Platonov—both of whom were half-heartedly rehabilitated as a result of liberalisation and then hurriedly dropped again. Secondly, established and 'official' writers also turn up in *Samizdat*, many of whom are grudgingly acknowledged by the authorities but in practice find it difficult to get their works published. The problem here is that the censorship has been in a period of uncertainty and change. The swing from Stalinist freeze to liberalisation and back again has confused everyone, censors and writers alike, and the arbitrariness of decisions has meant that no one is quite sure which side of the fence certain works will end up on. Part One of *Cancer Ward*, for instance, was accepted and part of it set up in type before being suppressed, while many other works, known only from *Samizdat* editions, have clearly been written with official publication in mind. Thus well-known authors such as Voznesensky, Aksyonov, Nekrasov, Akhmatova, Zabolotsky, Akhmadulina, Bulat Okudzhava and a number of others can be found in both sorts of publications simultaneously, i.e. official and *Samizdat*. And occasionally even the same work will appear in both.

It would be a mistake, therefore, to deduce some sort of direct confrontation or opposition between writers whose work appears in *Samizdat* and those who are officially published. The lines are blurred and indistinct and always changing. There are 'liberals' among the accepted writers, who may be party members even, and there are conservatives. The attitude of the liberals is that they support most of what the *Samizdat* editors and distributors are fighting for, namely greater freedom for literature (though not only literature) and the independence of art from the state, but are not usually prepared to move into open opposition, though they do occasionally sign protest letters. The conservatives, on the other hand, line themselves up fully with the state and seek repression not only of *Samizdat*, but also of the liberals.

It can thus be seen that Soviet literature is again, for the first time since the 'twenties, in a state of some fluidity. Gone is the monolithic solidarity and stupefying conformity of the Stalinist era. Instead there are camps, manœuvrings, struggles. Motion instead of stasis. And as was noted with regard to the 'twenties, motion, debate, dissent imply at least a degree of freedom, even in the present conditions of semi-freeze.

The second part of the equation is the Russian emigration. The emigration had become virtually dormant during the Stalinist era, that is to say not internally, in terms of its own development, but in relation to the Soviet Union. Links were cut, further emigration stopped and there was little that could be done about it. The war interrupted this temporarily with its mass movements of population. Millions of Russians found themselves outside the boundaries of the Soviet state for a time and large numbers of them took advantage of it and fled. But once Stalin had clamped down again it made little difference to relations between the émigrés and Russia: the influence of the former remained minimal.

With the policy of liberalisation in the Soviet Union, however, accompanied by the general loosening up of society there, the small but nevertheless significant increase in population mobility and the development of a modest tourist trade—in both directions—the emigration was enabled to gain a new footing. Stalin's airtight seal had been broken and Soviet Russians were eager to see and learn about the world outside. How better than to read about it in Russian, to seek Russian sources that were an alternative to the censored and heavily biased versions available at home? Thus it was that new links were established—tenuous and tentative, but nevertheless real. As a result the emigration emerged from its isolation and once again became a factor in the life of the Soviet Union. This is not to say that its role became a major one, or even perhaps as important as it thinks it is or would like it to be. Nor is the situation simply a return to that of the 'twenties. For one thing, most of the personal connexions are gone, the former sense of community is weaker, and the 'balance of talent' is too one-sided. But there are parallels. For instance, there has been a revival, or a reaffirmation, of the *idea* of a single community. Reviews founded in the West to promote this outlook have had self-explanatory names like *Bridges* and *Aerial Ways*, and in the latter an influential émigré critic recently wrote: 'Russia is a spiritual, conceptual entity, changing in time and coloured for each of us in a slightly different way, yet outlined sufficiently clearly and existing not only in the past, but through the bond between the future and the past. . . . The efforts of the new generation are directed—whether it is clearly or only dimly aware of it—towards restoring this bond.'[1]

Then there have been important defections to the West in recent years, including those of writers like Anatoly Kuznetsov and the critic, Arkady Belinkov[2] Svetlana. Alliluyeva (Stalin) has links rather with the Soviet intelligentsia than with political circles, and there are numerous journalists and less prominent cultural workers who have come out in recent times.

Movements such as these have a twofold resonance. Friends and colleagues in the Soviet Union become aware of an alternative life and system 'over there' and feel a personal link with it, even if unable to act in any way. This strengthens any independent leanings they might have. The emigration, on the other hand, receives fresh forces, fresh information, and is confirmed in its efforts—or persuaded to change its emphasis—by what it learns.

In this way we have reached the situation obtaining today. *Samizdat*, although an amorphous, shifting, disorganised and un-

[1] Wladimir Weidlé, quoted in Professor Gleb Struve's contribution, 'Some Reflections on Soviet Literature Today', to a symposium published under the general title, *Soviet Literature in the 'Sixties*, edited by Max Hayward and Edward L. Crowley (Methuen, London 1965).

[2] It is sad to report that Mr Belinkov died of a heart attack in May 1970, after these lines were written.

definable phenomenon, has won for itself a position as an alternative press in the Soviet Union. What doesn't get published in the official journals or by official publishing-houses—be it letters, diaries, stories, novels, collections of verse, memoirs, manifestos—is almost sure to turn up sooner or later in typewritten copies and be passed from hand to hand. Much of this in turn finds its way to the West and is published there: in *Grani* and in sister journals in the Russian language, and in translations into most of the major languages. Some indeed go on to become films and even box-office successes, witness *Doctor Zhivago*. A film is even now being made of *One Day in the Life of Ivan Denisovich*. Meanwhile the flow of manuscript continues. And although there are signs of an increasingly efficient drive to suppress it, *Samizdat* appears to be surviving with a resilience worthy of its energetic and resourceful propagators.

How, then, do the stories in this anthology fit into the general scheme of things? They are, for the most part, shorter works that have appeared either in one or other of the *Samizdat* journals, or else as separate items. The longer and better known *Samizdat* works of prose literature have appeared in translation in separate volumes, beginning with *Doctor Zhivago* and ending with *My Testimony* by Anatoly Marchenko. A great deal of poetry has also appeared in English, including a selection of poems from *Grani* published some time ago in a companion anthology to this volume,[1] while documents have appeared either separately or in collections. Examples are the books on the series of literary trials in the Soviet Union, while another companion volume to this one will contain documents, essays and articles on the social, economic and political aspects of dissent in the Soviet Union.[2] The present anthology, however, represents the first attempt to collect some of the best of the short prose from *Samizdat* and present it for its literary interest.

The collection is of necessity a miscellaneous one, but none the less adds up to a representative sample by virtue of its very breadth. For the sheer quantity of works unacceptable to the censorship makes generalisation difficult and dangerous. What we have is a sort of cross-section of the literature of nonconformity in the Soviet Union. 'Dissent', though clearly applicable to some of the stories, would be too strong a word to apply to all of them. Works here such as 'The Fleecy Jacket' or 'Before Sunrise', for instance, could hardly be

[1] See note 2, p. 9.
[2] *Russia's Other Intellectuals*, edited by Peter Reddaway To be published shortly.

called hostile; they offend, possibly, because of their subject-matter. As for the two stories that have not appeared in *Samizdat* form ('Hard Times' and 'My Sister's Applegarth'), although unpublishable in the Soviet Union, they could not by the wildest stretch of the imagination be termed subversive. They testify, rather, to the wide diversity of theme—and even style—that is considered beyond the pale by the Soviet cultural establishment.

It should be borne in mind, therefore, that although the ideas and forms of dissent will loom large in the ensuing discussion of individual works, such an approach has been dictated by their origin in *Samizdat* and by the obtuseness and repressiveness of a ponderous system of censorship, rather than from any deliberate choice. In such conditions, nonconformity is frequently pushed into dissent and even open rebellion, depending upon the personality of the writer. But dissent is rarely the point of departure for the writer and even less is it the purpose of his work. It is, rather, a by-product of his fidelity to his personal vision and of the consistency with which he adheres to his own perception of the truth at the expense of more public or more generally accepted 'truths'. In a monolithic or repressive society, the area of dissent becomes greater, but the extent of this area is dictated by society itself and not by the writer working within it.

Thus the stories translated here then represent various aspects of unacceptability and cover various periods, beginning with the twenties and ending with the late 'sixties. From the 'twenties come two stories totally different in style and subject-matter. The first of them, 'The Fleecy Jacket', is by a hitherto obscure writer, Anton Ulyansky; it became the title story of a collection of Ulyansky's stories published in the mid-'twenties. Ulyansky, who otherwise had not been published or mentioned for decades in the Soviet Union, re-surfaced recently in some memoirs by Konstantin Paustovsky. According to Paustovsky, Ulyansky began life as a compositor in St Petersburg before the First World War. Having been taken prisoner by the Germans, he returned to Russia a tramp in the midst of the civil war and somehow found his way to Odessa. It was there, in 1922, that he began to write, his first published work —a Dickensian sketch (shades of Boz) of an English steamer in Odessa harbour. In it Ulyansky apparently revealed the 'terrible skeleton of England'. The officers' macintoshes were 'supercilious and cold, like English snobbery', the captain's purple neck 'recalled England's colonial policy', while the whole ship 'overflowed with Christian hate and emaciated truths'. In fairness to Ulyansky it should be pointed out that he was half-starving at the time and was desperate for the five roubles which *Lighthouse*, the seamen's newspaper, was proposing to pay him. In the light of the prevailing ardour of that time, he presumably followed the only wise course. That he can in fact write, however, is more than proved by 'The Fleecy Jacket', a humorous story of the lower depths reminiscent, in many ways, of O'Henry (who was very popular in Russia in that period). In the course of time Ulyansky was to see two collections of his stories appear, before dying, it is thought of starvation, at the beginning of the 'thirties.

The other story from this period deals with the opposite end of the social spectrum. 'Hard Times' is about the rich and the well-to-do at a similar point in time. But their fate, curiously enough, is in this case the same as that of the down-and-outs: they are robbed by an impersonal and unfeeling superior force. It is impossible, I think, to regard the fate of Victor Rostopchin's unfortunate family as some sort of historic earthshaking tragedy; it would be a mistake to oppose the Soviet extreme by another extreme. One's heart goes out more to those nameless, dispossessed millions who died obscurely squalid deaths in the war, the Revolution, the civil war and the terror of that time. But equally it would be fatuous to pretend that the suffering depicted in 'Hard Times' was not real, that because it was 'for the good of the cause' it either did not exist or was not important. One would have thought that even a moderately robust philosophy of revolution would face up to such truths without flinching. There existed, after all, plenty of theories to account for it. But even in the early 'twenties, soon after it was written, 'Hard Times' was rejected by the censor for inclusion in an anthology of short stories: 'The story is artistically written, but because of its tendencies [intellectual whining, a pathetic lament for bourgeois-aristocratic impoverishment] it can on no account be included in the anthology'.[1] Victor Rostopchin was able to publish hardly anything during his long career in the Soviet Union. Recently, however, he was able to take up residence in Holland and is now engaged in sorting and publishing his extensive collection of works in manuscript.

A very different sort of writer and one who, at the period of his life represented in this collection, very decidedly embraced dissent was Osip Mandelstam. His presence here might seem odd to some experts: a carp among minnows. But it is motivated by several considerations. Firstly, Mandelstam is a favourite and indeed archetypal *Samizdat* author. Unreservedly acknowledged by cognoscenti as one of the greatest Russian poets of the twentieth century, fit to

[1] I am indebted to Mr Rostopchin for this information.

stand beside Blok, Esenin, Mayakovsky and Pasternak, he is yet derided in official circles and his work almost totally suppressed. He is a writer of such stature, however, that almost everything he wrote is of interest, particularly when, as in the case of the 'Fourth Prose', it has been hitherto unavailable to English readers. The particular circumstances of its composition and its place in Mandelstam's *œuvre* are discussed elsewhere by its translator, Professor Clarence Brown, who is the leading western authority on Mandelstam's work and has published a selected edition of Mandelstam's prose in a separate volume.

An additional interest of the piece, at this time, is the extraordinary percipience which Mandelstam showed about the trend of Soviet literature and the progress of censorship in Russia. Writing in 1930 or 1931, before the First Congress of Soviet Writers the following year (when Stalin's curtain finally fell), he described most Soviet writers as having 'sold out to the pockmarked devil for three generations to come', and characterised those who accepted censorship as follows: 'Writerdom is a race with a revolting smell to its hide and the filthiest known means of preparing its food. It is a race that wanders and sleeps in its own vomit, one that is expelled from cities and hounded in villages, but it is always and everywhere close to the authorities, who grant its members a place in red-light districts, as prostitutes. For literature always and everywhere carries out one assignment: it helps superiors keep their soldiers obedient and it helps judges execute reprisals against doomed men.' Mandelstam had his eye very much on the careerists and cynical yes-men, of course, and he goes on, in 'Fourth Prose', to amplify his concept of the role of these writers: 'A writer is a mixture of parrot and pope. He's a polly in the very loftiest meaning of that word. He speaks French if his master is French, but, sold into Persia, he will say "Pol's a fool", or "Polly wants a cracker" in Persian. A parrot has no age and doesn't know day from night. If he starts to bore his master he's covered with a black cloth and that, for literature, is the surrogate of night.' Nowhere has a clearer picture been painted of the condition of the writer in a totalitarian society and such opinions naturally made Mandelstam anathema to the authorities. His words elsewhere in the story could have been inscribed on the masthead of *Samizdat*: 'I divide all the works of world literature into those written with and without permission. The first are trash, the second —stolen air.' *Samizdat* deals in stolen air.

We come now, with a bound, to the post-war period. This is represented by some seven items making up the bulk of the volume.

Least is known about 'Before Sunrise' and its author, V. Goryushkin. The story is quite simple and very much in the tradition of Russian 'compassionate' or 'humanitarian' literature: an armless, legless and dumb cripple somehow, in spite of everything, finds happiness in life and retains his wife's love and respect. An ordinary tale, and with an optimistic message that should certainly be acceptable to the censor in general terms. But here too one must reckon with the pernicketiness of an uncomprehending bureaucracy. The predicament of an armless, legless and dumb cripple is in itself 'distasteful' and unfitting for the women's magazine concept of literature held by the censors, while there is also the Chekhovian schoolmaster with his gloomy opinions: 'Did you say "sanctity of labour"? What does "labour" mean when, because of it, we scurry about all over the place like ants and before we've time to look round it's winter, time to die. . . . I studied, dreamed, thought I would see a better world. But when I sit down to mark my tests, my hands are covered in dung.' To voice such thoughts is heretical, even when they are balanced by other elements in the story. And the situation is made even worse when the schoolmaster continues: 'I thought the purpose of life was work, serving other people. . . . But that's just dogma! Terrifying, life-killing dogma. And you're allowed no doubts, and no confirmations either. You're like a horse bitted and bridled, shafts on either side, and as for turning left or right—no hope, not a hope, that's what the whip is for.' The point is that even though the schoolmaster's despair is not uncommon, even though it could apply in almost any country at any time, such thoughts must not be uttered.

Doubt, questioning and despair are common ingredients in the best of these stories. 'Lord, we are at God's mercy! And when will it all end? And how will we live till the end?' asks the market woman in 'Hard Times'. And in the same story the family contemplate with loathing those fat-bellied lice and that 'hopeless feeling of the heavy power of these dirty-bodied, irrepressible, freely roaming creatures' in their lives. Despair it is that drives Velsky to his abortive attempt at escape from the Soviet Union as related in his 'Apologia', despair it is that slowly seeps into Lashkov's soul in 'House in the Clouds' and hastens his death, and despair is the backcloth against which Shalamov's dramas of camp life are played out.

Shalamov, in fact, is operating in a realm almost beyond despair, for his subject is the savagely inhuman forced labour camps of Stalin's time (those same camps that feature in Ivan Denisovich's story), where human life was so cheap that even despair was an inadequate response. Shalamov himself spent a large part of his life in those camps, chiefly in the notorious camps of Kolyma, before, like Solzhenitsyn, being rehabilitated sometime in the 'fifties and returning to Moscow. Since then his career has been typical of that air of unreality that pervades so much of the Soviet literary world. Known officially as a minor poet, with three slim volumes to his credit and occasional appearances in the official literary reviews, he is at the same time something of a literary lion in private circles and among readers of *Samizdat*—but for his prose, all of which remains unpublished. His best known work is an extensive cycle of stories of camp life under the general title, *Stories of Kolyma*, to which the two in this collection belong.

Shalamov, like Solzhenitsyn, has grasped the point that in order to portray horror, in order to speak of the unspeakable, the use of understatement is absolutely essential. So compressed are his stories, so tightly organised and controlled, that it is sometimes difficult to divine their meaning at a first attempt. The two stories represented here, 'Caligula' and 'A Good Hand', are excellent examples of his elliptical style and terse approach.

At this point it is worth noting the high standard of technique displayed in these stories. Not one of them is loose or slipshod in any way and it should be pointed out that in general the standard of literary craftsmanship is very high in the Soviet Union, where the self-conscious and hardworking approach of serious writers is closer to American practice than to the appearance of casual amateurism so cultivated in Britain. This is particularly noticeable in the form of the short story, which, as also in America, is a much more flourishing genre than in Britain. The stories in this collection, with the exception of the experimental pieces by the youthful Bukovsky, conform to this high standard. Mandelstam, Shalamov, Rostopchin, Goryushkin—they all are meticulous craftsmen; Velsky and Maximov, as we shall see shortly, are even more so, as also is Alla Ktorova—a special case in more ways than one.

Of all the authors represented here, in fact, she has the lightest touch. Of course, her situation is different from that of the others. Contemplating her homeland from the safety of America, where she now lives, she reacts to it with the bewildered amusement and sly satire of a voluntary exile. 'My Sister's Applegarth', begun in the Soviet Union and completed abroad, is a pointed picture of the wiles and deception needed to succeed in a clumsily organised society ridden with bureaucracy and shortages. A literary descendant of Gogol, Ilf and Petrov and Zoshchenko, Miss Ktorova is following a fine Russian tradition, yet in other respects she is quite unusual. Her self-conscious technique, with its knowing nods and winks to the reader and its Sternian asides, looks back to Russian prose of the first two decades of this century and to a tradition established by another outstanding writer, Andrei Bely, that has since been stifled by Soviet orthodoxy. It is this, perhaps, that has led to the extravagant paeans of praise addressed to her by émigré Russian critics. Certainly she brings a welcome breath of fresh air to the stuffiness of traditional Russian realism (be it socialist or otherwise) and has the makings of an exciting, original talent.

The most curious personality of all is undoubtedly Victor Velsky. His 'Apologia' is presented to the reader as an apparently unvarnished account of the 'truth' (it is part of a longer work called *My Confession*) with no tricks of style or narrative. Whatever may be the basic 'truth' or otherwise of the events narrated—and they are certainly commonplace enough to be at least thoroughly plausible—this assertion cannot be accepted unconditionally, for the 'Apologia' is undoubtedly a highly self-conscious and artfully constructed piece of work. Witness, for instance, the disingenuous disavowals of style, the quotations from Pushkin, Nietzsche and Anatole France, the arch asides ('as they say in novels'), the tightly organised pattern of themes and the beautifully managed peripetia at the end: Velsky, after realising his dream of arriving in the West at last, suddenly becomes disillusioned and decides to return to 'captivity'.

The pervading literary presence in the Apologia is Dostoevsky, particularly the Dostoevsky of *Notes from Underground* and *Crime and Punishment*. Like Raskolnikov, Velsky studies Nietzsche and ponders the necessity to 'commit himself' to a fatal act. (The Russian verb *prestupit* also means 'to step over' and by extension 'to commit a crime', and is the verb used by Dostoevsky in *Crime and Punishment* to describe Raskolnikov's decision to murder the old woman.) In Velsky's case it is to turn traitor and informer on his friends. He is motivated in this by fear and by egotism, but his reaction to it is typical in its Dostoevskian complexity. It could so easily be Raskolnikov or the Underground Man: 'I went out into the street with a strange, incongruous feeling of relief . . . I strolled about carelessly, feeling free. Inside, perhaps, in my innermost self, I had shrivelled up and hardened and my youthful greenness and naïvety had vanished forever. I was half damned already. But now that I'd actually committed myself, everything was allowed. Yes, it was exhilarating to feel no fear of heights—to look down and not be afraid. To test myself, I visited a girl I knew, who always made me feel shy. I was worked up, animated and bold. . . .' Later this is superseded by disgust and fear, but how thoroughly Dostoevskian a progression it is.

Velsky also connects in surprising ways with some of the other stories in this volume. When he gets a job as a journalist he is asked by a colleague: 'Do you know what journalism is? Do you know about the "Second oldest profession"?' And he meditates à la Mandelstam: 'The oldest profession is, of course, prostitution, and we members of the second oldest were cheap, vagrant, intellectual whores . . . self-seekers and money-grubbers.' He is also something of a snob: 'I was the only one among them who had ever heard of Cima di Conegliano, but of course I kept it to myself.' Or: 'There is no longer an aristocracy or an élite. There are too many people. In this savage, kaleidoscopic anthill the value of the individual human being and the significance of his experiences have been lost. Everything has become commonplace, vulgar, available.'

It would be wrong to labour the point, but there seems to be a vein of latent snobbery running through many of these stories—a vein that one rarely comes across in Soviet prose. There is the inference in 'Hard Times' that virtue somehow resides not only in the old-fashioned values of the poverty-stricken family, but also, perhaps, in their 'good' linen and plate and expensive possessions. There is a hint of something similar in the implied comparison between the high-class Soninka and Morizchen, in 'My Sister's Applegarth', and the vulgar Soviet family who seek to take over their flat. And in 'House in the Clouds' the old residents, who in some ways are held up as examples of the 'old intelligentsia' and contrasted favourably with the new order, show many signs of a similar disposition. The disdain of Meckler and Kozlov and the loving attachment of Mrs Khramov to her possessions are highly typical, while the outbursts of Lev Khramov, who often acts as a spokesman for the author, come perilously close at times to a species of snobbish petulance. There is nothing basically surprising about this when one contemplates the effects of a proletarian revolution. It is more surprising, perhaps, that so little has manifested itself in literature. But it is so rare a phenomenon that it strikes the habitual reader of Soviet prose with the force of novelty.

In all other respects the 'Apologia' of Velsky is an excellent evocation of the suspicious, fear-laden atmosphere of the Soviet Union in the post-war Stalinist period, an exemplary study of the psychosis of the conforming intelligentsia. Here we see how the web of lies and corruption and denunciations gradually extended until it embraced everyone, even innocent students: 'The circle was closing in on us. What did it matter if the hares caught in that circle were harmless—who cared? . . . This sense of being accused without there being any cause for it was a terrible, desolate feeling. It seemed we were internally guilty. Although we did not give expression to our sentiments, we were against what was going on, or rather we were not "for" it, and also we stuck together to some extent. Someone already had his eye on us, that was clear. Maybe there was already a traitor in our midst. This was a constant nightmare. . . . There was no escape. There was just the fear. . . . The fear that was hanging over all of us achieved its quintessence in me. I couldn't stand it. I lost my nerve.'

Velsky is also good on some of the more elusive aspects of Soviet psychology, for instance the sense of disappointment and letdown that many people felt after the death of Stalin. This was not just the simple chagrin of hardliners, who felt that they had something to lose, for it also affected those who loathed Stalin and the type of society he had created. The ambiguity is beautifully formulated in the following passage, which gets right to the heart of much that has happened in the years since 1953: 'Under Stalin we had lived for the spirit (even if in a distorted way). The main thing was ideological values, communist ideas, enthusiasm—material considerations were insignificant in comparison. What of it if there was a shortage of accommodation, clothes, food—the main thing was our glorious ideas and the future in store for us, the main thing was that we had Stalin the Omniscient to lead us. Khrushchev's historical importance lay in the fact that he played down ideological values and substituted economic, material ones. Under him people did begin to live better, to live materialistically, i.e. for themselves and not for the sake of unrealistic goals. This again has another side to it. The concentration on material objectives led to a spiritual decline. If, under Stalin, this spiritual life had been monstrously distorted, now it ceased to exist altogether. Spiritually people had nothing to live for. No one was attracted by the official ideology and there was nothing new to put in its place. There was a certain revival of interest in religion and, to counter this, anti-religious propaganda was stepped up. But the main thing was that people wanted to enjoy life and get the most out of it, especially the young. Young people changed, became perhaps more egotistical, but also more courageous. An irreversible process of disintegration set in.'

Psychological penetration of this order is rare anywhere and is doubly unusual in the Soviet context. Velsky displays it again and again in his analysis of himself and his country, and nowhere to greater effect than in the climax of his narrative. Before departing for Germany and thence to the West he sums up his position: 'I cannot live in my own country. The existing order conflicts with my convictions and my dignity as a human being. . . . Even by the nature of my mind I am unfit for our . . . society. I cannot live under a dictatorship, in a slave society, where all the rights of thinking men are flouted.' And he rationalises his departure: 'I am a Russian European and my place is in the free world. . . . Man's home is the whole world and happiness exists where life is happy.' Yet when he arrives in the West, he is unable, to his consternation, to 'commit himself', to 'step over' the barrier: 'I couldn't do it, I lost my nerve, I lacked the will that gives a man the right to cross frontiers.' And again he rationalises: 'My only consolation is that no one has that will. Not even in the West.' He goes on to point out the spiritual barrenness of the West, its preoccupation with vulgar materialism, its own version of unfreedom, and has a nightmare vision of being interrogated, sent to a camp, employed in the Russian language section of a foreign radio station and becoming another sort of traitor—a traitor to his homeland.

Interestingly enough, the 'Apologia' of Velsky played a prominent part in the trial of Yuri Galanskov, a young student and writer who in January 1967 was tried with three other young people for illegal literary activities. Galanskov was a compiler and manufacturer of *Samizdat* editions and was specifically tried for compiling an unofficial journal called *Phoenix*. In it, according to the prosecution, were five 'anti-Soviet' compositions, of which the 'Apologia' was considered one of the worst. The defence disagreed with this view and held that the 'Apologia' could not be considered anti-Soviet, first because it was only a work of fiction (*povest*')—forgetting, perhaps, the uselessness of this plea in the Sinyavsky-Daniel case— and second because in it Velsky finally turns against the West and rejects it. 'It is no accident', said the defence lawyer in her summing up, 'that this tale has found no editor or publisher in the West.' Alas, that particular argument no longer holds good—it was in any case a straw for a drowning man. For Velsky's work is undoubtedly anti-Soviet in the way in which the prosecution meant it. But it is not only, or even mainly, anti-Soviet. Velsky is above all anti-Stalinist, and he is anti-materialist and anti-bureaucratic, 'anti' being a pawn in international politics, 'anti' an absence of spiritual ideals. A man with his character was bound to be against the repressive machinery of Stalin's state, just as he would almost equally certainly be 'anti-West' in many ways. Only the most simpleminded could assent to the court's proposition that he who is with *us* is against *them*, he who is against *us* is with *them*. The point lies elsewhere and is not subsumable under simple categories of for and against.

Finally we come to a consideration of the longest story in this anthology, 'House in the Clouds', by Vladimir Maximov. To my mind it is a minor masterpiece, one of the best works to come out of the Soviet Union since the war, and marks out Maximov as the most talented of the younger prose writers now living in the Soviet Union. It was a desire to translate and publish this story that initially led to the compilation of the present anthology.

'House in the Clouds' relates the history of a small block of flats and its inhabitants in Moscow from the time of the Revolution until some time after the Second World War. Its main protagonist is the caretaker, Vasily Lashkov, through whose eyes we see the heterogeneous inhabitants and watch events unfold. On its publication in *Grani* it was entitled 'The Caretaker Lashkov', but its real title is now known to be the practically untranslatable *Dvor posredi neba*, of which 'House in the Clouds' is an approximate rendering.

The title is important, for the story is so constructed as to make the house a microcosm of Soviet society, while its vicissitudes over a period of forty years are symbolic of the much wider life of that time. The story begins with the episode of 'compression', a post-revolutionary social policy whereby the wealthy and the well-off, or even simply the middle class (the 'bourgeoisie') were compelled to give up part or all of their living accommodation to members of the proletariat. In the present story it is the Mecklers, the Khramovs and the old army officer, Kozlov, who are 'compressed' in this way to make room for the Tsarevs, the Tsigankovs, the Lyovushkins, the Nikoforovs and the rest, not to speak, of course, of the expropriated owner of the flats, old woman Shokolinist. And it is this that accounts for the initial hostility between the two social 'layers' and creates a tension in the house that runs through the entire story.

With his account of the various families that move in Maximov gives us a vivid impression of the rootlessness of that time and of the great upheavals and wanderings that succeeded the civil war. Nearly all the new arrivals are misfits in some way, and, as events unfold, are made to feel this more and more keenly. With the arrival of the 'thirties arrests begin, people start to disappear and fear and distrust spread throughout the house. Here we see what a brilliant idea it was to show events through the eyes of Lashkov, for he it is who has to accompany the police or the Security officials to the particular flat each time, he it is who receives last messages, runs errands and acts as the helpless go-between in the vacuum between the authorities and the luckless inhabitants. Then, gradually, as the story unfolds, Lashkov himself is drawn into the action when he falls in love with the high-spirited, capable country girl, Grusha Tsarev. Abandoning his role of passive observer, he begins to act, to feel, to enjoy life. But no sooner has he proposed marriage to her than her brother is arrested in one of Stalin's purges. Lashkov is warned by his friend, the policeman, that he too is under suspicion. He takes fright and abandons Grusha, after which he lapses into a decline, becomes once more the unwilling and apathetic observer of other people's misfortunes and finally dies in an alcoholic haze. Broken in spirit by years of loneliness and poverty, he feels his life has been robbed of all meaning.

The tragedy and pathos of this central theme is paralleled by the lives of the other characters. Of the old inhabitants, Kozlov is arrested and presumably shot, the Khramov daughter goes insane and the son dies of a chronic illness, while both are survived by their hapless mother into old age. Only Meckler survives military service to remain alive at the end. Of the 'proletarians' Tsarev is arrested, Lyovushkin becomes an alcoholic, the elder Tsigankov is exiled to Siberia, his daughter is arrested and Grusha dies abandoned after having been married to Shtabel, an Austrian plumber, for a short space of time. The fate of Shtabel is, in fact, emblematic. The only truly 'positive' character in the story, he survives the Revolution and the civil war, marries Grusha and survives the purges, only to be rounded up as a 'German' during the Second World War and sent into distant exile. The last character of importance is Kalinin, the policeman, who, despite his unpleasant occupation, is also relatively 'positive', but ends by committing suicide in despair over the work he has been forced to do.

All this sounds like a thoroughly bleak picture—too much of a good thing, in fact, a propagandist's blueprint. But this is not so. It may not be the 'whole truth'—whatever that is—it may not take into account industrial achievements, social services and the like, but it certainly portrays one kind of very real truth: the price paid in terms of personal tragedy for all those achievements and changes. In this Maximov can be likened, perhaps, to Zola. And the grimness of the facts he chooses to portray is redeemed by art of the highest calibre. Maximov's powers of generalisation are such that he makes his house, its yard (the Russian *dvor* of the title is literally a 'yard' and Lashkov, the *dvornik*, a 'yard-keeper') and its inhabitants into vivid symbols of a whole society, a whole world even. Take, for instance, the following passage, when Lashkov is in the attic helping Kalinin hunt for the fugitive Tsigankov, suddenly catches sight of Moscow spread out below him and is carried away by his thoughts: 'Outside, beyond the panes of the dormer window and beneath a low January sky, the city lay stretched out. It was difficult to believe that somewhere down below, beneath that chaotically dark agglomeration of tin roofs, there lurked something called life. And Lashkov thought of how, living in his own yard and never going out anywhere, he had none the less seen a great many things that he had never suspected before. People were born and died, people were taken away by other people just like themselves, people fell in love and went mad. And all this had happened in his presence, before his very eyes. But then there was a lot more that even he didn't see. For people endeavoured to spend the major part of their lives either alone or with their nearest and dearest. And it came out that not even five lives would have been sufficient for Lashkov to know all there was to know about even one single yard. And how many there were, how many such yards in the city, in the country, in the whole world! And yet for all those yards there was but one sky. And was it really so difficult for everyone together to look up—just once—at the same time, and to feel, as he, Lashkov, was doing right now, a piercing sense of yearning for a kind word and a kindred spirit?'

Passages like these enable 'House in the Clouds' to transcend its place and time and transform it from a narrow indictment of a particular society into a passionate protest against man's inhumanity to man, and against his resulting loneliness and alienation in the modern world. Here and in many of his preoccupations, Maximov resembles another Russian master of our time, Solzhenitsyn. Maximov's choice of a simple, inarticulate working man to filter his narration is reminiscent of *One Day in the Life of Ivan Denisovich*, and has the same effect of both distancing the reader from events and yet making their impact all the greater through the disparity between their horrifying nature and the protagonist's limited response to them. In Solzhenitsyn's *Cancer Ward*, the metaphor for Soviet society is a hospital, while Maximov makes of his house a similar, powerful metaphor. Nikiforov, in 'House in the Clouds', plays a similar role in the story to the nasty party spokesman in Solzhenitsyn's work, Rusanov, while Lev Khramov is the 'raisonneur' in place of Kostoglotov. Typical, too, is the use of symbols. One of the most powerful symbols in *Cancer Ward* is that of the missing monkey in the zoo. The monkey is not in its cage any longer because 'an unknown man has thrown pepper in its eyes out of spite'—and this monkey comes to stand for the unjustly accused and condemned. In 'House in the Clouds' Maximov uses a similar device. In the course of a drunken conversation with Lev Khramov, Lashkov traps a fly in a glass: 'At last the fly was caught and began to buzz frantically, storming the sides of the glass. Viciously and with a kind of sadistic thrill Lashkov thought to himself: "Go on, round you go now, you bastard!" Exhausted the fly kept falling and springing up again in the vain search for a way out. And again Lashkov gloated darkly, but this time aloud: "Round you go-o-o!"' Khramov, meanwhile, is launching a tirade against the injustice and cruelty of the life he has experienced and in the complex counterpointing that Maximov establishes here the fly comes to stand for him and his misfortunes, for the unhappy Lashkov and for all the suffering people around them.

Such similarities are not, I think, the result of conscious imitation. They arise out of similar moral concerns and similar diagnoses of the ills of contemporary society. And they do not end there. Like Solzhenitsyn (and indeed many other Soviet writers), Maximov has a vibrant response to nature, has a tenderness and sensitivity to the simple joys of living that lighten his narrative with flashes of quiet lyricism. At the same time he possesses a calm stoicism that seems equal to all the stresses put upon it. But one must not push these comparisons too far. Maximov resembles most of all the Solzhenitsyn of *One Day in the Life of Ivan Denisovich* and the short stories. He has not that capacity—as yet—to pluck the major chord as Solzhenitsyn does in his longer novels. On the other hand he is in many ways a more delicate artist than Solzhenitsyn. The counterpoint of his narrative, the proportion of the parts, the almost musical harmony of his lyrical scenes, the freshness of his imagery and above all the gaps, the silences he leaves (see Mandelstam's hole in the doughnut, the punctures in Brussels lace) are evidence of a superior, distinctive talent that has few equals in the Soviet Union.

Having commended my wares perhaps more than I intended, it remains for me only to repeat the refrain that I took up at the start of this brief introduction. Politics and literature are separate areas of human endeavour. It is true, they overlap and touch at a thousand points. Both are concerned with man's nature and environment, with man and society and man in society. And each is able to make use of the other for its own purposes. But the methods and aims of the two can never be identical and any attempt by one of them to appropriate the other is bound to end in misunderstanding and self-defeat.

If such truisms seem self-evident, I hope I may be forgiven for perhaps excessive sensitivity. In dealing with translations from modern Russian it is my experience that the standards of Soviet critics are more widely accepted than most people suspect—if only in reverse. Furthermore, they seem to be receiving implicit support from current developments in our own society, where 'politics' appears to be expanding its sphere of action at an alarming rate, while 'art' displays an equally alarming tendency to contract its horizons and turn inwards upon itself. Finally, it is in the very nature of works connected in any way with Soviet Russia for them to be scrutinised, from both ends of the political spectrum, for their ideological content.

Let me conclude, therefore, by inscribing two quotations from Russian writers on my banner. The first of them is from Turgenev, who in the preface to his collected works answered certain of his critics in the following terms on the distinction between the poet and the publicist: 'The publicist sees his task with a publicist's eyes, the poet with the eyes of a poet. In the department of art, the question *how* is more important than the question *what*. If the things you repudiate actually exist in the writer's mind as images, repeat *images*, then what right do you have to cast doubt on his intentions? . . . Believe me, a genuine talent never serves alien ends, and it finds satisfaction in itself. Its content is supplied by the life about it—it is but a concentrated reflection of this. And it is as little capable of a panegyric as of a pasquinade. The point is that that sort of thing is beneath it. To subordinate oneself to a given thesis or to carry out a programme is possible only for those who cannot do anything different or better.'[1]

The other quotation comes from a near contemporary of Turgenev's, the critic Vissarion Belinsky, who was later to become almost the patron saint of Soviet criticism and whose views are alleged to have paved the way for ideological standards of literary criticism. Belinsky was, among other things, a champion of Nikolai Gogol, and he was much concerned by attacks on the latter for his 'lack of patriotism' and 'negative views' on Russian society. Belinsky answered these attacks in his 'Reply to the *Moskvityanin*' (a conservative literary journal) in words as true today as when they were written, and which were recently placed at the beginning of his *White Book on the Sinyavsky-Daniel Case* by Alexander Ginzburg:

'The greatest and harshest accusation which writers of the

[1] Quoted from 'Turgenev and the Life-giving Drop' by Edmund Wilson (*The New Yorker*, 1957).

rhetorical school bring against Gogol, hoping thereby to destroy him utterly, is that the characters he displays in his works are an insult to society. . . . Such an accusation merely illustrates the immaturity of our social education. In countries whose development has out-stripped us by whole centuries, people cannot even conceive of the possibility of such an accusation being made. No one can say the English are not jealous of their national honour; on the contrary, it is hard to think of another people in which national egotism is taken to such extremes as in England. Yet they love their Hogarth, who depicted nothing but the vices, debauchery, malpractices and vulgarity of the English society of his time. And not one Englishman will say that Hogarth slandered England, that he saw and recognised nothing human in it, nothing that was noble, elevated or beautiful. The English understood that a talent has the complete and sacred right to be one-sided, and that its very one-sidedness can be what makes it great. On the other hand, they are so deeply conscious and aware of their national greatness that they are not in the least afraid of it being harmed by the revelation of the failings and negative characteristics of English society. And that is the way it should be: the stronger a man and the more moral he is, the more boldly will he contemplate his failings and shortcomings. And this is even more true of peoples with a history spanning not merely a generation but whole centuries. It is a weak, ineffectual people so far past its prime that it is unable to go forward any more that loves merely to sing its own praises and fears more than anything to regard its wounds: it knows that they are mortal, that its reality has no rewards to offer and that only self-deception can provide it with those false consolations that are so tempting to the weak and the feeble. Thus, for instance, are the Chinese and Persians: to listen to them you would think that there was no better people in the world and that all other peoples, in comparison with them, were either knaves or fools. But this is not the way for a great people to behave, bursting with strength and life: the acknowledgement of its failings, instead of driving it into despair and forcing it to doubt its powers, endows it with fresh energy and inspires it to new achievements.'

The writers in this anthology are not all Hogarths, but it is true that they are more than averagely aware of their society's faults and shortcomings. At the same time the fact remains that the question *how* is the important one 'in the department of art', and it is on that basis that their works should be judged.

Biographical Notes

Vladimir Bukovsky (born 1941) has been prominent among youthful dissenters from Soviet literary and political orthodoxy. Having contributed to the underground literary magazine, *Phoenix 1961*, and participated in unauthorised public poetry readings and demonstrations, he was twice confined to mental asylums and in 1967 sentenced to three years' hard labour. The 'Miniature Stories' were published in *Grani* no. 65 (September 1967).

V. Goryushkin is a young Soviet writer living in Moscow. 'Before Sunrise' (together with another story, 'Petrusha') was first published, in Icelandic translation, in the Reykjavik newspaper, *Morgunbladid*, in December 1966. Both stories appeared in Russian in *Grani* no. 63 (March 1967).

Alla Ktorova (born 1930) is the pen-name of Victoria Kochurova-Sandor, a former Soviet citizen and translator from English now married to an American and resident in Washington, D.C. The author of eight stories of varying lengths that have appeared in Russian-language magazines in the West, she has been highly praised for her original talent and vivid style. Two of the stories have been translated into German and one into Danish. This translation of 'My Sister's Applegarth', which was published in *Grani* no. 55 (June 1964), marks her first appearance in English.

Osip Mandelstam (1892-1938) was one of the greatest Russian poets of the twentieth century. In his early career he was associated with the poetic movement known as Acmeism. In the 'twenties and 'thirties he came under increasing attack from orthodox cultural bureaucrats and in 1934 was exiled to Siberia, allegedly, among other things, for satirising Stalin in an epigram. In 1938, after his return, he was again arrested and deported to Siberia, where he died in a transit camp in Vladivostok. With the exception of a handful of lyrics, Mandelstam's works have not been officially published in the Soviet Union since 1933. 'Fourth Prose' was first published in vol. two of the two-volume edition of Mandelstam's Collected Works that appeared in the U.S.A. under the joint editorship of Professor G. P. Struve and B. A. Filipoff (Inter-Language Literary Associates, New York, 1966). The present translation has been made from the almost identical text that appeared in *Grani* no. 63 (March 1967), which in turn was reproduced from the underground literary journal, *Phoenix 1956*, edited by Y. Galanskov.

Vladimir Maximov (born 1932) is a member of the younger generation of Soviet writers who finds some difficulty in getting his works published as written. By an accident of fate he has had a few stories printed in the conservative literary review, *Oktyabr* ('October'), and a small collection of these stories was published in the Soviet Union in 1967. One of them, *Zhiv chelovek* ('A Man Survives') had by then already been translated into English and published in New York (translated by Anselm Hollo, Grove Press, 1964). A small fragment of 'House in the Clouds' was printed under Maximov's name in the Riga literary review, *Krugozor* ('Horizon') in 1967, but the full text has never appeared in the Soviet Union. It was published anonymously under the title, *Dvornik Lashkov* ('The Caretaker Lashkov'), in *Grani* no. 64 (June 1967).

Victor Rostopchin (born 1894) is a poet, prose writer and scholar who began writing before the Revolution. Soon after the Revolution his works were subjected to censorship and he abandoned literature to work in the textile industry, only to return much later to literary research, notably in the field of Pushkin studies. In 1965 he left the Soviet Union for good and now lives in Holland, where his health is very poor. A number of his poems and stories have been published or republished in the West and one of the latter, 'Dog on Ice', was translated into French and English. 'Hard Times' was written in 1920 and refused publication by the censorship. It appeared in *Grani* no. 61 (October 1966).

Varlam Shalamov (born 1907) is a poet and prose writer living in Moscow, whose biography is not very clear. He appears to have been deported a first time in 1929, and before his second confinement in 1938 he worked as a lawyer. He is known to have spent about ten years in the prison camps of Siberia during Stalin's time and to have described his experiences in his *Stories of Kolyma*, from which the two printed here are taken. Although his poetry is regularly published in magazines and in volume form, his prose has not, apparently, been printed in the Soviet Union. 'Caligula' and 'A Good Hand' appeared in January 1967 in *Possev* no. 1 (1076), the then weekly companion paper to *Grani*.

Anton Ulyansky is a forgotten writer of the twenties who began his career as a compositor and proof reader and took up writing only in 1922. Two volumes of his stories were published during the 'twenties, of which one had 'The Fleecy Jacket' as its title story. Ulyansky is thought to have died of starvation in the early 'thirties and his stories have never since been reprinted. 'The Fleecy Jacket' appeared in *Grani* no. 69 (November 1968).

Victor Velsky (?-1964) is a pseudonym for the author of 'My Apologia', whose real identity is not known. The Apologia represents the first part of a much longer work, *The Confession of Victor Velsky*, in which Velsky goes on to expound his religious and philosophical beliefs (see *Russia's Other Intellectuals*, ed. by Peter Reddaway, Longman 1970). According to an editorial note accompanying the second part of the text in *Phoenix 1966*, Velsky died in 1964.

Vladimir Maximov

House in the Clouds

If they say, Come with us . . .
My son, walk not thou in the way with them. . . .

Proverbs 1: 11-15

●

From morn till night Lashkov would sit hunched up in front of the
first-floor landing window of the wing, whence he had a bird's-
eye view as he surveyed the yard in his sorrow and sobriety. Apart
from the week in every month that he spent blind drunk, Lashkov
used to perch there every day, winter and summer. For Lashkov
was taking stock. Lashkov knew that he was soon to die.

Every brick, every little fret on the cornice of the house opposite,
every window frame, it seemed, he could have taken apart and
assembled again without a single mistake. The private affairs of
every resident were as familiar to Lashkov as his own. He had
accompanied them into the house, christened some of them and
seen others to the grave. Rivers of wine had been drunk and dissolved
in seas of drunken tears, and yet now it was not so much a question
of having no words to utter as having nobody to utter them to. And
so Lashkov feared not death—no, he'd learned to live with that
thought—but rather this crushing sense of alienation, this universal
and wordless feeling of isolation. Some terrifying force, it seemed,
was tearing people away from one another, and Lashkov, as he
yielded to it, also withdrew day by day deeper into his own shell,
into his misery. At times his throat would be choked with a wild,
almost animal desire to resist the inevitable, to scream at the top of
his voice, to fall to the ground in convulsions and bite the earth,
but then at once a feeling of exhausted numbness would settle
onto his shoulders and he would only wheeze tormentedly with his
sore throat:

'Let's have a third then, shall we?'

The vodka somehow soaked into his soul, filled it with the buzzing
warmth of holidays, and everything around him suddenly seemed
pleasant and novel. On days like these Lashkov would drag himself
into the central yard and there on the bench—the bench he had
built himself—get back that peace of mind, that feeling of oneness
with the past, that he was missing more and more with the passing
of each new day. His pension was immediately transformed into a
million-rouble fortune, and with grave liberality the retired caretaker would shell out rouble after rouble for a hair of the dog for his
cronies.

But even on these days, somehow snatched from perpetual misery, the gaudy alcoholic curtain would sometimes suddenly and unexpectedly be torn aside and before him, like a phantom, like a black blot on the bright blue of the past, would materialise the wispy figure of old woman Shokolinist. Still as nimble as ever, wearing a dark panama hat pulled down almost to the eyebrows, she would scurry past him with her swaying gait, invariably muttering something under her breath. She collected overdue books for the local library. She had been collecting them now for over twenty years. From house to house, from flat to flat she skittered, like a mouse, with quick, darting rushes, and every time she crossed his path a sort of chord would be set quivering inside him, a quick stab of pain that instantly died away again, and he would be left with a sense of uneasiness. For years he had had a gathering premonition that some sort of discovery was near, a revelation even. And—more important—Lashkov was growing more and more convinced that this discovery was connected somehow with old woman Shokolinist.

Who in this house could have realised then, thirty years ago, that she, its founder and mistress, who even in those times was more like a shadow than a creature of flesh and blood, would outlive so many of them? What is more, Lashkov knew for a certainty that she would outlive him too, if not the house itself. And in all this the old man sensed some sort of almost supernatural meaning.

More and more now he spent his time thinking, thinking, struggling to unravel the tangled skein of events and to find the thread that somehow linked everything together.

●

The first to move into number five on the ground floor had been young Ivan Lyovushkin, still but a youth, a firm-cheeked lad from Ryazan with his already pregnant Lyuba. A wee bit tipsy already, with his shirt unbuttoned over his dark sweat-stained chest, he had flashed his cheeky eyes at the 'compressed' Jew and dentist, Meckler, and said laughingly as he trampled over the latter's belongings:

'It's God's way, God's way. Not all for some, but share it round a bit, eh? The missus here is almost due, an' you can't expect her to bring a child of the proletariat into the world in some worm-eaten shack now, can you . . .? No, it ain't just because of the new regime—it's God's way, God's way. . . . Still, we'll rub along together. I'm a quiet bloke, an' as for the missus—you wouldn't know she was there. . . . And clean. . . .'

Meckler, wearing only a jacket over his string vest, was standing in the door of the room assigned to him with his hands clasped behind his back, and rocked springily back and forth on the balls of his feet.

'Don't mention it,' he said, and his low voice trembled slightly, 'don't mention it. Why should I object, particularly if it's God's way?' When the Jew pronounced 'God's way' he even caught his breath slightly, and it came out with a sort of lisp. 'Your children— my children. And that, so to speak, is where we stand.'

From behind the dentist's back and beneath his arms a number of pairs of absolutely identical eyes regarded the strange visitors. Those eyes were brown with bright nuclei in them, they rolled in time with Meckler's rocking, and it is probable that never in his life before had the carefree Lyovushkin attracted so much hostility at one go.

'I'm a *dentiste*,' said Meckler, using the French word instead of Russian, and the bright nuclei in his eyes were submerged by the dark fury of the brown eyeballs, 'a *dentiste*, you understand?' And by the way he stuck out his suddenly quivering chin at a sharp angle and the way his jaw muscles jerked convulsively under his dark skin, it was clear that it gave him great pleasure to utter a word that his new neighbour did not and could not possibly have known. 'But I rather fancy, young man, that I shall be of no use to you for many years to come.'

The eyes, several pairs of eyes, rolled once more, enveloping them all in a cloud of hostility, then the door slammed and Lyovushkin wilted, sighing vaguely:

'Nobs.'

Lashkov, who was helping Ivan to drag his humble chattels into the vacated corner room with its windows overlooking the yard, had already noticed that although he was putting a bold face on things and was laughing loudly as though he couldn't care less, Lyovushkin had no sense of proprietorial ease in all this hustle and bustle, there was no satisfaction in it, no genuine joy. Every now and then his movements, his words and his laughter would betray something that he himself was as yet unaware of, a feeling of anxiousness or rather dissatisfaction.

Only later, over a half-bottle, did Ivan suddenly turn sober in the middle of their conversation and say sorrowfully:

'I s'pose I'm glad really, but there ain't no relish in it. Nope, no relish, I don't care what you say.'

Lashkov thought to himself: 'He's just coming the old soldier.'
But aloud he said:

'You'll settle down, brother. It's always the same in a new place.'

'True enough,' sighed the lad and crunched his cucumber
abstractedly, 'even your missus tastes sweeter behind a haystack,
but who would have thought . . .'

While they talked Lyuba glided soundlessly and smilingly from
table to sideboard and sideboard to table, accompanying the serving
of the food with her singsong Moscow accent:

'Eat up, eat up, please, help yourself.'

There was something sort of catlike and soothing about her.
Drawing his wife to him, Ivan lovingly stroked her firmly rounded
belly.

'Lyuba's gonna give me a lass. I love lasses. Lasses are more
obligin'. A lass, another lass and then another lass.' Here his face
suddenly darkened and he compressed his lips, and at once the
peasant in him showed: 'An' now a son as well. So he can learn to be
a *dentiste*. A son, Lyuba, so—' He fell silent and with a single
movement emptied his glass. 'Come on, my friend, pass the hooch.'

When they went outside it was already past midnight. The
summer stars, huge in the centre of the bowl but melting and
disintegrating nearer the rim, twinkled, grew sharper and more
ethereal, looking from down here on earth like warily napping
birds. From time to time one or the other of them would fly up,
startled from its place, and score the inky darkness with its fiery
wing before disappearing somewhere behind the neighbouring
rooftops. In the next yard a gramophone sobbed furiously: 'Farewell
my gipsy band, I sing for the very last time,' and a drunken tenor
vainly tried to join in: '. . . a-a-ast ti-i-ime.'

The friends sat down on the bench in the yard. All of a sudden
Ivan butted the night with his head and groaned with sweet
nostalgia:

'Back home in Lebedyani the buckwheat's in bloom. . . .'

And although Lashkov had never in his life seen buckwheat
blooming and would have been hard put to it to distinguish buckwheat from millet, his soul was infected by Lyovushkin's delicious
languor and he too sighed almost lovingly in response to the other:

'In bloom . . .'

'An' the squeezeboxes . . .'

'An' the grass smells of new milk . . .'

'New milk.'

As they talked the stars continued to fly up, setting the dark night ablaze, and fall behind the neighbouring rooftops. On and on they went, up and down.

Their talk, at first glance, was totally trivial—about the weather, about their day-to-day affairs, about this and that—but the discovery of common interests affected them deeply and it suddenly seemed to Lashkov as though he had been sitting there with Ivan for years and years already: the stars flew up, burning themselves out on their path through the sky, and fell back again, while they sat on and on; the buckwheat bloomed and withered, while they sat on and on; Lyuba, Lyuba's daughters and Lyuba's daughters' daughters gave birth to yet more daughters, while they sat on and on there, beneath the very dome of the sky, at the very centre.

'It's lonely here in town . . .'

'You'll get used to it . . .'

'Crowded . . .'

'You'll catch on.'

'Tobacco's gone to the dogs nowadays—all stalks.'

'Yep. . . .'

A moonshadow cut the wing in two and began to creep over the wall; suddenly, as if triggered off by its touch, a lantern flared in the far corner window, snatching from the darkness the almost incorporeal silhouette of old woman Shokolinist. From below she showed up with painful clarity: the quivering, toothless mouth, the frenzied hands clasped high in front of her, and even, it seemed, those gelid eyes clouded with ecstasy.

'Who's that old witch?' asked Lyovushkin hollowly, then stood up, crossed himself and started to walk away. 'Jeepers, talk about St Vitus' dance . . . I'm goin' . . . Lyuba's waitin' for me. . . .'

'She used to own the place. . . . Praying for her sins.' Lashkov also stood up. 'Okay, be seein' you. I've got an early morning tomorrow.'

He stepped into the shadow of the wing, heading for his room, and just then he had his first experience of that nagging constriction under his heart that was just like a stitch, and a silent dread entered into him, a dread that was destined to grow irrevocably into the very marrow of his being.

●

Old woman Khramov in number eleven flatly refused to be compressed voluntarily. Big and bulky and wearing a soiled housecoat, she stood in the door of the kitchen, watching Lashkov and Shtabel, the plumber, drag furniture from the dining-room into her daughter's chamber and wailing furiously:

'Our daddy'—somehow it sounded absurd and pitiful the way she said it—'our daddy was often enough down at the police station, as you know very well, Lashkov. . . . Yes, yes . . . because of his beliefs. . . . Do you think that up there,' the old woman jabbed a sclerotic finger in the direction of the ceiling, 'all that has been forgotten? . . . Do you think you can plunder the family of a famous performer? . . . And what about young Lev, where's he going to rehearse? Where, I ask you, where? And my girl? My girl's so gifted. . . . Those fingers, does nobody need those fingers? Tell me,' and she rushed at police constable Kalinin, who was standing stock still on the landing, 'do you think nobody needs them—those fingers of hers? Where's she going to do her exercises, may I ask, where? Of course, quietness isn't so very important in a public-house or, begging your pardon, a brothel. . . .'

The constable merely scowled in reply and worked his sharp, phthisical cheekbones. It was clear that he had long ago grown sick to death of this whole tiresome business and that he personally had nothing whatever to do with it and couldn't wait to get shot of it and go back to his home.

Behind him, propping up a mountain of bundles and parcels, stood two of the Tsarevs: the wife, silent and colourless, wearing a baggy grey costume and with canvas slippers on her bare feet; and her sister-in-law, a buxom lass who regarded the world sardonically through eyes that seemed to smoulder behind an outer veil.

As for Alexei Tsarev, a pock-marked young man of about thirty, he was distractedly trampling in circles around the constable, his best boots squeaking, and every now and then for some reason he would thrust his permit into the other's heavy hands and say:

'It wasn't my idea, you know. It's all the same to me where I live so long as there's a roof over my head. I'm just obeying the law.' Kalinin would wave him away gloomily and then Tsarev rushed over to his wife. 'Why is she doing it, Fenya? We've got the permit!' Fenya raised her eyes dolefully to her husband and remained silent, but he was already seeking sympathy from his sister. 'Grusha, calm her down a bit, will you, calm her down! A fine sort of housewarming this has turned out to be. . . . Citizen, we're only obeying the law. . . . Look, here's the rubber stamp. . . .'

But Mrs Khramov had no time for him. The old woman was being forced to part with something that she couldn't possibly part with, not in any circumstances, otherwise her life would lose all meaning and sense. Every now and then she stopped resignedly by the kitchen window and gazed down into the yard with dimmed eyes, then she would sally round the flat again, hauling various knick-knacks out of the dining-room: glass-holders, china ornaments, family albums, etc., and stacking them in a heap on the kitchen stove. Then, suddenly, she would turn to her son and implore him:

'Lev, my darling,' he was standing with his back to her, frowning, with a pained expression on his face, and she tugged at the tail of his jacket. 'Lev, darling! You're an *artiste*! You must go and tell them about it up there!' and again her finger soared towards the ceiling. 'In the name of your grandfather! Every article here is dear to him! . . . They haven't the right! . . . Think of Olga! . . . What will happen to her? . . . To her fingers! . . . Remember what Taneyev said about her! . . .'

She tried to catch his glance but his eyes kept slipping away from her, his eyes gazed somewhere upwards through the wall across the yard and further. At the same time the son sharply pushed her hand away and quietly, as though fearing that he might be overheard, tried to persuade her:

'Mummy, Mummy, think what you're saying. What has happened? Nothing's happened. And anyway, I'm quite prepared to sleep in the corridor. Let Olga have my room. It'll be quieter for her there. . . . Come now, Mummy, what are you doing to yourself? . . . Mummy, that's enough now!'

Mrs Khramov again subsided, only to hang on her daughter a moment later.

'Just look at those fingers!' The old woman tenderly stroked the almost ethereal hands. 'No, just come and look for yourself! Taneyev himself admired these fingers! Olga darling, you mustn't smile like that! Olga darling, come, I beg you, please don't smile like that!'

Olga did not hear her. Leaning on the doorpost of the outer door, Olga rocked slowly back and forth, with a quiet and amiable smile on her face. She was standing directly opposite Kalinin. The constable scowled and worked his phthisical cheekbones, while the girl went on smiling. Needless to say, she saw neither Kalinin nor what was behind him, for the simple reason that she lived and existed in a world where it was apparently still possible to smile quietly and amiably. Now, however, the very sight of the two of them made Lashkov uncomfortable. In the challenging contrast between them he sensed some almost frightening resemblance: the rage of one and the bliss of the other both denoted a sickness, and there was no way out for them, nowhere they could flee to to escape this cruel kinship. So they stood there, thrown together by chance, one facing the other across this single landing, while at the same time both remained locked in their separate, private worlds—and both with their own truth.

Shtabel worked with a truly German solicitude for material objects. Before picking up an article he would carefully test it to see if it could stand the strain, then he would lift it cautiously and with measured steps, as though walking on ice, carry it into the girl's room, where everything was then ranged by him in perfect symmetry. But old woman Khramov was enraged by his very assiduity.

'Who puts chairs on the table, Shtabel? Who puts chairs on the table? Your German papa? Or maybe your German uncle? That's Hamburg furniture! Your whole life's wages wouldn't be enough to pay for that table! Not even twice your wages! Or three times! And you put chairs on it.' She followed at his heels, grey with helpless rage, swaying and trying the whole time to wound him as much as she could, to find a sore spot. 'Naturally they're not the sort of things you're used to! You don't have a brass farthing to your name—not even a country. And when you pass on to the next world it'll be on a pile of dirty rags in some boiler house or other. . . . Oh, Shtabel, and I took you for a respectable person. Ah, well— you're a German, I suppose.'

Shtabel kept his mouth shut. Shtabel knew how to keep his mouth shut. Why should she, this haggard old Moscow society lady with the cotton-wool cheeks, know anything about the road that lay between him and his motherland? Having arranged the next chair precisely in its place, he took a handkerchief from his trouser pocket and thoughtfully wiped his hands with it. Then, folding the handkerchief in four, the plumber thrust it back into his pocket and only afterwards began to speak:

'I, madam,' Shtabel took the old woman by the shoulders, spun her round almost effortlessly, so that she was facing away from him, and gently but insistently propelled her away in the direction of her son's room, 'am Austrian, madam. Austrian. I haff lissened you, and now you lissen me. I no idea vot your goffernment vants, but I used obey effery goffernment. They say: "Shtabel, do this" und I do it. But I don't vant that vorking pipple conk out in boilerhouses. Forgive me, madam.' He pushed her over to a chair, turned her to face him once more, gently pressed on her shoulders and she sat down. And once sitting there she somehow subsided all at once and sagged low in the chair like a heap of melting putty. Turning back, the plumber touched young Lev on the shoulder. 'Lev, take sister your room. She mustn't stay like that. She really really mustn't.'

Lev started with fright, then suddenly bestirred himself, seized his sister by the hand and in the same quiet voice as he had used earlier to his mother, began to wheedle her:

'Let's go, Olga, you have to go now. It's time you took a rest. And besides, we're in the way here.'

Still smiling, she refused to yield to him:

'But why, Lev dear? It's early still. And there's so much sun out here. Look how much there is. You can hear it. Listen, can't you hear it? And we have those curtains. Those horrible curtains. And there are so many people out here. Are they going to live with us? What does Mummy want with them? . . . And then those curtains. Can't we take them down?'

'Yes, I'll take them down. I'll throw them out and open the windows wide. Come on, Olga. That's the way.'

The brother drew her after him and she yielded listlessly, still not ceasing to smile and still eager to talk to someone. The corridor emptied and noiselessly, without comment, the Tsarevs began to move in. As they bore the things in, Alexei and Fenya trod carefully, as though a corpse were laid out in the flat. They were somehow embarrassed by their success, and only Grusha lost no time in establishing herself as mistress in their new home, commencing to demonstrate by every detail of her appearance and behaviour that everything here had long been hers by right and that there wasn't long to wait now before justice would triumph unconditionally. She moved about briskly and noisily, peremptorily issuing orders to her wordless brother and sister-in-law:

'Come on, Fenya, move that table of theirs into the corner. Ours can go by the window. What's up with you, Alexei, has somebody clouted you across the earhole or somethin'? Move the ruddy thing. Gosh, they haven't half spread themselves. . . .'

Lashkov immediately took a liking to this buxom lass with the look of a fish-wife and the muscular, not at all womanly arms. She had about her a powerful homely aura of fresh, not yet stale sweat and of fresh new laundry. The young caretaker was about to put his arm round her in the space between the kitchen and the corridor leading to Olga's room, but all she did was shrug her shoulders, just shrug her shoulders, and then stare at him in such a way that he flushed deep red and became embarrassed. Something, nevertheless, suddenly melted and stirred inside him, and later, when

Tsarev was treating them all—Lashkov, Shtabel and the police constable—to tepid, sourish beer in a nearby bar, he couldn't help himself and said thoughtfully:

'That's some sister of yours, Alexei Mikhailich, I must say. First rate, if I might say so, quite a lass. Absolutely de luxe, in fact.'

Tsarev shifted his feet and his department store boots squeaked as he snickered into his mug:

'Well, she's got good Tsarev blood in her.'

Shtabel thought for a moment and then added in confirmation:

'A voman like that in house'—at this he raised his index finger aloft significantly and made big eyes—'O!'

Kalinin kept silent. In his condition it was a long time since girls had interested him. The constable was heartily depressed both by this wicked heatwave, with its unspringlike persistence, and the warm sour beer, and this dreary conversation that seemed as if it might never end. With stubborn concentration he listened only to his insides, or rather not his insides but his illness. Kalinin could feel it growing and spreading inside him, weaving its way in pore by pore, nerve by nerve, so that sometimes it seemed as though he could even hear its very movements—the rustling melody of creeping death. And therefore everything else in the world, in comparison with this melody, inspired in him only a black boredom that was as glutinous as molten pitch. Listlessly the constable tore off a piece of smoked fish with his almost black teeth, chewed it, drained his mug and curtly concluded the meeting:

'Home.'

That night the intoxicated Lashkov dreamed a dream.

He was walking through Sokolniki park arm-in-arm with Grusha. And the two of them were decked out in linen and crêpe-de-chine. And the trees, as though flying somewhere, hummed overhead and were hung with bright lights, and everybody turned to look back at them and smile: what a pair! Faces, faces, they were smiling after them. How many faces! And suddenly he felt scorched: all the faces, every single one of them, like peas in a pod, were identical with the face of the beatific idiot girl, Olga Khramov, from flat eleven. Lashkov wanted to shout at them, to shout out angrily and derisively. But the dream clouded over. . . .

Waking up, the caretaker thought with puzzled irritation: 'What was all that in aid of?' and then decided the question in the way most propitious to himself: 'Maybe it's to my advantage?' And finally, but not without a certain coquettish regret: 'Could be your bachelor days are comin' to an end, Lashkov.'

●

Snared in a labyrinth of washing-lines, Sima Tsigankov darted
hither and thither about the yard like a mouse in a shopping net.
A hunt was in progress, conducted by her two brothers, a nean-
derthal pair with compressed foreheads and swart locks hanging
low over bushy brows; they were hunting with such drunken
abandon that a good half of the washing already lay trampled in the
squelching mire, while Sima still somehow contrived to elude them
and every now and then attempted to make a dash for the gate.
Each time she did so, however, one or other of the brothers would
intercept her and the whole process would start all over again from
the beginning. With cold fury and in total silence the two brothers
were stalking Sima like a wild beast. All that could be heard was the
jerky wheeze of their breathing and the whining crackle of snapped
washing lines.

Lashkov knew from experience that it was better not to meddle
with the Tsigankovs. They had moved into number nine only
recently and their very first day in the yard had been marked by a
relentless, typically Vologda-style punch-up, rounded off by
ambulances and the police. The family had crippled the elderly
philologist, Valov, who lived next door, and at the same time
completely done for that uninvited champion of all underdogs,
Ivan Lyovushkin. On the next day already Stepan Tsigankov, the
father, having taken all the blame on himself, left to spend the year
in the cells prescribed by the criminal code, while the philologist,
after putting in an official application for an exchange, moved in
with Meckler. As for Ivan, he proudly paraded the yard with his
battered skull, which had been hastily bandaged for him at the
emergency ward, and indignantly complained to every passer-by:

'Now is it God's way, I ask you, to take it out on an old man in
broad daylight? That's not what we want to encourage, is it?
Conscience is what you need, eh? We're all God's creatures, but
conscience is hard to find nowadays. . . .'

Sima was as different from the other two Tsigankovs as chalk from
cheese. Slender and frail, almost a schoolgirl in her laundered blue
polka-dot cotton dress, she picked her way about the yard with eyes
lowered, as though treading on broken glass, and also as though
not really running at all, but apologising for the whole of her dis-
graceful family. It was sufficient, however, to see the way in which
all the bachelors (and married men too) used to look at her to learn
truth: Sima was a prostitute—with the face of a Botticelli angel.

Lashkov was still in the act of pulling on his jacket in order to run for the constable when somebody shouted from above:

'Hoodlums! Get your great clodhoppers off my lace! What in hell brought you to plague us in the first place! Haven't you got no common decency? And look at my lace, what about my lace, eh?'

Down in the yard the hunt was almost at an end when Lashkov arrived. Tikhon had managed to drive his sister into the corner formed by the wing and the boilerhouse. Sima fell to the ground, rolled up in a ball and covered her head with her hands. A mud-bespattered boot was already aiming for her speckled dress when the space between them was suddenly filled by the person of Lev Khramov.

'Don't you dare touch her! You ought to be ashamed to hit a woman!' He waved a pale, undersized fist under Tsigankov's nose. 'Don't go near her, I mean it!'

The whole thing looked ridiculous, of course. The bull-like Tikhon needed only to give the skinny actor a shove, let alone strike him, and an ambulance would have to be called. Tikhon stood stock still for a moment, like an elephant contemplating a rabbit: ought he to tread on it or go round? But by the time he had made up his mind to tread on it and began moving his lowering bulk forward, the heavy hand of Shtabel descended on his shoulder.

'Lissen here, friend. You see this?' Otto raised his free hand, in which was grasped a length of piping. 'You vant your pension, hit him, you not vant pension, go home.'

Gloweringly, Tikhon measured Shtabel from head to toe, as if weighing up the cost of a fight with the burly Austrian, then briefly exchanged glances with his brother; the latter nodded sullenly and they both moved off, and it wasn't until he got to the front porch that Tikhon threatened drunkenly:

'I'll pin your ears back one of these days, you German swine!'

Shtabel smiled with his eyes alone, then put his arms round the shoulders of Sima and the actor and drew them towards the boiler-house.

'Come sit vith me. You haff much to talk. Ve,' he pointed at Lashkov, 'vill haff smoke. Ve tink,' he nodded in Lashkov's direction again, 'tink very much. And talk, talk.'

Lashkov maintained a patient silence while his friend, puffing on a clay pipe, studied the darkening sky. Lashkov knew Otto Shtabel: the longer he thought, the more serious would be his words.

The caretaker had run into the Austrian accidentally at the labour exchange, where at the request of the house manager he had gone to look for an efficient plumber and stoker. Shtabel had caught his eye immediately. He was grave and painstaking—he'd think ten times before speaking once—and it was precisely this painstakingness of his that won Lashkov over. You wouldn't have thought someone was living in clover once he had to go to the labour exchange, but nevertheless Otto Shtabel, mixing German with Russian, had interrogated him meticulously and laboriously about the location (what was the transport situation?), the conditions (how many days off?), working clothes (would it be for long?) and even about the residents (what sort of people were they?). And Lashkov, ignoring all the traditions of those thin—at least where manual workers were concerned—and difficult times, praised his merchandise and tried his hardest.

The caretaker knew that the house manager would surely stand him a drink for a plumber such as this, and not only one, either. Transport? Right under your nose. Wages? You won't grumble. Special clothes? We don't go without. The residents? Angels in residents' clothing.

Not long afterwards the new plumber had taken over Lashkov's cubby-hole in the boilerhouse, while the caretaker himself moved into a room belonging to the compressed Madame Nizovtsev, a dressmaker, on the first floor of the wing.

The evening suspended its first, still tentative star over the rooftops. The star swelled and throbbed as it filled with pale twinkling blueness, and the rustle of the poplars beyond the gate blended with the sound of two voices rising from inside the boilerhouse:

'Mother's never awake. Nor those two either. And all the time it's money, money. I give them everything as it is. Goodness knows what brought us to this awful hole in the first place. They took our forge away, but what of that, there are other things in this world besides a forge. We could have managed. We were all healthy. . . . Home on the Volga it was so nice—and plenty of space. . . . "Factory, factory!—" Well, here's the factory for you! . . .'

'How horrible, how horrible! Horrible. . . . Horrible. . . . Horrible. . . . My dear, dear girl. . . . How horrible! What's behind it all, why do they do such things to us? Go on, go on.'

'It sounds horrible to you, but we have to live somehow. . . . Old people say it's for our sins.'

'But who of us ever sinned enough to deserve such punishments as these?'

'They say it's in the family.'

'Good heavens, good heavens, in what family and in what

century? Little girl, little girl, dear girl. . . . Please believe me, there is no such family and no such tribe; and no such century ever was. And even if all families in all centuries had committed the most terrible and monstrous sins, the most we should be punished with is death. But this is simply horrible!'

Then she said in a low voice:

'Shush, you mustn't. You can't pity everyone. And what about me, why did you do it? They could have thrashed you, you know. And thrashed you to death. You're so kind-hearted . . . and that's what makes you so mild. It's always the weak ones who are kind-hearted.'

'You're quite, quite wrong, my dear. It just seems that way to you. I shall always protect you.'

'Protect . . .'

'I will look after you. We'll live together. Oh, don't get me wrong. As brother and sister.'

'If that's what you really want, I shall be your slave. . . . And there's no need at all for it to be as a sister.'

'My girl, my dear, dear girl. . . .'

'Your hair's just like flax, so soft and smooth. . . .'

The poplars rustled beyond the gate and a pale blue star and two soft voices floated high over the world.

●

Sima sat on the bench, swinging her legs and eating bread and mustard heavily sprinkled with salt. To her it must have been far sweeter than the sweetest of shop-bought cakes she had ever been given, otherwise she wouldn't have been swinging her legs as she sat there on the bench in the yard or laughing so lightheartedly, with her face raised to the sun, choking on what she ate and almost gasping to get her breath back.

And it wasn't for nothing that Shtabel had been even quieter than usual that other evening. Otto didn't much care for empty or superfluous words, and so it was only when they parted that he had said to Lashkov:

'Lissen here, Vasya. Your dressmaker's got boxroom. Now tell me, Vasya, vot a dressmaker vant with boxroom? Two pipple—vun boxroom. Great. Mrs Khramov sure von't let 'em live vith her.'

Having said it he descended into the murmuring darkness and Lashkov could only shake his head after him: a strange sort of fellow. They had been talking about the dressmaker's boxroom since the previous winter. The caretaker himself had spied it out for his friend. The boxroom was so-so, not much on the whole— nine by six, but the beauty of it was that almost a third of one wall was taken up by one side of the flat's big stove. Making the boxroom fit to live in would be child's play, they were merely waiting for the summer, but then Shtabel had gone and twisted the whole thing round in his own special way. And Lashkov, when all was said and done, agreed with him.

That was why today Sima was sitting on the bench, swinging her legs and eating bread and mustard heavily sprinkled with salt, and laughing lightheartedly, with her face raised to the sun, choking on her food and almost gasping to get her breath back. A room was waiting for Sima. God knows what sort of a room you could expect to get out of an old boxroom, but then home comforts were not the point. Especially when her future quarters were being subjected to the simultaneous exertions of so many people: three Tsarevs, two Lyovushkins, Shtabel, Lashkov and now her own, her very own husband—Lev Arnoldovich Khramov. True he was merely walking round in perplexed and unnecessary circles, not knowing what to start on, but what could that possibly matter to Sima now? A room was being prepared for Sima.

In a corner of the yard, directly opposite his own window, Ivan Lyovushkin had constructed a workbench, and now a pungent aroma of fresh resin rose from the shavings that sang and streamed under his plane. And as he worked he smiled to himself over some-thing secret and personal, as though the wood was telling him the most amazing and cheerful stories. And yellow panels for Sima's happiness, one after another, formed in a line along the wall. And from the window of Lyovushkin's room came the smell of cakes to fill the whole block, and Lyuba, flushed with warmth and as a result looking suddenly prettier, kept flitting back and forth between the house and the wing; every time she passed she would exchange glances with her husband, and he would wink at her and they would smile coquettishly at one another.

Alexei Tsarev, with sleeves rolled back to the elbows, was deftly and swiftly painting the ex-boxroom the cornflower colour of spring, while his silent Fenya gazed up at her sorcerer of a husband almost with awe as the paste brush in her hand sketched out the most fantastic pretzels.

Grusha, her skirt tucked up country fashion, was raking out the last of the rubbish; when she bent over too far her calves were set gently quivering and Lashkov's heart raced and a delicious contraction took place in the region of his throat.

He and the plumber were dragging derelict furniture from the attic and giving it over into Lyovushkin's benevolent hands for repair. Lashkov kept as close as he could to Grusha. She, for her part, sort of didn't seem to notice the young fellow and sort of let it be understood that so far as she was concerned he was just like all the others, but then she did after all make a tiny distinction—a half-glance here, a slight smile there—in his favour. He felt himself in seventh heaven. The sun was flooding the yard with the light of one-hundred-carat June gold, and in his buoyant bliss everything around him seemed filled with some kind of special design.

'Lord, lord, what does a man need?' he thought. 'The smallest trifle, a mere scrap. And yet what peace of mind that scrap brings! All is provided, all is given, live!'

That evening a refined courtesy held sway at table. Each of the guests wanted to show that he too was no country bumpkin and was well aware of what was what when it came to *bon ton*, and that even if he himself wasn't all that well educated, still, he knew how to behave himself in educated company.

So they refrained from filling their glasses of red wine to the brim before emptying them, wiped their lips on ultra-clean napkins and always left just a tiny morsel of food on the edge of their plates: we don't starve round our way, you know. And to crown it all they contrived in that indescribably small space to dance to 'The Waves of the River Amur'. And before they dispersed Ivan Lyovushkin even managed a short speech.

'It should always be like this, brothers.' His voice shook a little. 'We live like wild beasts. But we're all of us people. I used to think a lot of things about my neighbour. But even dentists, it turns out, are people as well.'

Taking their leave, the guests glanced meaningfully at one another and gravely shook the young pair by the hand. Moved to tears, Lev Khramov, standing in the door, called into the darkness after them:

'Come and see us, don't forget to come and see us, we shall always be very, very pleased. Just call in any time you like. Everything here is yours!'

Lashkov invited Grusha to go for a walk with him, and she agreed and herself took his arm, and everything was exactly as in his dream: the light-strung trees of Sokolniki park hummed over-head and many people turned to look after them.

They sat on a bench in a dark avenue and Lashkov put his arms round Grusha and kissed her. And she did not resist. And patting her hair into place afterwards she declared:

'All right, but first the register office, the proper way.'

He said: 'Of course.' And then added: 'Absolutely!'

And the trees up above them floated away somewhere. Though maybe it wasn't the trees floating at all, but they themselves—Lashkov and Grusha. And that indeed is probably what it was.

●

Nikiforov moved into number seven—that's on the first floor—with Colonel Kozlov, the military specialist, late on the evening of November the seventh. The new resident wasn't very tall and was scraggy to look at, but he turned out to be a pernickety, pigheaded sort of fellow. Still on the stairs already he was breathing like a prickly young bull and rubbing his hands voluptuously in anticipa-tion of a scandal.

'We'll put paid to your little game, master general, sir.' Nikiforov was obviously putting it on when he raised the rank of his new neighbour. 'You're the cuckoo in the nest, yes, but you'll soon chirp a different tune. You've outlived your day, sucked the blood of the workers. And you, Comrade,' he nudged Kalinin, 'you can be a witness if anything happens. He won't get away with it, it's not the old regime any more.'

The constable didn't even twitch his ear. He merely squinted sideways at Nikiforov and the jaw muscles under his grey skin swelled and collapsed again.

The door was opened by the occupant himself. Despite the late hour, Kozlov was dressed not in his dressing-gown but in the meticulously pressed uniform of a military specialist, and his gleaming white moustache, kept up in the best traditions of the guards, had been provocatively waxed.

'Good evening, gen . . .' Kozlov stopped short, and then immediately extricated himself from his predicament, '. . . erally speaking we welcome guests here. I know,' he interjected as Kalinin reached for his pouch, 'you've brought me a new neighbour. How do you do, young man.' The old man bowed politely in

Nikiforov's direction. 'The inspector has already informed me. So you see, Vasily,' he shrugged his narrow shoulders, turning to Lashkov, 'you were disturbed for nothing, my friend.'

Even an expert, and one who was far more pernickety than Nikiforov, would have had difficulty in pinning down a single false note in this irreproachable manner, and yet the exaggerated politeness with which Kozlov polished every phrase and the ceremoniousness with which he accomplished every gesture—these so transparently displayed his lofty contempt and even loathing for the new neighbour that even the totally indifferent Kalinin permitted himself an ironic grin of approval.

The disheartened Nikiforov was about to fly into a huff, but the old man, lowering his white lids, cut off his splutter at its source.

'It was proposed that I vacate the dining-room. But I am an old man and an old man needs a minimum of space in which to live out his last days. Moreover, I have discharged my charwoman. Therefore, with the permission of the authorities,' here he performed a slight bow in the direction of the constable, 'I am retaining for myself only the study. The remainder is yours, together with all the furnishings . . . At my age a man needs only a few sticks.' Here Kozlov turned to Nikiforov and for the first time a mocking glint danced in his faded eyes. 'Isn't that so, young man?'

The latter was aware, it seems, of this mockery, but the prospect of taking over extra rooms, and fully furnished to boot, had a soothing effect on him:

'I came without my family for the moment, on a reconnaissance, so to speak.' He flashed a glance in his neighbour's direction as if to see what impression he had made with his knowledge of army terminology, and having assured himself that he had been correctly understood, continued further, though now Nikiforov's tone of voice was softened and conciliatory: 'Here, you may see for yourself, everything's quite above board. . . . No, please, I'd be obliged if you'd take a look for yourself.'

'Not at all, not at all, young man,' Kozlov languidly pushed aside the documents that the visitor was trying to hand him, 'do come in. And make yourself comfortable, this is *your* home now.'

The word 'your' was pronounced with such particular emphasis that they all felt suddenly somehow discomfited and it occurred to Lashkov that in any other circumstances it would have been better for Nikiforov never to have met the former colonel.

Kozlov hospitably opened the door to the dining-room and switched on the light.

'Do come in.'

And even if the new tenant had been bristling a moment ago and had rolled himself into a prickly ball again, now, at the sight of that carved dining-suite and the almost untrodden carpet on the parquet floor, everything inside him was restored to its former equilibrium and it even called forth an answering gesture of magnanimity.

'Well then,' as though as a mark of class reconciliation he extended his hand to Kozlov, 'in that case, let me wish you a happy holiday, respected citizen colonel.'

'Young man,' said the old colonel, now taunting him openly and thrusting his hands behind his back, 'I am a deeply religious man and I recognise only the Christian holidays, together with the birthday of the heir to the throne, Alexei Nikolayevich Romanov. Please excuse me.'

Making a smart left about turn in regulation fashion, Kozlov turned his back on the visitors, disappeared into his study and with a double turn of the key barricaded himself off from his future neighbour once and for all.

'Ouf, the old fox.' Having been struck dumb for a moment, Nikiforov again flew into a dudgeon and even seemed half ready to dash after the old man. 'That's only the first fart as far as your troubles are concerned, master general, you . . .'

Wearily and with hostility the constable cut him short:

'All right, quit dancing up and down. Let's go.'

Framed in the first snow and the stars, the yard seemed tiny, toylike and abandoned. Only the coloured rectangles of the windows gave warmth to the icy silence, so that the silence itself seemed coloured: each window had its own kind of silence.

The new tenant was still seething when they got to the yard:

'Well now, Comrade constable, we ought to report this, oughtn't we? That amounts to having a declared enemy at large. Today it was only me, but tomorrow he'll say it in public.'

'Yes, I suppose he will,' Kalinin lit a cigarette and inhaled furiously. 'And in public, I suppose. And now scram.'

'I don't quite get it,' Nikiforov backed away threateningly, 'a representative of the law and . . .'

'Scram, I said. And go easy on your wife—don't put it in too far the first time.'

'I . . .'

'Scram.'

This was said curtly, quietly and through clenched teeth, but even Lashkov, who had got used to the rare outbursts of their local constable, felt a stab in the pit of the stomach, and at last it flashed upon him why the latter was always so reluctant to talk about his work in a special punitive detachment during the civil war.

Nikiforov did not dare to argue, but even in the way he strode off, as though driving nails into the snow with his heels, one could sense a threat and a warning.

Lashkov sighed indistinctly:

'The old man's let himself in for something now. That one won't forget.'

The red eye of a cigarette butt described an arc in the darkness, fell into the snow and went out.

'I'd rub him out myself, of course, for talking like that,' said Kalinin, and his voice still trembled from his recent upsurge of hostility, 'but at least his sort know how to kick the bucket decently. That other one's not fit to shake hands with. . . . Oh well, so long.'

He strode off into the night—tall and bent—and the snow crunched deafeningly beneath his boots, and Lashkov's soul, perhaps for the first time in his life, was cut to the quick by the sudden thought: 'Why does everything have to be this way? For what reason?'

●

Just before the new year Kalinin knocked on the caretaker's door again. Once inside he took off his cap, leaned his chest against the stove and for a long time just coughed and retched. Then he said without turning round:

'Got a drop of something to drink?'

Emptying the glass at a gulp, he merely squinted sideways at the proffered gherkin and sat with his head bowed.

'Listen, Lashkov,' his face, peakier than usual from the frost, was now smothered in blotches, 'we're going to take in Sima Tsigankov. I've got a warrant. That family of hers has been at work.'

Lashkov waited for the catch: the Tsigankovs were not the sort to give up easy money so readily. Several times already he'd caught the brothers gloating at one another whenever they bumped into Khramov and their sister. But this he hadn't foreseen.

'Yes, but what for?' he almost shouted. 'What for?'

'Article one-five-five of the criminal code, point "a": professional

prostitution. Anyway those skunks,' and the constable banged the
table, 'have found witnesses! Actually found witnesses! Those sons
of bitches have had their whack and now they're putting the finger
on her!'

'But she's married!'

'Yes, but the point is, they're not registered.'

'Maybe she can go away for a while?'

'Pounding pavements?' He lifted his head and then lowered it
again. 'It's possible, I suppose, there's a demand everywhere.'

'Yes. . . .'

The conversation petered out. Lashkov poured himself a drink
and also downed it in a single gulp. A superhuman weight descended
on his shoulders and he could not, *would* not be the first to stand up
and go to the Khramovs' boxroom. Only a few steps lay between
them and the boxroom, but how obviously painful that distance
had suddenly become for him. Dearly would he have paid not to
have to see the Khramovs today, not to have to look them in the
eyes and talk to them. And the irrevocability of what was to come
made it still more painful and hard to bear.

Once more Kalinin's sinewy fist rose and descended forcefully onto
the oilcloth.

'Let's go.'

Their knock was answered by Sima.

'Who is it?'

'Open up, Tsigankova,' snapped the constable hollowly. 'It's me,
Kalinin. On business.'

There came the sound of whispering: anxious, hasty, in various
tones. Then, part shout and part groan, muffled by trepidation:

'Just a minute.'

The latch clicked and Sima Tsigankov, wrapped in Khramov's
overcoat, stood immobile before the untimely visitors with a look
of mournful inquiry on her face: with some it wouldn't have been
so easy, but *she* didn't need telling that early visits from police
constables had nothing to do with an excess of politeness.

'Yes?' she breathed, and then again, like an echo, repeated it:
'Yes?'

'The fact of the matter is, Serafima Tsigankov,' Kalinin for some
reason removed his cap, looked down at his boots and began to
stroke his hair, 'you will have to come along with me to the station.
I've got a warrant. That's the fact of the matter.'

'Yes?' her heart sank, and then again, no longer a question but
an affirmation: 'Yes.'

'What's the trouble, Alexander Petrovich?' Lev Khramov peered out over Sima's shoulder. He was in the act of hastily dragging a shirt over his head. 'What's the trouble?'

Sima turned to face him, took his hand in both of hers and began to stroke it as though he were ill.

'I'll be back, soon, Lev dear.' Her voice was as quiet as the grave and if her chin hadn't been trembling a little one might have thought she was absolutely calm. 'You'll see, I'll be back soon. You lie down now, you've got a rehearsal today. Just don't forget to pick up the bread . . . Don't, Lev darling, I'll go straight there and back again.'

Sima endeavoured to smile, but instead of a smile it came out as a grimace, crooked and pitiful.

Lev, however, had already lost his composure:

'But won't you explain at least what it's about, Alexander Petrovich?' he groaned, grasping at the lapels of Kalinin's greatcoat. 'What harm has she done to anyone? Do you mean to say you can arrest a person for no reason?'

'There's a reason,' Kalinin obstinately inspected the toes of his boots. 'But I'm not telling you what it is, Khramov. Go and see the investigating magistrate and find out for yourself. My job's to bring her in.'

'Then I'm not giving her to you!' Lev stepped in front of Sima and stretched out his trembling arms to either side. 'I won't give her to you and that's that, do you hear, Alexander Petrovich? My God, what's going on?—I'll find out everything!'

The constable replaced his cap, stepped back from Khramov's door and said to the caretaker in a hoarse weary voice:

'Go and call two militiamen, I'm damned if m going to get into a fight with them.'

Lashkov hung about, not wishing to contradict but not hurrying either. 'Who knows,' he thought, 'perhaps it will still come out all right in the end?'

'Get going!' repeated the policeman, but this time more harshly and insistently. 'It wasn't me who signed the papers. It's useless, Khramov,' he flung this over his shoulder at Lev, 'it's the law.'

He went out into the yard, with Khramov's frenzied yell ringing in his ears:

'Then to hell with your bloody laws! And to hell with the people who made them! To hell, hell, hell!'

When Lashkov returned, the wing was surrounded by a tight semi-circle of tenants. The fragile morning snow crunched under dozens of feet, while the soft rustle of apprehensive whisperings floated overhead.

'Oh God, oh God, nobody gives a tinker's . . . Crazy! Just when the girl's been set on her feet.'

'Ha, ha, ha. . . . Now she has to answer for her sins—if not to God then to the people's court.'

'They say her family did her the favour.'

'Swine, and no mistake about it.'

'Boy, oh boy.'

Ivan Lyovushkin circled among the other tenants, dressed only in an overcoat slung straight over his vest and with galoshes on his bare feet. The ribbons of his underpants stuck out from under his trouser-legs and trailed over the snow.

'What's goin' on, citizens? What sort o' slaughter is this? Is this God's way? We can all get together an' make a protest. We can go higher. They were livin' all quiet and snug together, they weren't interferin' with nobody. . . . What's goin' on, brothers?'

Lyuba was tugging him by the sleeve to make him go home, but he, indignant, broke away again and again began to seek support from his neighbours.

'Alex,' the carpenter fastened onto Tsarev, 'you were at the wedding. Were they interferin' with anybody? You wouldn't know they was there. You're a Party man an' you've got your rights. Protest, I say. Protest. Have a heart, Alex.'

But Alex shivered, hunched his shoulders, looked away from Lyovushkin and muttered inaudibly:

'They'll sort it out all right, Ivan, we're not living in the jungle you know. You should go home and get dressed. . . . You'll catch cold. . . .'

'A-a-ah. . . .' Lyovushkin gestured with his hand in hopeless disgust and rushed over to Shtabel. 'Shtabel, why don't you say somethin', Shtabel? You can bend pipes with your bare hands when you want to, Shtabel, an' now when you're needed you're not there. How's that, Shtabel? All they wanna do is live an' that's what they get for it, eh?'

But Shtabel kept quiet: Shtabel could bend pipes into shape, but Shtabel knew that it was just as easy for the authorities to bend him, Shtabel, into shape.

The Tsigankovs were gathered in a tight little knot away from the others. With an air of gloating triumph they gazed at the wing in anticipation of the end, while the mother, a thin, stringy peasant woman, was combing the crowd with her lacklustre, fishy eyes in search of support and screeching from time to time in a slurred voice:

'Now the bitch'll learn the bloody s-s-score in this world! No more gaddin' round bloody restaurants with all those fancy lover-boys of hers!'

Hanging about in the entrance to the vestibule was Nikiforov with a business-like expression on his face, and although not addressing anyone in particular, it was obvious he wanted to remain in the centre of attention for as long as possible as he hastily and loudly proclaimed:

'We have to cut it out. Cut it out at the root. Ease up on that sort of thing and red lights'll go up all over the district.'

Meanwhile the wing was filled with cries. While Sima got ready, Lev was kneeling and clinging to the hem of Sima's dress, stroking her legs convulsively, pressing his cheek to her hand and talking, talking, talking:

'Little girl, they're all against you . . . But I'll go, I'll go just the same. I'll tell them. I'll tell them everything. . . . I don't give a damn for their barbarous laws. You'll see, they won't dare. They won't dare! . . .'

With her free hand she was tousling his hair, while tiny little tears, one after the other, ran down her cheeks and gathered on her chin.

A militiaman tugged cautiously at Sima's sleeve.

'Enough.'

Sima shuddered, tensed her whole body as though trying to recall something that was extremely important and necessary to her, and then composed her blue, resisting lips.

'Forgive me, Lev Arnoldovich, for everything. After you, no mud will stick to me now. I'm pure now. Pure, and that means everything. But somebody,' and her face suddenly became drawn and alien and fearful, 'will be made to pay for my tears.'

Khramov dashed towards her, but the constable intercepted the actor and put a full Nelson on him, while the latter thrashed about like a landed fish, wheezing hoarsely. The two militiamen made a grab for Sima, but she slipped out of their grasp and fastened on to Kalinin.

'Don't touch him, you filthy creep, don't touch him! Beat me and take it out on me if you like, but don't you dare touch him. He's sick! You always were a rat, Kalinin, and a rat is what you still are. Don't touch him!'

They dragged Sima to the door. Sima kept resisting, but they pulled her after them, tearing her away from doorposts and window-sills, until at last they shoved her into the van brought specially to the entrance for that purpose, though even inside she continued to resist them.

The crowd gave way before the van and when it had disappeared beyond the gates closed up in a semicircle once more round Lev Khramov as he lay there in the snow. Lev was ironing the snow with his head and groaning and weeping, and his cloudy tears sank into the snow without trace.

'Sima, Sima, my little girl, what will they do to you? What will they do to you?—I love you, little girl! I love you! . . . I love her, I love her, I love her!'

He shuddered for the last time and grew still, with one arm thrust awkwardly behind his back. Shtabel silently scooped him up in his arms and carried him through the crowd, which stepped back to let him pass, to his room in the boilerhouse. And a moment later there was nobody left in the yard but the caretaker, the policeman and Ivan Lyovushkin.

'Here, take this,' Kalinin undid his pouch, took out a twenty-five-rouble note and handed it to Ivan, 'send the missus for a litre of vodka while we sit in Lashkov's place and warm ourselves up a bit.'

When he had finished speaking he was overwhelmed by a fit of hollow, persistent coughing.

●

That spring seemed to Lashkov to be possessed of some sort of special scent and special airiness and colour. Everything around him appeared extraordinarily vibrant and at the same time somehow weightless. And he saw himself from outside as unprecedentedly young and astonishingly light. And if Vasily Lashkov had been reminded—hour by hour, minute by minute—of everything that had happened to him in the past, he would not have believed it or else would have endeavoured there and then to forget it. He was filled to overflowing with an acute sense of the novelty of what was happening to him. Typhoid? Trench warfare? Starvation? Those were dreams! Night-mares on a sultry night! But even if they weren't dreams, he was ready to repeat his life thrice over for the sake of such a spring—spring, did he say?—for a day, for the sake of one such day!

Sitting opposite one another at a table in the open-air café of

Sokolniki Park, he and Grusha drank beer in smiling silence. Somewhere beyond the birch trees, thickly spattered with budding foliage, a band was sighing in waltz time for the 'distant mountains of Manchuria', while every now and then, to the accompaniment of its groaning strains, a cloud of chattering birds would soar up into the sky and dissolve in the piercing azure.

The beer foamed and bubbled and through the foam, on about the level of Lashkov's eyes, floated Grusha's two arms, looking like two great white fish. He endeavoured to touch them, but they would slip away—supple and almost ethereal. Her slightly slanting eyes glinted invitingly, dissolving in the bubbly foam into a myriad azure droplets.

Grusha pleaded with him:

'Come on now, silly-billy, don't be daft, come on, don't be daft, I say!'

Lashkov only laughed in reply and stayed silent. Anyway, what was there to say? No matter how hard he struggled he would never be able to find words to express all the things that now quickened his heart. Thirty-three—he was no longer a stripling, of course, but then she was no spring chicken either, and anyway, when it's the first time it always seems as though eternity lies ahead of you. In his case, and in hers too most likely, there had certainly been affairs in the past. But what difference did that make? The acrid smoke of satisfied desire had only lightly singed them in the past, but had still not set them on fire, perhaps precisely because they had been saving themselves for each other.

Then he led her through the trees and the trees hemmed them in closer and closer until a young birch copse suddenly cut off their path. Then Lashkov spoke to Grusha his first completely spontaneous words:

'Let's go over there,' he waved vaguely in the direction of a narrow footway through the birches, 'over there where there's open sky.'

'Silly-billy, there ain't no sky over there.'

'What if we go anyway?'

'Silly-billy, you've overdone it a bit.'

'I ain't drunk. I jus' wanna go over there. With you.'

'All right, let's go, silly-billy.'

'We'll walk an' walk so's the trees never end. We'll walk a hundred miles, right up to the sky, an' through trees all the way, all the way. . . .'

'But this is all the trees there are, silly-billy.'

They emerged in a shallow ravine, on the far side of which stretched the boundary fence of the park. Lashkov took off his new worsted jacket and spread it on the grass:

'Come on, Grusha, let's sit here for the rest o' the day, an' all night as well.'

'We'll catch cold, silly-billy.'

Nevertheless Grusha sat down and he lay beside her with his head in her lap and gazed at the sky. And suddenly it seemed as though the sky had descended so close to him that he need only stretch out his hand and he could write on it, as on steamed glass, any word of his choice. And he stretched out his hand and wrote, and it came out 'Grusha'.

'Your lap's so lovely and warm. . . . An' I can hear your heart beatin'.'

'Silly-billy.'

'No, really.'

'Silly-billy.'

'Grusha, why should we wait for a place to live? My room's big enough for the time bein', let's settle in there.'

'And when the kids come?'

'I dunno, we got stacks o' time till the kids come.'

'A year's enough. . . .'

'Grusha. . . .'

'What is it, silly-billy?'

She bent over him. And the sky disappeared. And he drowned in her eyes, and she melted in him. And the world around them ceased to exist.

Standing up, she said to him with tender indulgence:

'An' you talk about kids.' And a moment later she added sternly: 'But don't you make a fool of me—I'm a bad enemy.'

'Oh no, Grusha!'

'You all say the same to begin with.'

'Oh no, Grusha!'

'Silly-billy. . . . Get up, it's time to go home.'

'To my place?'

'To your place. . . .'

That day Grusha entered Lashkov's room for the first time. Once inside, she looked about her proprietorially and at once rolled up her sleeves:

'I dunno, you blinkin' bachelors. Up to your knees in muck and still you stick your noses in the air.'

She set to work energetically, swiftly and with gusto, but at the same time without fuss. Somehow she communicated her own firmness of purpose to the things and objects around her, and under her light touch the room gradually took on a sensible, workmanlike appearance. As she worked it was as though Grusha was also admiring herself from outside, and as though she could sense with what pleasure Lashkov watched her now, so clearly did she betray in all her movements a queenly grace. And Lashkov was truly watching her with the delicate bashfulness of a newly-wed, and smiling happily and guiltily.

That night they lay side by side and Grusha said to him, gazing thoughtfully at the ceiling:

'It's a short enough life I've lived, but if somebody dreamed it he'd wake up with grey hair. Eleven I was when I became a woman. . . . God knows what tortures I been through. . . . An' now I wants me own little nook somewhere, an' badly too, so that if you does the dirt on me I'll turn tart an' never trust a man in my life again.'

'Don't say it, Grusha.'

'I jus' wanted you to know.'

'You can stay here if you like.'

'No, let's keep to our bargain. Alex is a serious fellow, he won't stand for no shilly-shallyin'. He does what he does for my sake. So you jus' be patient a while. Back home in the village they have to wait even longer.'

'I'll be patient.'

'Silly-billy, it's not that I don't want it, it's just that it's the proper thing. We have to do things properly . . . come here, silly-billy. . . .'

A moonbeam slid round the room, from door to stove; and through the open window came a trickle of music. Lashkov used to hear it every time the Khramovs left their windows open, but whereas before it had sounded weird and incomprehensible to him, provoking only irritation and bad temper, now, inexplicably, he felt like crying, just crying, for no reason at all.

Grusha went away at dawn, leaving behind her the indestructible scent of laundry and soft echoes of nocturnal music.

●

They came in the middle of the night at the end of May. There were three of them: one with a shaven head in civvies, one a faceless taciturn major, the third a red army soldier with a vague-looking and apparently permanently sleepy face. Shaven head encompassed Lashkov's room with a rapid glance and without greeting him announced:

'We'll start with number eight, Kozlov. You'll be one of the witnesses. Can we find a second one there?'

The house had not escaped arrests even before, but usually they were made by the police and mostly by Kalinin himself. This, however, obviously had a smell of the secret police about it. The civilian stared unblinkingly into the occupant's face, and in his slightly mocking and even almost amiable expression there lurked something that suddenly made Lashkov feel tiny, insignificant and totally vulnerable, as in some miserable dugout when a shell comes whistling over.

Nikiforov needed no explanations of what was going on. With barely a glance at the visitors, he assumed a forced frown and correspondingly became all ingratiating, as a result of which he managed to somehow associate himself with what was about to take place.

'This way,' nodded Nikiforov in the direction of the corridor. 'The old boy's asleep.'

He stole a glance conspiratorially in the direction of shaven head, but the latter didn't deign to notice him as he strode straight in. The visitor had barely managed to take three steps, however, when the door to Kozlov's study was flung open and the occupant himself came out to meet him, fully dressed in his usual, tightly fitting uniform and with his trousers tucked into brilliantly polished knee-boots.

'Good evening, gentlemen,' this time the old man didn't break off and clearly accentuated every single syllable in the word 'gentlemen', giving them to understand quite unambiguously by that very act that he was fully aware of what lay before him, but for that very reason intended to make no concessions, 'I'm ready.'

It was his voice, his bitter hauteur and this ironic sense of fatality that set the tone of his arrest: the visitors became quieter and more economical in their movements and speech, working swiftly and efficiently. And every time the least need arose, the civilian took great care to address the old man politely by his full name, which in itself was intended to distinguish the ex-colonel and military specialist, in the eyes of those present, from mere ordinary mortals. And when Nikiforov, with a caustic grimace, started to examine the cover of a book he had taken out and was about to make a remark, the civilian came up to him, silently took the book out of his hand, put it back in its place and with a single, swift, scalding glance from beneath frowning brows, compelled him to retreat to the door and make himself scarce.

While they were compiling a description of the articles being confiscated and the major acquainted the witnesses with the rules of evidence, a short sharp exchange took place between the old man and shaven head, like a pistol duel:

'What shall I take with me?'

'A set of underwear.'

'Is that all?'

'What's the use of more?'

'Are you in such a hurry?'

'There's no time, colonel, no time.'

'Toilet gear?'

'As you wish.'

'Spare collars?'

'You're a serious man, colonel,' the visitor grinned heavily, 'what use is a prick to a monk?'

'That's something you can't understand, of course, young man. You're a materialist. But Russian guards officers prefer to die in clean collars.'

In two hours everything was finished. Before leaving, Kozlov slowly gazed all round the room, piece by piece, during which time his sharp Adam's apple jerked several times as though he were trying to swallow something that wouldn't go down.

Outside on the landing the civilian nodded to the major:

'Take him along. Up there,' and his eyes indicated a destination further up. 'I can manage on my own.' Then he turned to the two witnesses: 'And you come with me to number nine.'

The blood rushed to Lashkov's head and there was a hammering in his temples: 'It can't be the lunatic girl Khramov!' he thought.

Two flights. Twenty-four steps exactly. A minute's climb. But that minute threaded his brain, like cotton through a needle, with such a searing, urgent whirligig of thoughts as would have sufficed him not for one, but for a whole row of sleepless nights.

He had pitied the old soldier, of course: an inoffensive, slightly eccentric old man. The caretaker could sympathise with him, wonder at his self-control, and in the last analysis feel an active compassion for him, but the plight of an ex-colonel could never touch him in the same visceral way as the fate of the working man, Alexei Tsarev. Their calluses had the same colour and smell. They had eaten the same bread and drunk so many pints of beer together—

with a dash of smoked fish to go with it. It was on the cards that they were soon to become relatives. And so when this man in civvies just kicked carelessly at number nine with the toe of his boot, instead of knocking, Lashkov for the first time felt such a wave of choking rage well up in his throat, higher and higher, and was so seized with an almost overwhelming desire to hurl himself upon the shaven head and trample him underfoot, together with that cockiness and that superior feline smile of his, that he turned away and clutched at the banister in order to master the temptation.

Meanwhile the civilian was facing Tsarev:

'Get yourself ready, Tsarev. Somebody wants to talk to you and it's going to take a long, long time.'

Here he took far more liberties than at Kozlov's place. He rummaged noisily through the chest of drawers, leafed through books from the bookcase while still moving back and forth and tossed them onto the floor, glanced briefly into the wardrobe with offhanded disgust and then sat down opposite the tenant and chivvied him on:

'Look lively, Tsarev, we're in a hurry.'

But Tsarev, in the act of putting on his boots, somehow couldn't manage to get his foot into the opening. The boot kept stubbornly slipping out from under his foot.

Fenya, pressing herself back against the strip of wall between the two windows, was gently trembling all over, while Grusha watched her brother sternly and even, as it seemed, accusingly from beneath a blanket drawn almost to her very eyes.

Licking his dry lips from time to time, Alexei comforted his wife:

'They'll sort it all out, Fenya, they'll sort it out. The main thing is to bear up. As for me, I'll . . . soon . . . You'll see. It happens. They'll sort it out. . . .'

But from the air of concentration with which Tsarev did up the buttons on his blouse, avoiding his sister's eye, it was evident that he was comforting himself as much as his wife, and that he himself had little faith in his speedy return.

Little Seryozha, the Tsarevs' firstborn, woke up, but did not cry. He merely examined, in infant incomprehension, each of the nocturnal visitors in turn and wrinkled up his nose resentfully. His father went over to Seryozha and ruffling his hair said:

'Go to sleep, Seryozha, we'll go to the zoo on Sunday.'

The son accompanied him to the door with a glance that was stamped with suspicious questioning, the way children look at the dead—not yet comprehending but already insensibly divining the awesome mystery of what has occurred.

On his way down the stairs Tsarev turned to his friend Lashkov:

'Vasily, keep an eye on them for me, please. I'll settle up with you. Our paths are bound to cross.'

'Quit it, there won't be nothin' to settle.'

'They'll sort it all out. . . .'

'They'll sort it all out,' agreed Lashkov, but then, intercepting the mocking glance of the shaven head, again said, this time without any particular confidence: 'They'll sort it all out. . . .'

The night smelt of smoke from dying stoves and of blurred poplars. From the goods station behind some neighbouring houses came the echoing cries of the locomotives as they called to one another. The lamp over the gate snatched an island of pavement, wet from the recent rain, out of the surrounding darkness, and the whole street, from end to end, was strewn with similar islands in diminishing order of size. Shadows danced, fluttering and flickering, on their gleaming surface. A night like any other, like any other, like yesterday, the day before yesterday, or like five or ten years ago at the same time of year, but when the car's number plate, swaying jerkily, had melted into the night, Lashkov was pierced to the marrow of his being by the sense of a far more momentous and irrecoverable loss than simply that of Alexei Tsarev.

Nikiforov, still in transports over what had just happened, murmured in Lashkov's ear:

'We'll get 'em all at the root, the lot of them. Wipe 'em out. We had to fight, to spill our blood, and now their nose is out of joint. If you don't like it, my cocksparrow, here's a bullet for you.'

Lashkov began to experience difficulty in breathing. Let Nikiforov say just one more word and the caretaker, in the grip once more of his former rage, would almost certainly have trampled him underfoot. But the other fell silent, as if guessing that trouble lay in store, and Lashkov strode away into the night. From behind him, from that island of light, Nikiforov's invitation burst through the furious buzzing in his ears:

'Listen, Lashkov, why don't you drop in for a glass of tea some time! We can have a chinwag and maybe a game of lotto.'

'Skunk' thought Lashkov to himself and did not reply.

●

As Lashkov drew the door shut behind him he was engulfed in a rumbling babble of voices from the human goulash that thronged the low vaults of the Butyrka Prison reception hall. A mighty force, it seemed, was stirring this motley mass round and round within the four dirty-grey walls of this huge semi-basement, where one would have been hard put to it to make out a single intelligible word or distinguishable face. Like leaves on a pointed stick, all words were threaded on a single note, and all the faces had the same unbroken form: it seemed as if calamity itself were writhing here, caged in by iron bars and thick brick walls.

Working vigorously with his elbows, Lashkov cleared a path for Grusha and Fenya to the requisite window and they took their place in the queue. It was only here, perhaps, submerged in this sea of groaning tribulation, that the two women became fully aware of what had happened to them. And even if yesterday, or not even yesterday but an hour ago, they had still retained some slight glimmer of hope, now not a trace remained: their own loss now appeared too tiny and insignificant for it ever to occur to anyone else, apart from themselves, to care about it. Fenya somehow faded entirely in a single instant and grew even more silent and colourless, while Grusha, retiring into herself, sagged visibly and became submissive.

In front of Lashkov stood a woman in a beret and wearing a dark silk dress whose collar was edged with fine-textured lace: a buried island of severe silence in this uproarious sea of grief. There was something icon-like in her immaculate simplicity and grandeur. She surveyed the room calmly with her big prominent eyes, but their (as it seemed) forever settled imperturbability must have been charged with something that prevented other people from wanting to start a conversation with her. Only the woman beside her in the queue, a pallid pipit in a man's jacket, her frantic eyes volleying rapid glances this way and that, twittered away at her side:

'And so he got caught, the mangy devil, and I have to get by with three kids on my hands and all of them grizzling for bread, bread! And where am I going to get the damned bread from? Where, I ask you? Pulled all the veins out of me, they have. And I'm still on the young side as yet.'

Her tiny, bowed face grew tense and the veins stood out prominently on her birdlike neck, so that it was possible to think that indeed someone had taken hold of them and pulled and pulled.

The woman in the beret said in a low voice:

'What are you saying? You mustn't. It's even harder for them in there.'

But it seemed the other woman had just been waiting for a word of reply in order to give full vent to the rage that was eating away at her like rust on scrap iron:

'It doesn't mean much to you, of course! Silk dresses don't exactly amount to being at the end of your tether. And look at those lilywhite hands! Try putting yourself in my shoes and you'd soon change your tune. It's nothing special if your sort are inside—you're scrapping for what's already yours, at least, but why did mine have to go and get mixed up in it? Looking for the good life? Some hopes. . . .'

Her neighbour cut her short briefly but sharply:

'My flat is sealed. I'm sleeping with friends. So this dress is all I've got. . . . And even so, can't you forget, even in time of trouble, about who has most of what? Better in that case not to live at all.'

'With money tucked away. . . .'

'I have no money tucked away,' said the woman in the beret, spacing her words deliberately, 'I am a poet.'

'Oho,' the little woman looked her up and down uncertainly, 'what does that mean?'

'I compose verses,' explained the first woman and fell silent, and fatigue crept into her prominent eyes. 'You must excuse me.'

'Ah!' the pipit drew out the word slowly as if in disenchantment, but when the sense of these words finally got through to her she bristled again and then, her face unexpectedly darkening, she asked simply, without her former resentment:

'And can you write about—this?'

Before replying, the first woman slowly passed a hand over her face, as though removing a veil that was invisible to all the others, and only afterwards did she reply quietly and simply:

'I can.'

And there was such meditative assurance in her voice and so much inner conviction that it was at once as if she had fenced herself off from the uproar reigning all around her, and everyone in the vicinity grew silent and preoccupied, as though regarding her from some further shore.

Back at home Lashkov found a note: 'Come and see me. I've got something to tell you, Kalinin.'

The constable lived on the other side of the street, in an old wooden house with props all along the front of it. When Lashkov entered, Kalinin was pacing about the room in pumps and plus-fours and every now and then raising a two-pint enamel mug to his lips.

'Sit down.' He brought forward a chair for his visitor. 'The old man sent me this dog lard from the village, look. I'm trying to get it down. They say it helps. . . . Filthy stuff, God help me if it isn't.'

The very fact that, contrary to his usual custom, Kalinin was beating about the bush led Lashkov to expect the worst, but suddenly he made up his mind to take the bull by the horns:

'All right, Alexander Petrovich, quit hedgin'. Get it off your chest—we're not kids, you know.'

The other sat down at the table with a heavy grunt. Pushing the mug to one side and finding difficulty in marshalling the reluctant words, he began:

'You see, it's like this, Lashkov. . . . How shall I put it to you? . . .'

'Stop beatin' about the bush, Alexander Petrovich!'

'Well, someone came in here and started asking this and that about you, who you were and what you were. . . . And what connection does this man Lashkov have with the Tsarevs? I straightened him out, of course, as to what, but you know yourself that there's not much you can say to those sort of people.'

'I've got nothin' to hide. I copped a pair of bullets at Chardzhou. You should know me better than that, Alexander Petrovich!'

Kalinin wheezed gloomily:

'Stow it, Lashkov, it's not just the likes of you that go up against a wall nowadays. They don't ask in there about whether it's bullet wounds or shrapnel and how many. All they're interested in is when and where were you recruited. You know what they mean: by the "enemy". And you know *how* they ask. That's the long and the short of it.'

Lashkov suddenly recalled that memorable May night, the civilian with the shaven head and his mocking amiability that made the blood run cold, and a chill spasm of terror paralysed his spine. Swallowing hard on the bitter lump that had risen in his throat, he hoarsely asked the constable, or rather himself:

'But what about her? What will she do?'

'Well, tell her it's just till things are sorted out. . . . Will it be any better for her if they take you away? She's a smart girl, she'll understand.'

'Maybe it will just blow over?'

Kalinin even spat in his anger and stood up:

'In that case—so long. And don't ask me for advice. But when you go on your knees to them to beg a bullet in the head, just remember this conversation. That's all.'

The constable took to pacing about the room again—dry and ruffled, like a woodpecker in spring—and although he was obviously infuriated, he made an effort to restrain himself and called out after the caretaker:

'Use your brains, Vasily, I'm on your side!'

Lashkov sat on his bunk, his head clutched in his hands until late that evening. 'Oh mother, mother!' he thought, 'Why should all this happen to me? Haven't I had enough already? Haven't I earned a drop of happiness with my past sufferings? Whose way am I in?'

And many things came back to him then: old Shokolinist's nocturnal vigils, and the Khramov affair, and Tsarev's arrest, and many more things. And he was possessed by the agonising thought that there must exist some *Being*, at the touch of whose vengeful hand all semblance of peace collapsed. And Lashkov was filled with unendurable terror by the sense of his own helplessness before *Him*. He was engulfed by a wave of leaden desolation. And he sank into a bleary reverie.

'Daydreaming?' Grusha came in and switched on the light, filling the room at once with her person, the smell of laundry and her own self-confident bustle. 'Or are you sickenin' for somethin'?' She sat down with an arm around him. 'Well, what's up?'

He pushed his head into her warm lap and blubbered shrilly, like a child. She ruffled his hair.

'What is it, what is it, silly-billy? A drop too much always brings out the tears in you.' Grusha pronounced these last words without her former confidence, as if sensing that something was amiss: 'You shouldn't drink so much.'

As if gasping it out after choking he announced in a strangulated voice:

'We've gotta hang fire a bit. . . . Stay away from each other. . . .'

'What for?' she gasped. 'What d'you mean, stay away?'

Getting all muddled and hot under the collar, Lashkov told her the gist of his conversation with the constable. Grusha listened in silence, without interrupting. She stared out of the window into the night with unseeing eyes and it seemed she was paying no attention to the sense of what he said. But hardly had he stopped talking when she stood up abruptly.

'I see, Lashkov, I see, Vasily,' she rapped out crisply. 'I see. So you're lookin' out for your own skin, are you? An' what about me?' She was involuntarily repeating the question that he had asked of Kalinin. 'What will I do? You've had your way with me, an' now you wanna call it a day. And the top of the mornin' to you, I s'pose. Thanks, Vasily, but I ain't got the least intention o' hangin' fire an' waitin' for you. . . . Keep your head down if you like, but I shall go my own way.'

Grusha stepped over the threshold and Lashkov was about to hurl himself after her when she suddenly turned and scorched him with a look of bitter hatred:

'Don't come after me, Lashkov. Even if you was to crawl through the yard on your belly I wouldn't come back to you. Just look at you, red hero!'

It seemed it wasn't the door but something inside him that slammed at that instant. And fast shut. Forever.

●

Lyovushkin came stumbling into the caretaker's room barely able to stand and from the very doorway fell on his neck:

'Vasily, friend! One livin' soul at least in the whole damn box. . . . Forgive me, brother, I've just been scrappin' with Khramov. Sima got five years. . . . So that's the way it's all turned out. I can't go on, I can't go on. Here,' he struck himself under the heart with his fist, 'here's where it hurts. I'm homesick, Vasily. A co-op on the Volga has asked me to go back an' work for 'em. An' I'm going! I'm sick, Vasily, sick to death. . . . I reckon even wolves must live better'n we do. Forgive me, brother. . . . Anyway, come on, me and Khramov have got some booze. . . .'

The carpenter's clouded lacklustre eyes, heavy as lead, took on a feverish glaze, his tousled head jiggled on his shoulders and the whole of his body, as if deprived of that foundation which lay at the very heart of its being, sagged feebly and drooped.

Lashkov sighed mournfully:

'Why must you, Ivan?'

'I'm sick, old friend, sick to death!'

'An' how d'you think the rest of us feel?'

'I feel sorry for the lot of us. . . . Our souls are furring up. . . . It ain't God's way. But what can we do?'

'Well, if they're callin' you back to the Volga you might as well go. Maybe you'll feel better there. Like this you'll end up with the D.T.s afore long.'

Lyovushkin put a finger to his lips:

'S-s-sh, Vasily, that's what worries me too. . . . But then we only live once! Come on, Vasily, be a friend and keep us company.'

'Okay, let's go.'

Khramov's boxroom was in a shambles. Enthroned in solitary splendour behind a table equipped with a whole battery of heterogeneous bottles and miscellaneous snacks sat Lev Khramov himself, with his chin sunk in his hands and muttering drunkenly to himself:

'So there you are, Lev Khramov. They don't measure love by Shakespeare but according to the criminal code. They've no time, they're in a hurry. There's still too much to be changed in this world. Why should they care about you, Lev Khramov, much less about Shakespeare! You can't make porridge out of Shakespeare, or new boots. . . . And all they're interested in is something to eat. So let 'em guzzle your heart, Lev Khramov! Or even your soul. . . .'

At this point he started up to greet his visitor. 'Ah, Vasily, come in, my friend, don't be shy. It's just a little wake that Ivan and I are holding for Russia. . . . Self-service is the order of the day, pour yourself a drink.'

The three of them emptied the vodka bottle in two quick snorts and Khramov fished a red tenner out of his jacket and held it out to Ivan:

'Ivan, do me a favour, will you? I'd go myself, but I don't think I could make it . . . this empty bottle's giving me the creeps. . . .'

While Lyovushkin was turning to leave with the ten-rouble note, the actor surveyed the caretaker with the half-closed eyes of a sleeping chicken and expatiated on his relations with mankind:

'You see, Lashkov, you and I are, how shall I put it, living in the stagnant bywater of a mighty current. We are linked with its general process, we are an inalienable part of it, but the current itself flows on while we stick here and stagnate—and disintegrate. . . . Do you see what I mean, Lashkov?'

'Yes,' sighed Lashkov in assent, not understanding a single word.

'And what has doomed us to this disintegration? Sima says: sin. But then every punishment spawns a new sin, and so on to infinity. The simplest sort of geometrical progression! Do you see what I mean, Lashkov?'

'Yes,' sighed the other once more, unable to follow the sense of Khramov's words: he was trying to trap a fly with a glass and was totally absorbed in this manœuvre. 'Sure thing.'

At last the fly was caught and began to buzz frantically, storming the sides of the glass. Viciously and with a kind of sadistic thrill Lashkov thought to himself: 'Go on, round you go now, you bastard!' Exhausted, the fly kept falling and springing up again in the vain search for a way out. And again Lashkov gloated darkly, but this time aloud:

'Round you go-o-o! . . .'

'What?' Khramov was perplexed.

'I was just talkin' to meself.'

'O-oh . . . So you see, Lashkov . . . Wait a minute, what was I talking about? Oh yes! Well, in general all this philosophy's not worth a brass farthing. Sima was here and now she's gone, and that's all the philosophy you need. . . . And even if a million more Shakespeares are born, it's not the poetry writers who have right on their side, but the people who write the laws. And the people who write the laws are shallow and worthless, people who don't have passions but bodily urges, who instead of love talk about family cells. . . . Christ, what a word they dreamed up, as if we were bugs. And look who writes them! Half-baked seminarists, five-minute lawyers, lunatic inventors of perpetual-motion machines. Try asking any one of them: and what can you do? And he won't answer. Won't answer! They can't do anything. Never in the whole of their pitiful lives have they made anything with their hands. They fan the flames of the mob's most disgusting passions and the bestial roar of this mob is balm to their unsatisfied figgy self-infatuation. They say: take from the full and fill yourselves, take from the well-to-do and clothe yourselves, take from the rulers and rule. . . . And the mob takes. The mob in its hungry blindness isn't aware that this doesn't bring any more bread into the world, that clothes don't grow on trees and that power doesn't get any sweeter. Filthy, stinking, crawling Smerdyakovism has engulfed our Russia. Make way for his majesty, mister Smerdyakov. . . . Everything is permitted, everything is allowed! The Foma Fomiches have come out to make politics. Politics! Politicians! . . . But what sort of a profession is this, I ask you, what kind of a trade? If all the blood spilt on their behalf were gathered together, you'd have enough for another flood. . . . And they'll still manage to burn the world down. You'll see, Lashkov, they'll burn us down. . . . They even make up laws on the basis of their own paltry lives. They couldn't give a damn for the lessons of history. The impulse behind their laws is primitive emotionalism. If, for example, one of them's got haemorrhoids, then you can bet he will introduce some sort of special dispensation for sufferers from haemorrhoids. If he has one wife, then it goes into law: "Thou shalt have but one wife and no more." If he's soft on kids: "Bring forth, oh women, as many children as you can." If he has none—get an abortion; if he drinks—enjoy yourselves, we only live once; if he doesn't—let's all be dry, by law! And if a eunuch should turn up among our chief lawgivers, then by God they'll castrate the whole nation! Castrate them! And what do they care about some Sima Tsigankov! People for them are counted in millions. . . .'

Growing more and more sober with every word, Khramov uttered this last sentence firmly and distinctly with eyes wide open. It was as though Lev could actually see with his own eyes everything that he was predicting, and Lashkov, who till now had been staring inanely at the doomed fly, suddenly shook himself, infected by Khramov's grief. The caretaker didn't exactly understand the actor, no. The strange words, like dry leaves, whirled somewhere overhead, but the tone and mood of his companion somehow communicated itself to him and he said abruptly:

'For two years I chased counter-revolutionaries in Central Asia. Look,' he tore open the collar of his shirt and revealed two lumpy scars just above the collarbone, 'I didn't buy those. An' now it looks as if I even have to breathe by special decree. Is that right?'

The friends talked for a long time, each in his own way. There was no chance of them understanding one another, life appeared too differently to them, but united by the pain of a common doubt, they involuntarily yielded to the self-preserving instinct of mutual trust, and so each listened to the other without interrupting.

When Lyovushkin returned, Khramov was in the act of rapping his knuckles on the table and bending over to Lashkov, saying:

'The nation is perishing.'

While the other was stubbornly asserting:

'Let 'em have a taste of my kind of life an' then they can start pokin' their noses into my affairs.'

After his very first drink the heavily loaded carpenter dropped his head onto the table, blubbed like a child and struck up:

As I went a-ploughing . . .

Breaking down at the second line, he fell silent and for a space of time shuddered all over, then repeated the words again:

As I went a-ploughing . . .

Khramov stroked his head affectionately and comforted him:

'What are you crying for, Ivan Lyovushkin? What are you crying for? You're a class god. Everything is yours—and you're crying. You should be dancing for joy and singing for very bliss. The earth is yours, heaven is yours. St Isaac's cathedral too. And you're crying, Ivan Lyovushkin. Or isn't this enough for you? St Isaac's isn't enough? Take the metro as well. You're crying? The Russian peasant is crying. Before it was the knout, now it's from sheer misery. What has happened to us, Ivan Lyovushkin? What has happened?'

Lashkov poured glass after glass into himself, hardly feeling any bitterness but still not getting drunk. Only his head swelled with a leaden heaviness, while round and round in his iron-bound brain went the sluggish aching thought: 'What has really happened to us? And why are we crying?'

The fly in the glass at last collapsed, rolled over on to its back and grew still.

Lyuba started scratching at the door pleadingly, like a cat:

'Ivan, Ivan dear, come home. You'll feel awful tomorrow. Come and sleep it off, I'll get you some more tomorrow. . . . You've got children at home, take pity on them at least.'

Ivan merely mumbled unintelligibly in reply, while Khramov, still anxious to wag his tongue, attempted to excuse him:

'What's the matter, Mrs Lyovushkin, what's the matter? Surely Ivan Nikitich Lyovushkin can be allowed to hold a wake for his homeland? It's his duty, even—to be represented at the funeral of the old lady he murdered himself. . . . You'd do better to come in, Mrs Lyovushkin, and adorn our company. It's dull here without a woman. Dull and depressing. . . .'

Lashkov felt an urge for fresh air, he got up and went outside to where Lyuba was. In the darkness they collided and Lashkov involuntarily put his arms round Lyuba's shoulders, and was about to release her again after this initial confusion when she, interpreting his action in her own way, yielded completely to him and muttered submissively:

'All right, be quick. . . .'

There was something repellent in this submission and therefore, overcome by a feeling of desolation, he was only able to say to her: 'Okay, get going. He can't stand up, I'll bring him over myself.'

Lyuba went away and he dragged himself over to the flower garden in front of the wing and lay down right in the flowers, which were wet with the first dew.

Through his feverish stupor Lashkov could still hear the carpenter crawling on his hands and knees beneath his own window and groaning:

'Lyuba, salt water!'

Khramov chimed in mechanically:

'The nation is perishing!'

'Lyuba, pour me some!'

'The nation . . .'

'Salt wa-a-ater!'

And that was the last thing Lashkov heard before lapsing into unconsciousness.

●

Pressed down almost to the very housetops by the low sky, columns of birds were streaming over the town. From morn till night the day brimmed with their throaty cackle. And rustling flocks of brittle leaves whirled about the yard. Lashkov stared through the window, listening to the stealthy tread of September, and was slowly saturated, like cotton-wool in water, with a leaden indifference to the whole world. The days dragged on slowly and drearily and he killed all his free time playing cards with Shtabel, though without the least trace of enthusiasm or interest. The world slowly disintegrated before his very eyes, objects lost their individualised features and everything around him merged into a shifting chaos, in which Shtabel came to resemble the king of diamonds and a poplar leaf the ace of spades. And vice-versa.

Shuffling the cards one day the plumber complained:

'I not unnerstand vot kind of man is Rossian? Yesterday he said: "Vere my girl study music?" Today he drag out piano and sell it. . . .'

Merely in order to keep the conversation going Lashkov answered glumly:

'People need grub. You can't fill your belly with music.'

'Hands you got, head you got?'

'That girl tops the ace and the jack, brother, and she weren't no use to nobody neither winter nor summer. She needed a whole worker to herself. . . .'

'Selling thing no vay out. He sold it and now vot?'

'Well, there's still plenty of pews to go round, thank God.'

'Pews?'

'Well, the church, I mean.'

'Ayee,' Otto clucked his tongue disapprovingly, 'that's no good. Daughter of great maestro a beggar. . . . No good at all. She giff me tenner und say: "Help me, Shtabel, take piano avay." I vouldn't. I couldn't. I looked girl's eyes und I couldn't. Old voman locked up girl, but I said no.'

'And then she went and sold it anyway. And a tenner's not to be sneezed at. You slipped up there, Shtabel.'

The plumber blinked his prominent eyes angrily and tossed the pack away from him.

'Vot you are, you Rossians? Vot I vant vith tenner? I don't vant tenner! Take girl's music avay for tenner? No good, Vasily. You got good heart, Vasily, vy you talk like that? You hear how she cry?'

'Yes, I did.'

'My ears voll o' them cries. Poor girl.'

Yes, Lashkov had heard the screams of Olga Khramov, locked in by her mother, as they carried the piano away, but the sufferings of others, which in this case he saw simply as a piece of upper-class nonsense, could no longer evoke any response in him: he was too deeply immersed in his own grief. The caretaker answered Shtabel so as not to offend his friend, but the sense of the conversation barely got through to him.

He was mechanically dealing out two piles of cards for a fresh hand when a brand new Moskvich came crawling into the yard like a black beetle. Lashkov grinned ironically as he watched the car laboriously and clumsily manœuvre back and forth, trying to draw up alongside the main entrance. The extent of the yard, however, proved to be too small for its broad wings and just as one front wheel crashed into the flower garden immediately opposite Lashkov's window, the car halted and its motor died. The caretaker leapt across to the window to swear at the driver and was about to fling open the window when he was brought up short with a jerk: climbing out of the Moskvich and supported on the arm of a moderately bald and immoderately drunken brigadier came Grusha Tsarev.

Intoxicated beyond all reason and dressed in a dark crêpe-de-chine dress that had obviously belonged to somebody else, and wearing high-heeled shoes, she suddenly turned and clutched at the garden fence. And her eyes, blazing with hatred, rooted Lashkov to the spot:

'Have a good look, Vasya, make sure you get a good eyeful. You thought I'd go to the dogs, I suppose? Well, I ain't, see. I got cars to ride in now, an' chocolates to eat an' liqueurs to drink. An' it's not for the likes o' you to come sniffin' around me now. I got officers hangin' round me now, out of your class. Still, no hard feelin's. You can empty my pisspot for me from now on.' She launched into a drunken recitative, but soon her voice broke querulously and turned to a shrill screech: 'You can chew your nails up to the elbows if you like, Lashkov. You an' your poxy face, you only dreamed you ever had a girl like me. You won't get me now!'

'Miss Tsarev, Agrafena!' glancing around him apprehensively and noticeably soberer now, the brigadier began tugging her away from the fence. 'Come, what's the point of this? Such a polite girl and now suddenly all this silliness. You were the one who invited me, yet now . . . Agrafena, please. . . .'

The brigadier fussed around her like a distracted roly-poly ball, but Grusha impatiently shrugged him off, so that he retreated, and under a withering crossfire of opening shutters and windows began to look up and down with a hunted expression on his face.

Fenya Tsarev ran out, bedraggled and pathetic, and stroking Grusha's back imploringly whined in a slurred gabbling voice:

'What are you doing to yourself, Grusha? You ought to be ashamed. . . . Hold on to me, Grusha dear, let's go home. I'll make you some tea. . . . People are looking, Grusha!'

'Who cares about people!' snorted the latter, not even bothering to look at her sister-in-law. 'Do I owe 'em summ'at, or what?' Her dulled and glazed eyes swept the yard with a challenging stare. 'What are you gogglin' at, like a lot o' sad old owls? Well, let the saint among you spit on me first. . . . What about you, Nikiforov? How many more souls have you managed to sell? What about you, old mother Tsigankov? Have you learned to live with the idea of turnin' your own daughter in? Or do you still go to church, the same as to the party committee, to beg a bit o' money off 'em? And what are you chewing your gums for, you old crow? Waiting for the tsar to come back, eh, want to kick us all out without a penny again? Yes, like hell you will, you'll peg out first!'

The shutters started to slam shut again as though punctuating each separate outburst: with respect to the management of personal morals there were few supporters of publicity among the residents in the yard.

Lashkov was somehow paralysed as he stood at the window, seeming incapable of stirring from the spot or moving away from Grusha's words and eyes, and shame, hot choking shame, inexorably filled his being, so that he would have preferred the earth to open and swallow him or to die.

Shtabel touched him on the shoulder.

'No hard feelings, Vasily. I vent. I speaking to her.'

A moment later Lashkov saw the plumber emerge in the yard, go up to the military man, take hold of one of the buttons on his tunic and start to twist it round and round, at the same time earnestly assuring him of something. The latter backed away indignantly, waved his arms about and even attempted—in his turn—to squash this uninvited mediator, but with his elbow locked in Shtabel's vice-like grip, he suddenly went limp and moved uncertainly towards the car. Otto continued his incantations for a minute or so at the driver's window and then the car moved off, enveloping the plumber in clouds of blue petrol fumes as it crawled out of the yard.

The plumber gently propelled Fenya Tsarev in the direction of her flat, to which she went without resisting, then cautiously put his arm round the shoulders of the suddenly docile Grusha and led her over to the bench, where he seated her beside him. At first Grusha remained listless and impassive, listening to him; then, with obvious reluctance, she began to answer him and gradually she grew more and more interested until in the end the two of them were deep in friendly conversation.

Twilight had forsaken all corners of the yard for Lashkov's window when Shtabel rose and took Grusha's arm, and she obediently accompanied him into the boilerhouse. The caretaker strained to follow them with his eyes, still hoping in his heart of hearts that Grusha would have last minute second thoughts and turn back and go home, but she had no second thoughts and did not turn back, and Shtabel's broad back cut her off from Lashkov's view. And this time it really was for ever.

He even winced at the stab of anguish under his heart. Then, stepping back from the window, he collapsed on to his face on his bunk. From the neighbouring yard, as from another world, a high-pitched caterwauling voice sobbed over him to the accompaniment of a triple-banked concertina:

. . . Vanya sits on the stove,
Smoking an old felt boot. . . .

●

'Vasily, Vasily, open up, dear boy, Vasily!'

Old woman Khramov was drumming on Lashkov's window pane, which was coated with drifting snow. He jerked open the little ventilation trap and caught sight of his neighbour's watery face, quaking like jelly and dodging about in front of him:

'Help me, dear boy, I'll pay you for it. . . . Pay you well. I can't handle her. She has to go to hospital. They're on their way now, I rang for them. She's yelling and thrashing about. Fenya's children are there. They're yelling too. And I'm alone. . . . Help me, dear boy, I'll pay you for it. . . .'

Number eleven was in a bedlam. Olga Khramov was prancing

about the flat with her arms spread wide and calling out shrilly:

'Look, I'm a bird, I'm flying! Look how high I can fly! Keep out of my way! Go away all of you—I'm flying away.' She stumbled over the objects in the flat as if blind and things were falling and crashing all around her. 'I'm flying away. Stop banging nails into my head! It hurts! . . .'

From behind the closed door of the Tsarevs' part of the flat a conscientious accompaniment was being provided by Fenya's two children squalling a duet.

Olga did not even glance at them as they came in, but disappeared into Lev's old room and then reappeared again in the kitchen.

'Give me my sky back again, I want to fly away. . . . Oh, my God, why have you taken my sky away?' And suddenly, with no transition: 'Why is everything so still? Why has everything gone quiet?' She put her ear to an old cupboard, then to the wall, to the stove and the main door, repeating each time in anxious bewilderment: 'Not a sound! Not a sound! Not a sound! . . .'

Her mother went off in pursuit of her, trying to catch at her hand and wheedling piteously:

'Olga darling, my precious, my pet, you can have everything, everything you want. Only please, please go into your room. . . . I'll sing to you if you like, and you can go to sleep. You always used to like it when I sang to you. . . . Olga darling, look at your mother, I'm here, with you. Sweetheart, let's go to your room. . . .'

Olga kept slipping away from her and the old woman looked back helplessly at Lashkov, still unable to bring herself to resort to his help, and then again took up her refrain:

'Olga darling, my little girl, take pity on your mother, listen to me! Tomorrow, if you like, we can go to the woods. You like the woods, don't you? Olga dear, don't break my heart, go to your room. That's a clever girl. You always were a clever girl. It just comes naturally to you. . . .'

The squalling behind the Tsarevs' door reached a crescendo.

The poor idiot girl resisted capture with desperate fury. By the time Lashkov had managed to pinion her she had succeeded in scratching his neck all over, tearing the buttons from his jacket and even in biting him twice on the shoulder, but once tied by the hands and feet with bath towels, Olga soon calmed down, her face cleared, and only the snowy white foam in the corners of her mouth remained to remind them of the crisis just passed. Lashkov looked at her face, completely drained by the fit, and her deep-sunk eyes, and with every moment his inexplicable sense of anxiety grew and grew, until it crystallised finally into a thought that lit up his mind with a flash of prophetic insight: 'Oh, Lord above! There ain't nobody without his own special element. Take that element away an' all you're left with is a helpless an' savage husk.' And Lashkov suddenly understood, with almost physical force, that inner blight that had been ravaging him of late.

In the kitchen the old woman handed him a greasy five-rouble note:

'Thank you, dear boy. Heaven knows what I've done to deserve such punishment in my children! What have I done wrong?'

'To the devil with you and your five roubles!' thought Lashkov, but unexpectedly, even for himself, he took the money and on top of that even thanked her politely for it:

'Thank you. If there's anything else, just give me a shout.'

Down in the yard he bumped into Lev Khramov, who, with feverishly glittering eyes, latched on to the lapel of his jacket.

'How are things up there, Vasily? Better now?'

'She's calmed down. They'll be coming to take her in a minute.'

They sat down on the bench. Rubbing at his temples ferociously, Lev fixed his eyes on the ground and wallowed in front of Lashkov:

'I'll go, I'll go up there right away. . . . After all, she won't eat me if I go. I'm her son! Yes, I'll go on my knees and beg forgiveness. . . . Oh, Olga my darling, how are you feeling up there?' He struggled to get up, but Lashkov silently took him by the shoulders and made him sit down again.

'It's all my fault! It was because of me that Mother sold the piano. Didn't I know they had nothing to live on, couldn't I have managed to give them something? It's true I thought Mother still had a little something—but what does "thought" mean? A self-centred monster!'

'You can hardly make ends meet yourself.'

'But then I'm alone, and besides, I'm a man. Oh, how terrible it all is.'

A motor horn sounded outside the gate.

'They've come,' said Lashkov, standing up, and went to open the gate. 'All right!' he shouted and then, turning round at the threshold, called back to Khramov: 'You just sit there, friend, an' don't try anythin' on, otherwise I can see us havin' to call the ambulance a second time.'

The yard came to life. To the quickfire rattle of opening windows and shutters, a muttering round-dance rolled round the well of the yard:

'Who's that for?'

'The idiot girl's gone berserk.'

'About time they came. That piano's been deafening all of us. Time for a change.'

'But she's so quiet.'

'Quiet! For two days now our ceiling's been shaking and banging!'

'She's still so young!'

'Bad blood. Gentry. . . . Don't even have time to enjoy their youth.'

'They're bein' paid back for all that champagne.'

'God have mercy on her! Oh, the sins, what sins we all have.'

'Take all the children indoors, she might accidentally bite one of them.'

Lev sank his head between his knees, put his hands over his ears and sat there thus, rocking steadily back and forth. Then he sprang up energetically and ran into the middle of the yard.

'Shut up!' he screamed in fury. 'Do you hear me, shut up! Else I'll smash your filthy mugs in, do you hear? Just let me hear a single squeak out of any of you! Pigs, pigs, pigs! Dung worms!'

Lashkov had barely succeeded in seating him again and he was still trying to yell something when Olga was carried out of the main door. She was covered, like a corpse, with a regulation hospital sheet, and as the stretcher drew level with the bench, Lev, forgetting everything else, shudderingly stretched out a hand to his sister:

'Olga darling, what has happened to you? Olga darling, we were going to appear at concerts together.' He stumbled after the stretcher. 'And still I, still I . . . O-olga-a-a!'

But at the ambulance a tall, broad-shouldered man with fair hair interposed himself between Lev and the stretcher—to judge by his double-breasted white coat he was a doctor. Chewing on his fleshy lips, he condescendingly took the actor by a button of his cloak:

'You, my dear fellow, shouldn't really be here. You're only a hair's breadth away from the same sort of thing yourself. A maximum of quiet, please, and a minimum of emotion.'

Khramov seized hold of his hand:

'Tell me, doctor, she'll soon be home again, won't she? Heavens, I've got so much to answer for in her life.'

'Who knows, my dear fellow,' said the other, his face darkening, 'who knows? Miracles have been known before.' And as he slammed the door shut behind him he added: 'But take it easy. I'd hate to have to come back a second time. You've still got a good half of your life before you. . . . Let's go.'

Lev took a few steps in the direction of the departing ambulance, then turned and was about to wander back again when he collided with his mother, who throughout had been standing behind him. Somehow it happened automatically that he dropped his bowed head on to her shoulder and the two of them wept in wordless relief.

Watching the two Khramovs cross the yard hand in hand and disappear through the main entrance, Lashkov thought to himself: 'I s'pose I'd better get the boxroom ready for firewood again.'

●

Shtabel came into the room, banged a half-bottle on the table and without waiting to be invited sat down:

'Vasya,' his voice was firm and clear, 'I said: "no hard feelings". You didn't vant Grusha, you frightened. I no frightened. I say Grusha: "be my vife". Grusha agree. Now you taken umbrage.' He shook his head admonishingly. 'No good. You my friend. No good.'

Lashkov replied by dividing up the remains of a herring and mumbling sourly:

'There's not much left here to share any more, not much to share.'

'Lissen here, Vasya,' the plumber's hand covered his palm, 'be friends, help me build home. Vife in boilerhouse no good.'

Lashkov knew what Shtabel had come about. For a week now Otto had been bringing various visitors to the yard for consultations: one day it would be the technical adviser from the housing co-operative, another day the fire inspector and another day snoops from the co-operative. Conscientiously the visitors would measure the corner where the boilerhouse met the wall of the adjoining house, then descend to join the hospitable stoker below and emerge a short time afterwards looking noticeably more convivial. And the day before yesterday Lashkov had been given precise information by the constable: Shtabel had permission to build.

'Yes,' thought Lashkov to himself, 'that's put the kibosh on it all right! Now you can knock yet another nail in your coffin. And you will, Vasily Lashkov, you will!'

But aloud he said:

'It's not you but me I ought to take umbrage at. I won't try an' pretend to you it don't hurt here inside, but that don't come into it. When d'you reckon to make a start?'

'On day off. Cheers.'

Lashkov, getting neither taste nor cheer from it, emptied his glass in two quick gulps and said with a short sigh:

'I'll be there. . . .'

Lashkov had never seen Ivan Lyovushkin looking so solemn and serious before. Instead of digging a mere trench for foundations he appeared to be preparing himself for some long, distant and precarious journey—from which, despite his optimism, he might never return. Before picking up his spade he regarded the rest of the company with stern affection and remarked softly:

'This is sacred work we're beginning, brothers—a home. It's no laughin' matter. To make a mess of such a job is a sin. An' a heavy one.' He crossed himself. 'God be with us.'

He worked in silence, his lips compressed, and kept pace spade for spade with the stalwart plumber, while the latter merely grunted as he endeavoured not to yield an inch to the persistent carpenter. Opposite the plumber crouched Grusha, peeling potatoes. She was squatting in the boilerhouse doorway, and as he cheerfully wielded his spade his eyes lingered greedily on her lusty calves and shone with tender satisfaction. From time to time Grusha tried to cool his ardour by assuming a reproachful look, but she made no attempt to change her position and it was obvious she was enjoying this wordless exchange: thirty-eight-year-old Otto Shtabel was at that fortunate age for a man when, especially if he is strong and agreeable, he is attractive to all women from the ages of fifteen to fifty.

Lashkov was not jealous as he watched them, no, the sense of outrage had burnt itself out in him, but still he couldn't escape a feeling of some sort of loss. A loss that was big and important. It was as though he suddenly missed something that would have enabled him to put himself on the same level as all the others. And this sense of oppression did not leave him until late that evening.

At knocking-off time Ivan Lyovushkin leapt nimbly out of the trench, took a log from the firewood bunker, found two spare boards in the shed and with a few strokes of his axe and plane and three bangs of the hammer produced a table to stand before the bench in the yard—it was a sight for sore eyes to see him. And Grusha spread her hands in admiration:

'Ivan, my friend, if only those golden hands of yours . . . An' I was just wondering where we was gonna sit. I could make a real man of you, brother.'

Ivan merely guffawed good-naturedly in reply:

'God didn't forget the likes o' me. An' anyway, Grusha, a man can be clever in different ways. Some are clever at doin' an' others at explainin', and there's nothin' to choose atween 'em: this 'un does, t'other explains. And I'm a man already, 'cause here I am, look, walkin' about on my own two legs. So no offence, my dear, but you're just about wrong on every score.'

The last flickers of the dying day slid from the cooling rooftops. And quiet evening, pacific June evening, flowed into the yard and filled it with inky blackness. Faces grew more and more indistinct. Such evenings predispose to philosophical conversation, irrespective of more immediate pains and cares.

Drawing on a cigarette after the completion of their meal, Lyovushkin sighed dreamily:

'Yep, it means a lot to a man, his own home.'

'Sure does,' asseverated the plumber weightily.

Lashkov held his tongue.

'Nothing better, is there?' responded Grusha thoughtfully. 'Your own roof over your head. Not somebody else's. An' you're not beholden.'

'Mind you it's no palace I'm promisin' you,' announced Lyovushkin confidently, 'but I guarantee it'll stand a hundred years. An' that's more than you had in Vienna.'

Shtabel paused a while before answering, and when he did his voice remained evenly at its lowest register:

'Vienna nothink for me. Vienna front. Vienna prison. Civil var. Vienna nothink.'

'Don't you never get homesick?'

'No,' said Otto firmly, 'no.'

Grusha shivered and said laughingly:

'Dopes.'

'As for me, I can't help it,' said Lyovushkin sorrowfully. 'The minute I thinks of it I gets all churned up inside. Ev'rybody's so busy yellin' at ev'rybody else up here, or buzzin' about with nothing to do. . . . Just a lot of fuss, that's all it is. Back home, though, you've got peace an' quiet. An' work's a pleasure, not work at all. But here even the ground smells of rotting straw, I smelt it the other day. . . . Oh my God! I'm goin' away.'

Lashkov couldn't resist his chance and said tauntingly:

'An' what about your boy, Ivan? You said he was gonna be a *dentiste* like Meckler.'

'Meckler's Meckler. That's his affair, pokin' around in people's gobs, but my Borka's gonna learn the same trade as his dad.'

'Dopes,' shivered Grusha again, but this time without laughing.

Shtabel put his jacket round her shoulders and stood up.

'Ve go bed.'

Two dark silhouettes merged into one and dissolved in the gloom.

'I'm sick of it all,' said the carpenter and spat on the glowing tip of his cigarette.

Lashkov commiserated:

'Me too.'

'I'm clearin' out. But not back to the village. There's no place for me there any more. As soon as Shtabel's place is finished I sh'll clear out. Go on construction jobs. Go to the Crimea. By the sea. You ever seen the sea?'

'Nope, never.'

'Me neither, but I'd like to.'

'What for? It's only water.'

'You ain't the man you were, Vasily, no fun to be with any more. What are you doin' on this earth anyway? And why? Cheers.'

Ivan spat forcefully and strode away from the table.

Letting his head fall on to the table, Lashkov sat there thinking, and all his thoughts began with Lyovushkin's 'why'. The course of his recollections splintered into a myriad channels and streams that lost themselves somewhere at the very sources of his childhood.

And truly, how and why had he lived to his present thirty-four years? Where had he been going? What had he sought? Had he ever, even once in his life, tried swimming against the stream? Only once, as an adolescent, when he had left his uncle, a furrier, and gone to work at the railway depot. He had thrown up everything: warm home, a promised dowry. And became a fitter. When he picked up his tools his heart sang. He went into the army as though going to a birthday party. They sent him into the desert to chase the Basmaches.[1] The Basmach was the enemy. Beat him, crush him, show no mercy. But he managed to come face to face with the enemy only once. And this particular enemy was barely seventeen years old. And that same enemy was lying at his—Lashkov's—feet, shot through by a bullet from his—Lashkov's—carbine. And something then scorched inside him and grew cold for evermore. Dully he had gazed at the still wet beads of sweat on the young Turkmenian's hairless upper lip; and somehow, he remembered, he had been totally incapable of turning away. For a long time afterwards Lashkov had had visions of those beads of sweat. He was demobilised,

[1] The name of one of the counter-revolutionary groups that fought against the Bolsheviks in the Civil War. They operated in Central Asia. Tr.

discharged unconditionally with a deformed forearm and a leg out of joint. And some sort of nagging regret began to gnaw at his insides. In nineteen twenty-three he began to work as a caretaker. Was there no other work? There was. It was just that he happened to cross the path of some big wheel at the housing co-op, who threw him a broom and pinned a badge on his overall. 'Here, look after the yard, never despair.' No dreams—that was all finished, and no attachments either. And, then no sooner had he started to warm to his chance share of happiness than he had refused it, for fear of the consequences. And yet those consequences were worth hardly twopence. Or even less. . . .

The night rustled in Lashkov's ear: someone was wandering about the yard. A dark blob moved straight towards him and he became aware ever more clearly and distinctly of the characteristic mumbling of old woman Shokolinist:

'There's bound to be a nail or two I can snaffle, or a plank. . . . Heathens! A bit here, a bit there, I'll get it all back. . . .'

Lashkov had already known about this weakness of hers for collecting all sorts of rubbish and dragging it off home with her, but only now did he realise the full force of that passion and the ulterior motive that maintained so constant a hold over the old woman. And for some reason he at once recalled the tiny drops of sweat on the hairless lip of the young Turkmenian in his grubby cap. And for a blinding instant a frantic question blazed across his mind: 'Why, oh why couldn't we share? Why?'

●

Lashkov loved that part of the morning when the sun had not yet risen but when everything was already full of it. The sharp toots of shunting trains, the dawn chorus of birds, the clip-clop of hooves on the cobbles—all this he heard and felt with a kind of naked clarity: it was like a private dialogue between him and the world around. The street section he had to clean was only a small one, about thirty-five yards of pavement and the same of cobbled road—half an hour was more than enough to take care of it. And afterwards he would sit on his bench and literally immerse himself in the silence, and a deceptive feeling of peace would fill him to overflowing. Nothing had ever happened, it seemed, and nothing ever would. There was only—from time immemorial—this prolonged pre-dawn silence and him immersed in it.

But today, just as Lashkov had put his broom away, a tall stooping man with a beard strode into the yard, halted in the middle and gazed around him proprietorially. Judging by his motley and tattered attire he had just covered a great distance, and on foot. Leaning on a stick he stood where he was for a moment, swept the yard with his penetrating gaze and then nodded to Lashkov:

'Good day to you, Vasily Prokhorov! You haven't forgotten me, I hope?'

Lashkov even got to his feet in astonishment: Stepan Tsigankov was unmistakable, no matter how he was dressed. He had disappeared immediately after the Valov affair and for eight years seemed to have sunk without trace. True, Kalinin had once blurted out in passing that old man Tsigankov, so he had heard, had earned himself an extra stretch—and a big one—while inside, but he had never explained how, and soon they all forgot about him.

'Well, good day,' the caretaker wonderingly held out his hand. 'Forgive me, Stepan Trofimich, but you was thought dead an' buried a long time ago now. The missus even has masses said for you.'

He recognised and yet didn't recognise his neighbour. The Tsigankov blood showed in everything—in his bear-like burliness, his hastily but at the same time generously carved face, and in the spade-like power of his hand. But Stepan spoke now with uncustomary confidence and with meditative sincerity, and his eyes glowed with a quiet and steady inner light.

'I'll join you in a moment, Vasily,' he said and sat down, arranging his knapsack between his legs, 'then I mun be off. Moscow's only lodgin' for the likes o' me is the lock-up.'

'How come?'

'Wrong passport—mine's endorsed.'

'Why don't you nip in an' see the family? For the day at least. I can talk the constable round.'

'Where's the use on it? If they've already buried me, all well and good. They're well, I s'pose?'

'Yep, more or less. Only your lass . . .'

'What?'

'. . . is in the nick.'

Stepan received the news with the same steady resignation as before, as if it had all been known in advance and foreseen at the appointed time, so that it no longer seemed important. He merely clasped his hands on the top of his stick and rested his chin on them:

'Have they drawed in their horns a bit?'

'Just about. Tikhon's got married. His wife's expectin'.'

'Well, well.' Stepan wrinkled his eyes ruefully. 'So I'm to have a grandson, am I? Never mind, he kin do wi'out a grandad like me.'

'Shall I call the old lady out?'

'How is she?'

'Got very churchy nowadays.'

'An' what's this mansion doin' here then,' Stepan nodded in the direction of Shtabel's annex, which had already grown to a quarter of its height, 'on three legs?'

'The plumber's. . . . He got married.'

'Yep, that's how it goes, Vasily. They shake us all up, flummox us an' bamboozle us, an' we nat'rally lose our heads an' stampede in our blindness. Nor God nor the devil knows where we go flyin' to nor what it is we want. Then on a sudden you see ev'rythin' round you startin' up again, settlin' back in the old ways. Kids gettin' born, churches asingin', houses risin' up—everybody goes back to his own. The translation of the holy relics, so to speak, from the pub to the police station. . . . The holy men say it's allus bin that way with us: the top stays apart the same, the bottom stays apart the same. . . . An' only us that was shaken up in the first place have nowhere to go, nor country nor town. An' then another madman got astride us an' made fools of us an' disembowelled poor old mother Russia. An' all she could do was rise up in bloody revolt an' now she's normal again like a hunnerd years ago. . . .'

'But what about us?'

'You sh'ld think a bit less an' don't sit around so much in one place. How old are you? Wake up, cut yourself a good stout staff an' away with you to the Urals or the steppes.'

And it all suddenly seemed so easy to Lashkov, and so simple, that he gasped at this unexpected gift of revelation: 'Why don't you just take off and go somewhere? Even on your own, or else with Lyovushkin? There's nothing here to keep a son of a bitch like you.' But a tiny doubt plucked at this last thought of his and then a second and a third, and a minute later his erstwhile enthusiasm already struck him as a caprice.

'But where to? There's nowhere. Everywhere's exactly the same. And anyway you can't go far nowadays once they've found a job for you.'

'People out there manage to get by, don't they, an' out there you soon learn how to fend for yourself. It's only little children they scare with their "jobs". Look at me —I'm still in one piece, ain't I, nobody's eaten me.'

'So where have you been then, Stepan Trofimich?' Lashkov purposely evaded this uncomfortable theme and latched on to Tsigankov's last remark. 'Bin knocked about a bit by the look of you.'

'Yes, I bin around—and bin knocked about a bit,' responded the other vaguely, then closed his eyes, as if falling asleep, and his head began to droop. 'All sorts of things happened.' Suddenly he lifted his head once more, pierced his neighbour with a point-blank stare and rapped out abruptly: 'I took a man's life while I was there, Vasily Prokhorov.'

With this sharp confession Tsigankov seemed to be indicating that he had nothing to hide from his fellow-men and that his opposite number could come to a corresponding decision on how to regard him.

And everything that welled up in Lashkov at that moment flowed into the quiet question:

'And now what, Stepan?'

'Summer's on its way out. I'll head for where it's warm. Spend the winter in the Caucasus, or mebbe on the Black Sea.'

'How about comin' in to my place for a bite and a drop o' booze?'

'I ain't had no taste for it since that happened.'

Stepan's 'that happened' was charged with ruthful sorrow and again, just as a short while before, Lashkov was suddenly filled with a sense of the burden that this man, a complete stranger to him until a short while ago, was forced to carry with him through the world. 'I don't go without, though. I keep to the villages more, an' a man with my hands don't go hungry. Don't take umbrage, I wouldn't mind, you know that, but I'm scared. . . . They're livin' in peace and thank God for it.'

He leaned heavily on his stick, got to his feet and looked round the yard once more:

'There are times I can't believe that I ever lived here, that I got a wife an' had a forge once. It's like it never happened, like I bin a tramp, God's pilgrim, since the beginnin' o' the world. Strange!'

A force far more powerful than simple human affection thrust them into each other's arms and they embraced. And like mortally affronted children they felt, if only for a fleeting moment, that the world had become a warmer and more comfortable place.

Stepan, tall and loose-limbed, strode out on to the pavement; and, as if to escort the pilgrim on his way, the sun sailed out from behind the rooftops and splashed across his feet.

The plumber's house rose at a cracking pace, row by row, layer by layer. Moreover, to give honour where honour is due, only the best-quality firebricks were used, two and a half courses thick; and—to crown the whole enterprise—carefully pointed into the bargain.

Ivan paid occasional visits to a neighbouring building site, chatted up the tradesmen, stood in for one or two of them as chippy's or bricky's mate and lo—rejoice oh Otto Shtabel!—the plumber's residence simply soared under Lyovushkin's nimble fingers. Shtabel could only smile and shake his head in astonishment as he worked as Lyovushkin's labourer. Down below Lashkov mixed the mortar, while Lyovushkin looked down at his friend from his perch and winked, so that the swift ease with which the latter was able to master every craft was somehow communicated to his apprentices.

Lev Khramov, who had begged to be allowed to act as water carrier, now sat on the bench with his arms about his knees and was rocking delightedly to and fro in time with Ivan's movements.

'Ivan Lyovushkin,' he said suddenly, and his voice was infused with amazement and delight, 'why, Ivan Lyovushkin, that's an absolute symphony, not just work! You know, somebody should put up a monument to your hands. Really, Ivan Lyovushkin, I'm not joking, word of honour. It's as if you've got some kind of magic instruments instead of hands: all you need is to wish and they do it.'

'Well, yes,' grunted the flattered carpenter with self-satisfaction, 'an' they'll do it just like that.'

'There must be a Michelangelo somewhere inside you trying to get out, Ivan Lyovushkin, or a Cellini!'

Lyovushkin didn't understand, but realised that anyway it was some form of praise, and as a result his movements became even smoother and nimbler.

'How can we ever catch up with the foreigners!' he remarked coquettishly as he worked on. 'How can we Russians in our bark sandals compare to them in their rubber boots. All we can do is try an' make sure it don't fall down.' Grinning broadly at Grusha as she bustled about the table, he took a flying leap down from the scaffolding. 'A fag and forty winks!'

But before they had had time to seat themselves the constable and a briefcase-carrying fireman appeared on the far side of the yard, spearheaded by no less a person than Nikiforov. He was making straight for the unfinished house and as he walked—like a commander on the parade ground, one step in front of his escort—

he dug his heels into the ground. Each step he took was an omen of challenge and menace and his prickly eyes were full of determination.

'Hey,' Lashkov scratched the back of his head with sinking heart, 'look who's here.'

Shtabel rose to his feet, went to meet the visitors and barred the way to the building:

'At your service.'

Lyovushkin gently nudged the shocked and apprehensive Grusha to one side and also emerged from behind the table.

'What's this vulture up to now? Everything's in order here. You can't trip us up.'

Nikiforov barely measured the plumber from head to foot from the corner of one eye before turning to address the constable and fireman by turns, as though these were the only persons present who were worthy of his attention:

'I measured it myself last night, it's six metres exactly. A whole metre more than in the permit. Intentionally too—social irresponsibility. They're all out to grab something over the odds and to hell with the rest of us. Look at me, for instance. I want to build a shed—you know, for my bits and pieces, but how can I put it next to a cesspool?'

He got out his complaint in a single breath and only afterwards did he acknowledge Shtabel's pugnacious stance with a challenging look of triumph.

In dead silence the pallid fireman, his wobbly legs slapping loosely inside oversized leatheroid boots like pestles in mortars, opened his pancake-shaped little briefcase, took out a steel tape and painstakingly measured the front extent of the foundations.

'Six metres!' he said in an unexpectedly deep voice. 'Six exactly.'

Lashkov saw the oxlike neck of the plumber swell with blood and his massive fists, glinting with rust, bunch and tighten. The caretaker was already on the point of dashing forward to restrain his friend when, all of a sudden, Otto's shoulders sagged and he went all limp; hanging his head low and turning clumsily, he stumbled off dejectedly towards the boilerhouse.

Ivan emitted a long-drawn-out groan, butted the air with his head and advanced on Nikiforov:

'A plague, that's what you are, a plague,' he gasped out, choking with anger, and tears trickled down his dusty cheeks, scoring them with light furrows, 'havin' the time of your life, aintcha, and yet nothin' ever happens to you. Just what sort of filthy animal spawned you, I'd like to know, an' what scabby dog fathered a mongrel like you? Here, let me just spit at you an' I hope you drops dead, you dirty skunk! Who asked you to come and spoil our lives?'

The carpenter seized him by the front of his collar, Nikiforov waved his arms about helplessly, trying to get away, and there is no knowing how it would have ended had not Kalinin thrust an arm between them and separated them.

'Enough. Sit down, Lyovushkin, and cool off. And you,' he went up close to Nikiforov and stared him in the face, 'you clear off home. We can manage here without you now. And I won't answer for the safety of your hide.'

Nikiforov stayed on a little longer for the sake of prestige, hanging around and shifting his spiteful eyes from one to the other of them, but it was clear that the memory of Kalinin's harsh temper was still sharp in his mind and he was careful not to cross him. Nevertheless, he couldn't resist a last parting shot:

'Have you ever seen the inside of a prison cell, Lyovushkin? I've got witnesses. And I've done my bit for the Party. We can't let the mob go on the rampage. You there,' he jabbed a finger in the fireman's direction, 'you can be a witness. He grabbed me by the collar!'

The bewildered fireman blinked his rabbity eyes and kept turning to the constable in search of support, repeatedly lisping in various tones:

'Alexander Petrovich! Eh, Alexander Petrovich! Oh, Alexander Petrovich!'

'Ah!' frowned the constable in reply and abruptly turned his back on Nikiforov, as if to exclude him once and for all from the general conversation. 'Now look, boys,' he threw his pouch on to the table and sat down, 'you'll have to pull it down in any case. It's against the fire regulations. There's no point in getting on your high horse about it. The mortar's fresh, all you have to do is dismantle one wall—a day's work. And as for that whipper-snapper, I'll see he gets a rocket where it's needed.'

'Alexander Petrovich,' Ivan flew off the handle, 'it ain't just a question of one wall! There ain't no joy in it no more. As if somebody'd plastered crap over the whole damn thing.' He groaned in desperation, gave a dismissive wave with his hand and approached Lashkov. 'Be a pal, Vasya. Give us a fiver.'

Lashkov groped in his pocket and fished out a handful of copper and silver that came to somewhere in the region of three roubles:

'Here, this is all I've got. But maybe you better hadn't, eh Ivan?

Drinkin' yourself under the table again. . . . You're the man we all rely on.'

'I'm gonna drink my fill! And till I'm right under the table!' Ivan scooped up the money and rose. 'D'you think that stinkin' louse is gonna let Shtabel live in peace? Next thing he'll dream up is a piss-house in the yard, and then shall we knock it all down again? Lyovushkin ain't your man for that sort of work.'

'Wait,' the constable restrained the carpenter, unbuttoned his leather pouch, took out a fiver and placed it on the table. 'You'll only poison yourself if you try it on three, you'll end up pushin' up daisies. Take it, here, take it, I know, I can trust you. But take my advice and take the stuff home with you. It's safer.'

Lyovushkin made an indeterminate gesture, something halfway between 'I know what the score is' and 'here today, gone tomorrow', and disappeared through the gate.

The constable grinned after him with gloomy commiseration and then added briskly:

'Right, Lashkov. While Shtabel's getting over it you can make a start. I'll come and help you in a little while. We'll have that wall as good as new in a day or two. . . . Let's go, Konstantin Ivanovich,' he nodded to the wordless fireman. 'Inform your bosses that everything's okay.'

That evening Lyuba came running in to Lashkov.

'Come quick, he's calling you. What am I to do with him, I'm at my wit's end. He's got it fixed in his head that he's going away. He's even packed all his things in a trunk. Heavens! He'll go to the dogs! Turn into a drunkard. And what about me with two kids? Borka has to go to school now. I don't know what to do with him, I really don't. See what you can do, Vasya. He likes you, he'll listen to you. The only human being around is Vasya, he says. . . .'

The carpenter was waiting for him, ready dressed for the road. He was perched on the edge of his trunk, with his knapsack and case of tools at his feet.

'Sit down, Vasily Prokhorich,' he invited him ceremoniously, nodding in the direction of a freshly broached half-pint bottle on the table. 'What I've got to say to you won't take long.' Judging by his behaviour, Ivan, although he had been drinking, had kept it within reason and his intentions were evidently serious. 'Let's have just a quick snort to see me off an' then never again. It's better, they say, to travel sober.'

'Ivan, love,' wailed Lyuba in a nasal twang, 'forget about it, think of the children. What am I to do with them alone? What's got into you? Haven't I been good to you in some way? Ivan!'

It was as though Lyovushkin didn't hear his wife, as though she weren't in the room at all. Earnestly sniffing at an onion as he spoke, he thoroughly explained the situation to his friend:

'It's my kid I'm worried about, Vasily, about Borka. It's time for him to go to school, but I shouldn't like him led astray. Maybe you'd do me the favour, keep an eye on him, see he's all right, eh? If anythin' comes up, just stick the blighter across your knee. It don't hurt, do it? Just see what that Fenya's lad did, the little son-of-a-bitch, just ran off, an' he still ain't back yet. Be a pal, eh?'

'I'll do it with pleasure, of course,' Lashkov tried to cool the carpenter down, 'but mebbe it won't come to that, mebbe it's best to sleep on it! Things'll look different in the mornin'.'

'Vasily Prokhorich!' said the carpenter sternly, then stood up and strained forward like a roused steed. 'Here I am openin' my heart to you, the best pal I've got, an' all you do is hand me a tit like I'm some baby calf or somethin'. Now is it God's way, I ask you?'

It became clear to Lashkov that Lyovushkin had no intention of going back on his decision and so, anxious to get away from Lyuba's almost slavish grovelling, he said:

'I'll take him to Shtabel an' get him to keep an eye on him. Shtabel could teach a cockerel to play the squeezebox, as you know yourself. An' I won't be far away either.'

'Mm, yes,' said the carpenter with thoughtful satisfaction and picked up his bag, 'now my mind's at ease again. . . . Well, see me out, brother, as far as the gate. So long, wife! Don't be in a rush to bury me. I'll go when my time's up. Anyway, I'll be back soon. With presents.'

'Ivan, Ivan my love,' wailed Lyuba, 'don't forget us, don't abandon us, breadwinner!'

But Ivan at once cut her short:

'Enough, don't drag after me, we must say our goodbyes at home.'

He lightly embraced her and immediately pushed her away again.

'Enough,' Ivan went to the curtain behind which his two boys were sleeping, peeped behind it and then pulled it shut again. 'Don't spoil 'em with sweets—it'll give 'em scrofula. Let's go, Vasily Prohkorich!'

At the gate Lyovushkin hoisted his knapsack on to his back and held out a hand to the caretaker:

'All the best, Vasily Prokhovich, an' the same to Shtabel—say I couldn't stand it no more an' just took off. An' tell him he might as well piss off home as well. This promised land'll never be worth a . . .'

He swore obscenely and disappeared into the night, but when Lashkov turned to go inside, the darkness called back to him with Lyovushkin's voice:

'An' another thing, brother, I know all about you an' my Lyuba, aha!'

●

During the first few days there was no distinctive colour or smell to the war. Nothing, it seemed, would disturb life's regular rhythm, it was merely that gestures grew more restrained, words grew quieter and clothing darker. But by the end of the week a crack appeared in the yard's calm. Mrs Tsigankov in number nine suddenly let out a howl of anguish: both her sons were being mobilised, Tikhon and Semyon.

And at once doors and windows started to explode, like the steady popping of corks:

'Will they take 'em?'

'Yep.'

'The married one too?'

'The pair of 'em.'

'The women folk are in for a rough time.'

'It'll be the same for everybody.'

'They say it'll soon be over.'

'"They say!" Polotsk has surrendered!'

'Out of strategic considerations.'

'They'll be considering Moscow before long.'

'Anybody'd think they was bein' buried the way she's yellin' her head off!'

'Wait till yours goes and then we'll hear a thing or two.'

'Mine's got an exemption.'

'What, doesn't his fat face fit on the picture, or something?'

'He's got sclerosis.'

'Ha-ha, what from then?'

'He got in a draught after a bath, really!'

'Monsters! Haven't you got no shame? Poor people here are in trouble and all you can do is kick up a rumpus.'

'You started swearing at them yourself.'

'It's all they remember nowadays, who swore at who. . . .'

Army call-up doesn't give you much time. Within an hour the Tsigankov family, in full force and with a deal of wailing and bawling, had tumbled out into the yard. The brothers were noticeably tipsy and both in a filthy temper. Tikhon had hardly emerged from the main door when he immediately set his sights on Shtabel's house; precariously, as though stepping from one boggy hummock to another, he made his way across the full width of the yard towards it. Stopping outside the door, he spread his legs apart and after swearing till the air turned blue began:

'All right, you German swine, are you ready for your turn now? Let our lads at the front in for a bit of bloodletting, have you, in return for our hospitality? Yes, well we'll let so much of yours now that you can start up as a dyer. For a hundred years the peasants will be going round in red drawers from now on. Open your trap just once and I'll knock your teeth down your throat!'

Shtabel's door opened and Shtabel himself appeared on the threshold with the inevitable pipe clenched between his teeth:

'I lissen you.' He stood before Tikhon with his hands thrust deep into his trouser pockets and taking short sharp puffs on his pipe. 'Go on.'

'Herr Hitler wanted to know how you were getting on and how much you were selling Russia for.' Tsigankov was about to lose heart, but hearing his brother's breathing behind him again flew into a rage. 'Half a hundredweight a rouble, maybe? Or is it more? I'll make you a complete bill out afterwards.' He practically fell on the plumber with the whole of his huge bulk, but at once sagged ponderously and hung on the latter, with his wrists propped on Shtabel's arms. 'A-a-ah!'

Now their heads were almost touching and the plumber ground out his hatred straight into Tikhon's face.

'Lissen here, Tsigankoff. You had forge, me nothink. You kill pipple vith sawn-off shot gun, I fight for Rossia. You grabber, I vorker. Who Hitler? Me Hitler? No, you Hitler.' He let go of Tsigankov and again thrust his hands deep into his pockets, still sucking rapidly on his dying pipe. 'Leaff me alone.'

Tikhon's wife, her face still covered in tawny spots from the birth of her baby, plucked at her husband's sleeve:

'Stop it, Tikhon dear, forget it. They're all in it together, the crooks, and just looking for a chance to get rid of us. Look at 'em all coming out.'

She flashed a glance full of hatred at Grusha, who was standing behind the plumber's back, but Grusha didn't bat an eyelid: she knew that her Otto could stick up for himself.

The Tsigankov progeny set up a weird unearthly caterwauling and Tikhon, with both women clinging to him like pugdogs to an elephant, still raging and cursing, made his way over to the gate. In this manner they trundled out of the yard in a cloud of oaths and expletives.

On the day when the first newspaper crosses emblazoned the window panes Meckler's eldest son, Misha, knocked on Lashkov's door:

'Daddy wants you to come.' The lad's tawny eyes regarded the caretaker with unchildlike severity and sorrow. 'Daddy's been called up.'

The Mecklers were sitting in silence round a table that had just been laid for a meal. Nobody was eating anything and all had their eyes fixed on the head of the family, who in turn was gazing back at them. There was something oppressive, but at the same time also solemn, in this eloquent silence. From time to time a pair of them would exchange a few brief words, expressing but the kernel of an idea, and then the silence would descend again.

A chair was vacated and offered to Lashkov. He sat down. And the master himself poured him a glass of vodka and proffered a snack to go with it:

'As you see, Vasily, I won't have to make your false teeth after all. Now I shall be doing the opposite. Still, think how much work I shall have afterwards.' Meckler attempted to joke, but his jokes had the smell of the grave about them. 'So much work! Then Misha will get his bike at last, and Maya her doll that goes to sleep.'

Any words of sympathy in this room would have been superfluous and even hollow, but etiquette demanded something:

'They say our boys have crossed the Rumanian frontier. Who knows, Mr Meckler, maybe it'll all be over before you get there.'

'I'd wish your children the same, Vasily,' Meckler's eyes brightened ironically and became quite yellow, 'but there are so many roads to happiness.'

Lashkov was poured another glass, but this time he drank alone and the caretaker realised that in this silence he was an accidental visitor here on sufferance, and that it would be better for him to retire and leave them alone with their grief.

He quickly drank up:

'Thank you for your hospitality, Mr Meckler. If you need me for anything, I'd be glad to be of help. Just tell your wife to give me a call.'

'Good luck to you, Vasily!' said Meckler senior, and several pairs of identical eyes were lowered in tacit agreement.

Lashkov made his way out in deep and prolonged silence.

That night Lashkov was woken by the constable:

'Get up!' Kalinin was unusually agitated. 'We've got to get over to Shtabel's, quick!'

'What's up now?' wondered Lashkov to himself as he dressed. 'Have they bin robbed? Or has Grusha bin up to somethin'? You never know with her. Spends all day down at that junk market and now this, oh my god!'

A yellow rectangle of light from Shtabel's wide-open door was slicing through the darkness and lit up the front end of a battered jeep. The head of the driver, a soldier, sleepily nodded over the wheel.

Shtabel, his face still crumpled with sleep, was painfully poring over some document, while a young stripling of a lieutenant, who had yet to have his first shave, hovered impatiently on the threshold.

'We still have two more places to go to, Comrade Shtabel,' the cub lieutenant said in an impressively deep voice, and every now and then he checked his wrist watch, with its metal bracelet, against Shtabel's pendulum clock, or else coughed importantly into his hand. In general he was trying with all his main to look as businesslike as possible: 'It's all official, an order's an order. It's up to you and me to knuckle under. Anyway it's only a temporary measure and doesn't affect your civil rights.'

The plumber wasn't listening to him. He was wrinkling his forehead with the strain, striving to make sense of what lay before him and muttering under his breath:

'I fight for Soviet power . . . I haff vound . . . Kherson . . . Uralsk . . . Vy I to blame for Hitler? Vy I must leaff vife and home?'

'Your wife,' said the lieutenant in an attempt to break into his thoughts, 'has a choice: she can either go with you or wait for you here. You can inform her of this from your appointed domicile.'

At the mention of his wife Shtabel bristled:

'No! She go village haff baby. No need vorry her. Vat for? I vant healthy baby.' He jumped up and feverishly started throwing his things together. 'Vat can I take vith me?'

'Only essentials. It's a temporary measure. For the sake of your own security. You'll soon be back.'

'Yes, yes,' answered the plumber mechanically, as though trying to recall just where those 'essentials' could be and what, if anything, the word meant. He moved clumsily about the room, picking up first one thing and then another. But then suddenly he gave up in disgust. 'I take nothink vith. I vent so.'

'As you wish,' the cub lieutenant started up with alacrity and stood back for Shtabel to leave first. 'It's simply a brief military requirement.'

Seating himself in the jeep, Shtabel said to Lashkov:

'Vasya, say Grusha I soon, very soon, be home. Grusha mustn't vorry. I write letter very soon.'

Casting a glance over the suspiciously silent yard the cub lieutenant turned and confidentially, as though speaking to the only other man sufficiently initiated into the mystery of mysteries of state policy to understand him, advised the constable:

'In the eventuality of gossip you may inform the populace accordingly.'

'U-u-uhuh!' Kalinin made an indeterminate gesture with his hand. 'Sod it.'

The cub lieutenant's eyes floated off into the night and soon the winker of the jeep removing Otto Shtabel, the plumber, could be seen signalling at some not far distant corner.

'Alexander Petrovich?' was all the thunderstruck caretaker could think of to say.

'It's a government order,' responded the latter curtly. 'Persons of German extraction must be deported to fixed areas of residence.'

'But he's an Austrian, Alexander Petrovich, an Austrian, and Austrian is what he's got in his passport.'

'It all amounts to the same thing, Lashkov. Hitler's an Austrian too. . . . Anyway the whole thing's a fucking mess, of course.' Kalinin's face was difficult to make out in the darkness, but the policeman's fierce resentment could be guessed at from his loud and jerky breathing. 'Here, take these and give them to Grusha. Nothing's been touched.'

He abruptly shoved the keys of Shtabel's house into Lashkov's hand and for the nth time they separated into the night.

●

The constable sat by the white-hot stove in the caretaker's room, warming his cold blue hands and hoarsely thinking aloud:

'We can't catch the so-and-so with our bare hands. And anyway, who the devil knows whether Fenya was dreaming or not? People have dreamt worse on an empty stomach. Should we call the detectives in? But what if Tsigankov doesn't show up again, even if it was him the first time; surely he won't come back to the same place? That means we shall make mugs of ourselves, Lashkov. And that's the score. Wherever we've looked there hasn't been a trace of him anywhere. The two of us will have to try it on our own. . . . Can you use a weapon?'

'I didn't earn me medal with a popgun.'

'You can have this pistol. And some bullets. But it's only for an emergency. He has to be taken alive. Otherwise we'll never get the coupons back. And we might as well go whistle for his cronies. So that's that.'

But no matter how much Kalinin strove to get worked up about it, and no matter how much he fidgeted on his stool in forced indignation, Lashkov detected an inner disquiet in the constable. It showed itself not only in the way he was coughing more than usual, but also in the way he kept nervously and abruptly cracking his finger joints, and also in the way the thoughtful pauses between his sentences gradually lengthened. All this betokened, somewhere at the back of it all, a tiny worm of doubt. And the constable wasn't so much speaking as conducting an interrogation with himself.

Meanwhile the business was pretty clear. The day before yesterday the house manager's office had been broken into and about three hundred bread and ration coupons stolen. In actual fact this was entirely a matter for the special branch and Kalinin could easily have washed his hands of it, but that morning Fenya Tsarev had sworn she saw Semyon Tsigankov at the Preobrazhensky Market, and that before that, about a week previously, when going upstairs to hang out her washing, she had bumped into old woman Tsigankov on the attic landing, and the old woman had been carrying what looked like a basket of laundry but with a teapot spout sticking out of it. What is more, the Tsigankovs' new neighbour, a teacher called Miss Khlebnikov, had happened to remark one day that her neighbours seemed to be living pretty well considering it was wartime.

The constable had been informed last autumn already that a search had been instituted for the deserter, Semyon Tsigankov. And now by combining information known only to himself, Kalinin, entirely on his own responsibility, had established a connexion between these at first glance completely disparate facts and was preparing to do battle. Way back at the time of Sima's arrest the constable had vowed to rid his territory of this family, but now, when he knew for certain that he had one of the Tsigankovs in a trap, he was frowning with vexation and steadily lengthening the thoughtful pauses between his sentences.

'I've given all my own boys a going over. . . . Beat 'em up, even. . . . "Fish", "Dragon", "Boxer", "Merkula", "Serge" . . . I know 'em well: if they were in on the game somebody would have split by now. . . . There's nobody else, it must be him. But I want the pleasure of meeting him face to face. And I will. But it must be alive, alive. . . .'

He stood up and reached for his overcoat, but even as he put it on he still seemed to be deep in thought and even paused for a moment with his coat half on. Then his cheeks bulged with resolution and he took hold of the door:

'So this is what we'll do then, Lashkov. You block the roof of twenty-seven and I'll drive him towards you from here.' Nevertheless the constable turned yet again on the threshold and again halted in indecision. 'Or should we forget the whole thing, Lashkov? And let the detectives sort it out. Why should we hunt him down, like an animal?'

But these last words floated back from the passage already: Kalinin could no longer overcome the temptation to return to the fray.

In the yard they split up and Lashkov, experiencing an icy shiver as he felt the chill of the cold pistol butt in the pocket of his padded jacket, made off for the next house. The roofs of the two houses met and thus provided a convenient refuge, in all respects, for anyone having a temporary disagreement with justice.

Lashkov climbed up to the attic and waited. Outside, beyond the panes of the dormer window and beneath a low January sky, the city lay stretched out. It was difficult to believe that somewhere down below, beneath that chaotically dark agglomeration of tin roofs, there lurked something called life. And Lashkov thought of how he, living in his own yard and never going anywhere, had none the less seen a great many things that he had never suspected before. People were born and died, people were taken away by other people who were just like themselves, people fell in love and went mad. And all this had happened in his presence, before his very eyes. But then there was a lot more that even he didn't see. For people endeavoured to spend the major part of their lives either alone or with their nearest and dearest. And it came out that not even five lives would have been sufficient for Lashkov to know all there was to know about even one single yard. And how many there were, how many such yards in the city, in the country, in the whole world! And yet for all those yards there was but one sky. And was it really so difficult for everyone together just once to look up at the same time and then feel, just as he, Lashkov, was doing right now, a piercing sense of yearning for a kind word and a kindred spirit?

His last thought was interrupted by an abrupt sharp cry:

'Ha-a-alt!'

And at once he heard the clatter of hobnailed boots pounding on the next-door roof.

Releasing the safety catch, Lashkov leapt out of the attic, rested one foot on the iron gutter and fired a warning shot. From lack of practice he felt a sharp jolt in his shoulder and his hand went all stiff and numb, with pins and needles running through it. The roof went quiet a moment, but only for a moment, then the sound of boots again shattered the silence and a dim silhouette began to move towards Lashkov. He fired again and thought: 'Where's the bugger think he's going?'

'Halt, or I'll shoot!' Kalinin's hoarse command scattered into a thousand fragments and dissolved in the frosty air.

The irregular clattering stopped, the fugitive's steps took on a brittle distinctness: one, two, three, four. . . . And suddenly a sharp sound, half-cry and half-moan, floated up from beyond the iron ridge, as though a man were gasping with horror, and immediately afterwards there came from the same direction, from below, the sound of a great smack, like a resounding slap in the face.

Lashkov suddenly felt sick and empty inside. He knew in an instant what had happened. These two houses were joined by a single drainpipe to a third house at the back, which faced out on to a street that ran parallel with theirs. True there was a five-foot gap, perhaps even a little more. The local kids used to compete at jumping over and back again, but only in summer; in winter this was sure to be the performer's last trick. This was well known both to Lashkov and the constable and so neither of them had taken it into consideration. It had seemed like a good enough straw to Tsigankov only because of his fear. But, like all such straws, it had failed to save him. And so when they met where the two roofs joined, no explanations were necessary.

Down in the yard Kalinin said to Lashkov without emotion:

'Run to the station and tell them to send a specialist and an ambulance. In the meantime I'll warm myself up at your place. It feels a bit chilly to me.'

Having said it he walked off, and somehow his walk was passing strange—like a shadow, unsteady and jerky at the same time.

Lashkov returned about fifteen minutes later, but the moment he crossed the threshold he froze and stopped short in mid-word, and he could feel the tips of his fingers turning to ice, and a viscid nausea welled up in his throat.

The constable looked as though he were asleep, or listening to something with his ear pressed to the table. But from the way his arms hung limply beside his knees, from the shapelessness of his lips and that particular kind of silence in the room that always goes hand in hand with death, it was easy to guess what had happened. A thin purple trickle from the temple had formed a tiny pool beside his dislodged cap and already stained the nap.

The expression on Kalinin's face was gentle and slightly puzzled, as though at the moment that had separated him forever from this life he had had time to be surprised at how easy and simple it all was.

●

Lev Khramov was lying back with pillows surrounding him on all sides, and it was from out of this ocean of down that he held forth to Lashkov:

'Our weakness is in our desires. Give us everything now, at once, in our lifetime. And when they refuse us we always, in the last analysis, resort to force to satisfy our desires. And so it goes on from one generation to the next. Blood is spilt from century to century, while the ideals for whose sake this blood is allegedly spilt remain, alas, but ideals. It is far easier, of course, to redistribute existing wealth instead of increasing it. For that demands patience and labour. But patience is precisely what we haven't got, and we don't care for working. And that's that: strike, destroy, we only live once! Do you follow me, Lashkov?'

The caretaker hastily replied in the affirmative. It was all the same to him. He listened to the actor out of pity and in order to lighten his existence, however slightly. Khramov's organism no longer responded to morphine, and in his endless monologues Lev was striving with all his might to assuage the pain. With every passing day the cancer was shortening his path to the grave. Lashkov used to sit for hours by the patient's couch, and a better listener to these prolonged monologues was not to be wished for.

Lev and his old mother had long since moved into the wing, exchanging their flat for that of the hairdresser, Mme Nizovtsev, plus a premium, of course. Mrs Khramov herself had not exactly declined, but force of circumstances had caused her to look at things more simply and soberly. Having buried her daughter, she had started work as a hospital orderly and ever since then the caretaker had taken to calling in, simply as an old and kindhearted friend.

He and Lev were united by a lacerating sense of doom and the consciousness of their impending end. They didn't listen, but merely heard one another, and their loneliness, muffled in torrents of words, mysteriously receded a little, temporarily granting them an illusion of the fullness of existence. Each of them was necessary, each of them essential to the other, and nobody knows which needed the other most.

The actor's slender blue-tipped fingers nervously played with the binding of the blanket. Whenever he got excited he turned pale, his eyes grew even more sunken and dewy droplets would stand out on his upper lip.

'We have to begin all over again, Lashkov, do you follow me, from the beginning. Otherwise there will never be an end to the blood, otherwise we shall return to the jungle again. We must, do you follow me, we absolutely must learn to think in millenia, and not just in terms of a human lifetime. We must teach ourselves to rejoice at the happiness and well-being of our descendants and train ourselves to work for this end. Work, Lashkov, work! And let's have no more of these windbags, let's have no more of these Opiskins boosting themselves up as mighty statesmen. When he enters this life each man should be asked: "And what are you able to make yourself? What can you make with your hands or your talent? Bread, houses, books, art?" Let's have no more of these illiterate leaders! We can manage without their help! All we need do is work, work! Do you follow me, Lashkov?'

Lashkov agreed with everything, but meanwhile thought his own thoughts and even contrived, out of the corner of one ear, to listen to the quiet conversation in the kitchen, where Mrs Khramov was bidding farewell to the doctor.

She: 'Would he perhaps be better off in hospital?'
He: 'As you wish, ma'am, as you wish, but I don't advise it. No, ma'am.'
She: 'So you mean to say there's no hope?'
He: 'Now you and I, ma'am, have already got one foot in the

grave, so what's the use of comforting ourselves with high-flown illusions?'

She: 'I'd gladly go now if it would save him. . . .'

He: 'Oh, how they brought us up, my friend, in our day, to make the beautiful gesture! There's no need, ma'am. Times have changed. As for hospital, well, why not, he can go if you like, but our official hospitals are hardly the place for a man with his nervous mechanism. You should know what I mean, ma'am— heredity. . . . No, preserve him from that, my friend, it wouldn't help. Goodbye, ma'am.'

The outside door slammed and the old woman lowered herself heavily on to a chair and fell silent. Lev, meanwhile, was getting more and more excited and struggling to overcome the pain:

'But to begin with we need an artist, an artist who is not as we are —pigmies. We need a giant who will come and say: we are all men, we are all brothers. But how will he ever say it! Oh, how will he ever say it! Many have spoken of it. Christ did—and many, many more. But the wrong way, the wrong way! It must be simpler and easier to understand. Oh, how it needs to be said. . . . So that it enters into everybody. So that everybody suddenly falls seriously ill with it and begins to fight for a cure themselves. . . . Yes, yes, it has to be like an infection. So that everybody, everybody can suddenly see into themselves. And when they see they will burst into tears and embrace one another. And they will say: "Let's begin all over again from the beginning. . . ." We need an artist. Only an artist can produce harmony. With a word, with one single word. And he *will* find it, he will! And it will be as simple as drawing breath. . . . Do you follow me, Lashkov?'

The actor was gasping for breath. As he uttered these last words he thrust his head off the pillow, straining with every nerve, then at once went all limp and closed his eyes with exhaustion. A minute later his breathing had evened out again and his face, which had turned white with excitement, took on its usual muddy hue once more: Lev was sleeping.

Lashkov straightened his blanket and went into the kitchen. Old woman Khramov was sitting by the cooking-stove and gazing apathetically into space. She didn't even notice him and didn't move a muscle. He said:

'He's sleeping.'

'Eh?' she started up.

'I said he's sleeping.'

'O-oh. . . .'

Mrs Khramov assumed her original position and grew still. Going out into the passage, Lashkov thought to himself that it couldn't be all that simple to survive one's children.

●

Lashkov was sitting beneath the mushroom-shaped wooden shelter in Lyovushkin's garden, while the carpenter kept monotonously repeating the same snatch of song over and over again:

I'm still a young maid,
But my soul is a thousand years old. . . .

He was holding the accordion like a strange thing, on the edge of his knee, and his eyes, leaden with drink, were fixed on the rain-filled sky as he stubbornly reiterated:

I'm still a young maid,
But my soul is a thousand years old. . . .

The mushroom leaked, murky March raindrops shivered to pieces on his forehead and nose-bridge and started running down his cheeks, so that it looked as if Ivan was crying. But it only looked that way. In reality he was transcendentally and totally drunk. With Lashkov the carpenter rarely spoke. During their twenty-odd years of friendship everything between them had been talked out and thought out to extinction. Now they communicated by signs. The carpenter, for example, would stick his little finger out to the side, raise his thumb and glance interrogatively at his friend. The latter would nod silently and the two of them would turn out their pockets. After three or four of such sessions the friends would drink themselves into a solid stupor, and then Lyovushkin would pick up his battered squeezebox. He could play all sorts of things on it and stick to the tune too. He had acquired this accordion about ten years ago, during his wanderings in search of 'big money', and since then was never separated from it.

Lyuba usually banned them from drinking inside and they drank here, beneath the mushroom, and the murky March snow melted overhead, and everything they had ever had was behind them: youth, hopes, life—though surely life was hardly the right word to describe that long series of flashes of pain and despair? No, there was no longer any ache in Ivan's soul, he had long since lost even the habit of citing 'God's way'. It was as though he had wrapped himself in a skin of impenetrable deafness to everything, and nothing could extract him ever again from this dead equilibrium.

The sky overhead swelled with grey heaviness, everything around them, already soaked by it, seemed to huddle closer to the ground and it looked as though up there, beyond that grey bulk, nothing existed any more—neither sun, nor stars, nor even the sky itself—and there was only emptiness, murky and sticky, like this rain.

Listless Lyuba, like an ailing trout—her head a ripe melon plastered with dirty-grey tow—peered at them from behind her window with not a flicker of light in her eyes, and her furious muttering tumbled through the ventilation trap and down into the yard. But it would have taken more than her and more than her blistering rage to penetrate into Ivan's totally charred soul.

Just as the carpenter was entering upon his third bout of digital manipulation, Nikiforov entered the yard with his head bowed low, hastily accompanied by his sobbing better half. Unusually for him he was walking slowly, and his steps were heavy and his head lowered. Over the intervening years he had matured and filled out considerably. A captain's epaulettes sat comfortably on his plump shoulders. Drawing level with the garden Nikiforov suddenly flew into a rage: 'What's this, eh?' Nikiforov's fleshy jowls wobbled and were suffused with blue. 'What's the meaning of this, eh? Today of all days you choose to be swilling vodka! Why, you sons of bitches, I'd like to . . .' He ran short of breath, then hurled himself at Lashkov, took him by the shoulders and began to shake him furiously. 'Where's the flag? Where's the flag, God rot your soul, where is it, I say?' Suddenly he let the caretaker go, shuddered all over and burst into tears. 'Sons of bitches! Sons of bitches! Masha, Masha!' Nikiforov hung on his wife. 'The sufferings that *He* went through for the sake of this rabble. *He* lifted them out of the mud, out of the muck, made men of them, and they're swilling vodka![1] Wallowing in it!' Nikiforov started up once more and again flew at Lashkov: 'You scum, you scum! I'll send you to kingdom come this instant!' His trembling fingers were already fumbling with the button at the back of his riding breeches. 'Swine! Do you hear?'

And no matter how drunk he was, Lashkov realised at that moment that death was truly tickling him under the nose: not for nothing did the local Sokolniki crooks get the hiccups at the mere mention of the name of Nikiforov, Chief Officer at Butyrka Prison.

[1] The reference is to Stalin and the day of his death: March 5, 1953. Tr.

But all of a sudden the limp hand of Lyovushkin pushed the caretaker to one side and the carpenter himself took a step forward, thus shielding the other from Nikiforov, while his discarded accordion flew to the ground, emitting a brief wail.

'Here—me,' began Ivan softly and even imploringly, 'shoot me with your bloody popgun.' Then his face gradually suffused with blood and soon he was almost screaming into the face of the astonished Nikiforov. 'Go on, shoot! I ain't never seen life an' I won't see it now. So what do I need it for—life! You guzzled it down with your regulation soup. . . . I wanted my boy to be a bloody dentist an' where is he now, eh? An' all thanks to you. I've spent the best part of my life goin' through hell, and traipsin' round the harbours of Russia. An' just because of skunks like you. Go on then, fire!' He tore off the collar of his blouse. 'What are you waiting for?'

The Chief Officer wasn't exactly over-endowed with courage. Unable to endure the pressure, he lowered his voice a register:

'All right, all right, just don't go too far. I've got a spare cell waiting for your highness, too, if you're not careful. You drink yourselves under the table and then start blabbing God knows what. I'll talk to you later elsewhere.' And he was already moving away when he called back to Lashkov over his shoulder: 'It's a day of mourning, you oaf, mourning. I want that flag up in a jiffy. I'll check to make sure.' And he walked off. 'Bloody crew. . . .'

Lyovushkin picked his accordion up off the ground and bawled out after him in open mockery:

Down our end of town
Everythin's upside down:
We're posh people too—
Guzzle shit an' never spew.

'Here, try a bit!'

●

Earlier, before his illness, Lashkov had failed to notice a whole host of interesting things—like the sun, for instance. The sun had always existed for him as a prosaic, indissoluble part of his total surroundings, equally familiar as rain, wind and air. But recently it had started to live a life completely independent of Lashkov. He found that he could hear, smell and even touch it. The sun worked and the sun grew tired. The sun moved with astonishing aptness from place to place. The sun rejoiced and the sun waxed indignant. The sun had its enemies and friends. But Lashkov remained on one side, separated from all this beneficence by the mortal feature of illness.

It was as though Lashkov was discovering the world anew for himself. There couldn't, it seemed, be a single spot left in this yard that he didn't know down to the minutest detail, but objects and things—which now existed in their own right—began to appear just as enigmatic to him as they had been in early childhood. Take the boilerhouse, for example, where Lashkov had spent practically a quarter of his life and had become, so to speak, thoroughly impregnated with the odour of rust and soft ashes; yet now it loomed so darkly just across the way from his window, mysterious and beckoning, like the entrance to Hades. Strange as it may seem, the ageing caretaker, with all the zeal of a pioneer investigator, was engaged in a stubborn struggle to comprehend concepts that he had apparently assimilated a hundred, nay a thousand, times in the past: 'fence', 'tree', 'ball'. And each of them was now, for the first time, revealing to him its amazingly simple secrets.

'But it's allus bin like that,' he argued to himself. 'Surely it ain't death makes you notice and feel all that?' And he felt discomfited. And, as usual in such cases, he dragged himself down to the yard, hoping that a walk or a chance conversation would help to suppress or muffle that sudden rush of stark terror to his heart.

Down in the yard a bulldozer stood growling and trembling beside the pump. The driver, a gangling youth in a beret and canvas overall, was washing one of his gumboots under the tap. And the sky flashed in the gleaming mirror of the bootleg.

'Digging again?' asked Lashkov as he lowered himself on to the bench opposite the youth. Not that he asked out of curiosity, but simply for the sake of striking up at least some semblance of a conversation. 'This is the fifth time . . .'

The bulldozer driver didn't interrupt his task, nor even glance in Lashkov's direction. He merely jerked his head towards the corner of the yard, where Shtabel's abandoned shack clung to the side of the boilerhouse, and explained matter-of-factly:

'I've come to knock down the "colosseum". The office needs the bricks. Got it, Granpop?'

Lashkov at once lost all inclination to talk. For him this scruffy lean-to with the two windows was a part of himself. Together with Shtabel and Ivan Lyovushkin he had invested in it not only labour, but also a particle of that which remains afterwards—that residuum that survives all alarums and cares, all workdays and holidays, all wars and armistices. But now this matter-of-fact squirt had come in his canvas overall and what did he care for Shtabel or his shack? He couldn't give a damn about what survived of this haggard old man on the bench. The office needed the bricks, so what was the point of argy-bargy?

'Hup-la, Grandad,' the youth reached the wheel in a single bound, 'push back a bit, otherwise I might hit you by accident.'

The bulldozer shuddered, turned slowly and directed the steel wedge of its scoop straight at the target. Past Lashkov it came— first the long bonnet, then the cabin with its wide open doors framing a rubber boot, with the sky slowly drying in its smoky mirror.

The house met its death like a living creature. When the razor-edge of the scoop bit into the base of the wall, it swayed imperceptibly and stood firm. But the driver merely pulled one of the levers a fraction closer to him, the steel blade bit deeper, and at last the house toppled and fell with a crash, swallowing the roof inside. And only a cloud of dirty white dust smoked over its ruins, funnelling upwards into that same lofty, lazy bowl of June azure as had been there thirty years ago.

●

Lashkov left the beer parlour in that benign mood that always seizes the hardened drinker in the immediate aftermath of intoxication. Everything seemed so ridiculously simple and so utterly comprehensible: past and future, good and evil.

For a long time he stood and watched with drunken sympathy as a lean sturdy-looking old man in a canvas cap kept accosting people on the corner of Rybinsky Passage. One after another the old man would fasten his tenacious, arthritic fingers on to the elbows of passers-by and begin always with the same stereotyped phrase:

'Back home in Cherepovets . . .'

But they all shook him off fearfully, taking him evidently for a drunk or a madman. And anyway, who cares about another's troubles when he's up to his neck in his own? Nevertheless, one or two people did advise him:

'Why don't you go home and sleep it off, old feller?'

But the old man only dismissed them with a wave of his hand and continued his feverish gyrations:

'Back home in Cherepovets . . .'

And the whole business was repeated from the beginning. The policeman by the grocer's shop, who had been observing the old man's zigzagging, was already beginning to exhibit moderate signs of nervousness when Lashkov resolved to save this hapless son of Cherepovets from an unavoidable spell in the lock-up.

'Yep,' he reassured himself beforehand, 'I'll just give him a rouble, or maybe two. Once the old boy has a snifter he'll see things clearer and kin go on his way.'

But evidently there was something about Lashkov that didn't appeal to the old man, for his round gleaming eyes merely slid over Lashkov's face and he walked straight past him. Lashkov called after him good-naturedly:

'Well, what is it you've got back home in Cherepovets, spit it out.'

The old man turned and looked at Lashkov severely, with the gleam fading from his eyes, but then suddenly his iron wrinkles relaxed a fraction and with an expansive wave of the hand, as if to say 'what the hell', he fastened on to his elbow.

'You see, dear comrade, back home in Cherepovets there's no justice. . . .'

And the old man, as was more or less to be expected, related to Lashkov the old, old story: 'They sent my brother-in-law to prison for absolutely nothing at all. A shoemaker he was, and a war invalid, with a family of six kids—all young and close together. They said he had too much leather, but some hopes—boots for the legless was about his mark!' And so on and so forth. The old man told his story with a wealth of detail, providing corresponding evidence and testimony for each and every fact. Then for an hour or more he droned on about his own services to his country: 'Caught typhus in the civil war and generally did my bit.'

And then in conclusion the old man put the question point blank:

'All right, you live in the capital so tell me one thing: do we have justice in Cherepovets or don't we?'

And the force of his conviction was such that Lashkov, although he had been able to make neither head nor tail of what had been told to him, felt bound to agree:

'No, you don't.'

The old man sighed with relief, gave a pitted smile and stood up:

'You must forgive me, dear comrade, for the first minute or so I thought you were . . . As if you . . . That there wasn't much sort of backbone to you, if you see what I mean. You don't really look much like the sort who sticks at things very much. But now I see I was off the mark. You've got your own ideas about things and for that, dear comrade, I thank you. If you're ever in Cherepovets, ask for Fyodor Terentye7 Mikheyev, every man jack knows me there. We'll take a glass of tea together—and some hooch to go with it, of course.'

'Ha-ha, go on invite me, you can invite me all right, I won't refuse!' thought Lashkov mockingly to himself, but aloud said sympathetically:

'You're out of cash, I s'pose, an' a long way from home?'

But the latter grew unexpectedly stern again and explained to the caretaker didactically:

'I, dear comrade, am a craftsman, and there is no such thing as a craftsman without money. I've got more than enough cash, I can even lend you some if you like—and for keeps.'

Lashkov was taken aback, but still didn't retreat:

'I don't s'pose you've got a place to kip though, have you? You need to have your wits about you, brother, to stay in Moscow.'

The old man drew a wad of Moscow accommodation coupons out of his pocket and lovingly flipped them under Lashkov's very nose.

'Here, I've got the whole of Moscow in my pocket, and as for wits, I can chew not only my fingers but two-inch nails if need be. Still, I must be going. And many thanks to you for the friendly conversation.'

The old man strode jauntily off down the pavement in the direction of Sokolniki. Calmly he went, with a masterful air about him. And it suddenly occurred to Lashkov how good it would have been now to hurry after the old man and tell him all about himself and the yard, and about Shtabel and old woman Shokolinist, and about many, many things besides. And it also occurred to him that this was that kind word of Khramov's that could transform the whole world, and that indeed it must be walking the world inside every one of us if he, Lashkov, had just found it so easy to bring relief to the old man. And suddenly this piercing enigma made him feel quite out of sorts and he couldn't resist it. Walking into the nearest pawnshop, he took off his jacket and threw it on to the counter:

'How much will you give me?'

•

One sultry July night Lashkov was wakened by a tap at the window. He put his nose to the glass and couldn't believe his eyes. His heart stopped in a rush of suffocating heat: it was Shtabel.

Before embracing, the two friends groped uncertainly for each other with their hands, as if assuring themselves of their mutual palpability. Then it was a long time before their shoulders drew apart.

'Yes,' said Lashkov.

'Yes,' said Shtabel.

And again they repeated it:

'Yes.'

'Yes.'

And every 'yes' comprehended days and years, rain and sunshine, shared joys and shared pain, and a lot, lot more that could only be felt but in no way said or expressed.

Afterwards they sat at the table and Shtabel thoughtfully rubbed his palm over an ink-spot on the cloth, while he gazed into Lashkov's face with those same tranquil eyes of his, only their lustre was somewhat dimmed now, and said:

'Authority exist, order exist. I alvays respecting authority and order. But nineteen years not order. I abandon Siberia, I abandon family. Yes, yes, I married. . . . Siberia abandoned—and family. . . . Yes, yes, I married. Siberia hard vithout family. . . . I got kids. And I no vant them Siberia. I come to tell authority: nineteen years not order. I believing in authority. I believing in all authority. Authority is order. My kids Siberia not order.'

Lashkov looked at his friend and was amazed by his outer vitality. The plumber looked completely unchanged, except that the skin on his neck was slightly looser and his shoulders had grown a trifle rounded with the onset of age, but on the other hand they had retained their usual suppleness. However, it was noticeable from the way his thick fingers trembled as they grasped the meat safe that he too was paying for the years that had passed.

There was much that the caretaker wanted to tell Shtabel, so very, very much, but even though so much time had passed, his news turned out to be no more than would have gone on the back of a postage stamp.

'Grusha? Well yes, there's Grusha! She couldn't never get over it, o' course, not for ages and ages, but then she calmed down a bit an' moved in with Fenya. She's still livin', but keeps pretty poorly these days. Ivan? Oh yes, Ivan! He drinks a lot. Works as a hired labourer. His son's bin in the orphanage most of his life. The actor? He kicked the bucket, brother, ages ago. Kalinin? Well, er, he ain't with us any more. Meckler? Meckler's still around. Puttin' in crowns. An' false teeth. . . .'

111

Lashkov broke off: through the open window and filling the entire room with its sound came the familiar hum of Nikiforov holding forth. It streamed down from on high from the house directly opposite:

'What is labour? What is labour, I ask you, you sons of bitches. Labour is a matter of what, eh? Of what, I ask you, you gang of parasites? It's a matter of honour. And what else? Can't you answer, you criminal degenerates? It's a matter of valour and heroism. What happens to the man who doesn't work? Go on, I'm asking you, you hairy swine. He doesn't eat. And what about you? What about you, I say? You don't want to work? Bloody namby-pambies! Well, I'll make sure you knuckle under. I've got enough cells for the lot of you. I'll make sure the lot of you knuckle under.'

In the hushed benignity of early morning this voice seemed ineffably absurd.

'What's that?' asked Shtabel anxiously.

Lashkov grinned gloomily.

'Your patron's up to his tricks again. He's a bit touched. Havin' a hard time in his job and now this. . . . Every mornin' at dawn he practises in front of that window of his. Sometimes he's all right, but mostly he's like that. Caretakers come in from the other streets to listen to 'im. Some people enjoys it.'

Shtabel said:

'Yes,' and again this 'yes' contained a wealth of meaning for both of them.

Meanwhile Nikiforov was proclaiming from on high:

'What songs are those you think you're singing, you bloody degenerate, do you hear me? "Murka" is it? "The River Flows" is it? "I Have a Fine Fur Coat"? Prison camp songs? And what about "Behind a Brick Wall"? I've got enough troubles with you as it is, you bloody parasite, without you singing all that bloody crap! You get your grub, don't you? You've got a mattress? Baths? Eh? So what the hell are you singing about? Do you want five days on bread and water? I'll give you the national anthem to get on with. So you can learn it by heart. Got it?'

Shtabel made haste to go.

'I must to be off.'

'Let me go with you.'

'You don't need, Vasya, really you don't.'

They continued to argue thus for some considerable time, although both knew that in the end they would go together. Afterwards, as the friends walked through the dawn-lit streets towards the centre, Lashkov tried to convince the plumber:

'The main thing is to make a stand: I don't want to and that's that. There ain't no such law. The war's ancient history by now. Hitler's bin eaten up by the worms and here they are still holdin' families with children. The only thing it can be is that the local authorities are playin' up.'

But Shtabel had only to disappear through the doors of that building, ponderous as a giant cliff at the roadside, and a sharp pain contracted his heart.

They had agreed to meet at the spot where they parted, beside a tobacco kiosk on the corner. Lashkov wandered aimlessly about the streets, returned, wandered off again and again returned: there was no Shtabel. Lashkov talked with the tobacco seller about this and that and, one after the other, for the sake of trade, bought five packets of 'Byelomor' cigarettes. Still there was no Shtabel. Nor did he come after an hour, nor after two.

As he closed up his kiosk the tobacco seller stared at Lashkov suspiciously and took particular pains over locking it.

In the big building the windows started to go dark one after the other: one, two, three . . . Lashkov watched them and comforted himself each time with: 'This must be it. . . . This must be it. . . .' But Shtabel still didn't come. And when, somewhere high up under the very eaves, the last bright rectangle disappeared, all he could think was: 'It's all over.'

●

Grusha was buried late that autumn, when rooftops and ground had been touched with the first layer of hoar-frost. Pressed down from all sides by an icy sky, the yard seemed to Lashkov like a stone sack, with the yellow candle of the coffin lid burning in its middle. Quietly but confidently it burned, and there was no power on earth to quench it.

Then, like silent fish, a series of shadows swam out of the porch and past the lid. Across the yard they swam, and their swimming had neither beginning nor end. Then voices followed the shadows, also from inside the porch, but they, too, brought no warmth to the cold well of the yard.

They carried Grusha out and halted immobile, holding her aloft on their shoulders, beside the upturned lid. From his window above, Lashkov could see her entire, from head to foot—nobody's now, belonging only to herself. A ring of faces closed around her. He recognised them all. Old Mrs Tsigankov and Mrs Khramov. Ivan Lyovushkin and his Lyuba. Nikiforov with his whole family. Meckler and Fenya Tsarev. They stood in silence around her, and she somehow ascended over them and forgave them.

The silence grew thicker and thicker, tightening the nerve-strings to breaking point, and at last they could stand it no more and something snapped: Nikiforov's youngest daughter, Svetlana, burst into tears. And it was like a spark setting off the whole yard. Faces suddenly became wracked with sobbing. But this lament was not for her, not for Grusha. Such tears are shed for the living, not for the dead. Lashkov sensed, Lashkov knew that they were pouring into this lament the whole of that searing pain that now enveloped his own soul in readiness for its parting from earth and sky.

'What did we find by coming here?' he thought with their thoughts. 'Joy? Hope? Faith? What about you, Mrs Tsigankov, you who lost everything? And you, Lyovushkin? Where's your dentist son? And you, crazy Nikiforov? What did we bring with us? Goodness? Warmth? Light? And to whom? To Meckler? Mrs Khramov? Kozlov? No, we brought nothing with us, and we lost everything. Ourselves, our soul. Everything, everything. And for what? For what? Inside every one of us there must have lived a kind word, and maybe it lives on still. It lives! Lev knew what he was talking about when he said: "Weep, men, weep, for tears have their power too!" '

Lashkov even strained his body forward slightly and suddenly, in the depths of the yard, just where Shtabel's house had formerly stood, he caught sight of old woman Shokolinist. Black and tiny, she stood there silently moving her lips, and then she gradually began to grow, swelling in his eyes until she filled the whole sky before him, and he collapsed across the windowsill. And probably only the earth heard his last husky moan:

'Oh my Go-o-o-d. . . .'

Anton Ulyansky

The Fleecy Jacket

It is difficult now to say precisely what kind of material it was made of. Difficult, because it's gone. But even in its day this was a question I could never really get to the bottom of.

It was given me by my aunt before I left for Moscow. This good deed was accomplished hastily and almost without a word—rather more by dumb show than in conversational style—and naturally it was not for me to break the sad silence which accompanied the scene by asking questions. It was my aunt herself who broke it, but beyond advising me to brush the jacket often and on no account to loll about on a plank bed wearing it, she threw no new light on the matter.

In consequence, when the question of selling the jacket came up there was still a chance of having a word on this subject with the dealers at the Smolensk Market. But even then the question remained a vexed one, for the dealers' opinions differed.

'Sealskin,' said one and offered me seven roubles for it.

'Beaver,' corrected another and raised the price to eight.

'Blanket cloth,' frowned a third and wouldn't go above six.

Personally, I believe the third man was nearest the truth. For in fact, on the brown pile at the edge of the back there was a kind of selvage of a different colour from the remainder, which disappeared very cunningly, cutting a corner, into the left arm-hole.

Nevertheless, whatever the jacket's previous history had been, one must give it its due: it looked solid and respectable—you could go anywhere in it. I prized it, for it was the only capital I possessed at the start of my career in an unknown city, and if the circumstances of my life had permitted me to follow my aunt's advice, if conditions generally had been more favourable—it might, perhaps, have served me to this day: and if I had kept it the whole course of my affairs would, naturally, have been quite different.

With the jacket, unfortunately, things turned out badly for me. In Moscow at Yermeki, on the very first night it caught the attention of Vasya Praktik, my neighbour in the next bed. This man has stayed in my memory. I can say nothing about his physiognomy: the yellow ceiling light made it hard to examine. What I judged him by was his conversation and his hoarse, disenchanted voice, which I had ample opportunity to hear, for in that room Vasya was the chief source of background music, his voice a steady whine, now softer now louder, but always spiteful, always envious, and never a laugh or even a smile to go with it. Incidentally, a crook who doesn't know how to smile always creates a bad impression and puts people on their guard.

At the very beginning of the evening Vasya had quarrelled with some newcomer or other who tried to take the berth Vasya had reserved for himself. Vasya promised to 'plug' him. This put me in mind of Pomyalovsky and the tobacco with which they used to plug sleeping boys' noses at school, but then I realised that the plugging was going to be done with something altogether more serious and in a different part of the body. On Vasya's lips the promise sounded bored and routine, as if the whole thing were only a matter of time.

Vasya began by giving me a crooked and reluctant grin, not considering it necessary to disguise with a smile what was automatically taken for granted.

'A nice job,' he said, jerking his head in the direction of my jacket. 'Just the ticket for the autumn weather.'

I agreed, but involuntarily drew the jacket closer about me.

'A high-quality job,' Vasya went on, stroking the pile like a cat. 'Sova in the washroom would give you a tenner for it.'

'Maybe,' I said.

But I stealthily fastened my belt to the tab inside the collar and wrapped it round my hand, so that I should wake up when they tried to jerk the jacket off me.

Vasya and I had no further conversation on that occasion. I closed my eyes and prepared to await the sequel. But Vasya set off on a tour of the other floors in search of business.

Until late into the night shadowy figures roamed from room to room, all engaged on the same search, examining the sleepers, sizing them up, winking at one another, disappearing. Their eyes slid over the sleepers' feet—and what these feet were shod in—but they dwelt even longer on what the sleepers were wrapped in. For warm clothing was the order of the day. A wind had been blowing since morning—winter was setting in—and people who were not well wrapped up, who had frozen in the queue in front of the doss-house, went into it firmly determined to get themselves a skin at any price. In the murky light of the dosshouse the identically tattered figures all looked alike and reminded me more than anything else of the saying: everyone wears out in his own way.

That night, when they were already snoring in various parts of the room, a conference was held on Vasya's bed. A list was drawn up of the propositions in the different dormitories.

'There's a medium-sized service jacket in number sixty. . . .,' reported Kolya.

'In number twenty there's a fur coat that's not too bad. . . .,' said Syenka.

'Too far,' hissed Vasya. 'There's something nearer than that.'

'Where?' asked Syenka and Kolya eagerly.

'Over there. . . .'

The bed creaked and heaved under the three friends as they all turned in the same direction, and the breeze caused by their motion blew down my back.

'A nice bit of work,' said Vasya. 'Sova in the washroom would give ten of the best on the spot. . . .'

'I dunno,' responded Syenka after a pause and in a different key from his friends. 'If you ask me, it's not worth dirtying your hands on.'

This was useful to me, although insulting to my jacket, and from his first words my impression of Syenka was of a shallow person, ignorant of the value of things. Subsequent events, however, obliged me to change my opinion of this man and to regard him in a completely new light. For Syenka, of course, was well aware of the value of my jacket, and if he didn't want to soil his hands with it, this was only because his love of profit was overcome by somewhat loftier considerations.

'It's not enough just to take the thing,' said Syenka judiciously and earnestly. 'You need to know who you're taking it from. What sort of a man is he? What are his circumstances? Maybe he's on the rocks himself.'

Such were the views that have brought fame to Arsène Lupin, Cartouche and many other gentlemen thieves, and I was glad to note that the humbler practitioners of larceny, in far less favourable circumstances, were no strangers to them either.

'Those boots of his aren't much to look at,' went on Syenka, turning from the general to the particular. 'Maybe he's some kind of actor? Or a student? Or maybe one of us—in business? I don't touch those types. . . .'

'You're breaking my heart,' was Vasya's reply to all these observations. 'When did anyone ever take pity on you?'

'How's he worse than the others?' said Kolya, puzzled.

'He's not worse,' answered Syenka. 'It's just that he's not my line of country. . . .'

'Do you want to go it alone?' asked Vasya, finding a simpler explanation for his obstinacy. 'Go ahead.'

And Syenka said no more, got up and went off to look for his line of country elsewhere, while Vasya and Kolya continued their conversation about the jacket.

'God, we could just do with that tenner right now,' whispered

Vasya. 'First some long togs for you and me. And then clean drawers and the bath-house. What a treat that would be, Kolya, the bath-house.'

'Not half,' replied Kolya dreamily. 'I've got enough lice on me to suit a gypsy. . . .'

'We'll demolish those lice out of all recognition,' said Vasya excitedly. 'We can put our feet up, get a hot meal.'

Growing animated, he even stopped whining and spoke simply and with warmth. The prospect of even a bare minimum of human comfort—long togs to wear and no lice eating you—was enough for this hunted and half-wild outcast to forget his malice and the whining cynicism he affected.

'He's tied the inside of the jacket to his arm, blast him,' said Kolya. 'He thinks we don't know about tricks like that.'

'If he wakes up, we'll put a half-nelson on him and that'll be that,' said Vasya decisively. 'Right, Kolya, we'll take it in turns to sleep. First me and then you. And at five we'll go to work.'

'Right,' agreed Kolya.

And Vasya went to sleep on the spot, while Kolya, fighting against sleep, began to whistle softly. I lay there under my jacket and wondered why five o'clock should be so convenient for putting a half-nelson on one's neighbour. Was it because at five o'clock the doors opened and it would be possible to disappear without fuss after the deed was done?

I considered my cause already lost. At five in the morning my jacket would be stripped off me. If I heard nothing the operation would be carried out without fuss. If I woke up—they would put a half-nelson on me. My only defence against Vasya and Kolya was to run away: but where could I run to if there was no exit until five and all the rooms contained their own Vasyas and Kolyas? It would, of course, have been possible to attack on the moral front, to open my heart to Vasya, tell him about my affairs and advise him, for his part, to 'try going straight' and not to build his happiness on other people's fleecy jackets. . . . But, of course, God knows what kind of a hornet's nest would have been stirred up by such words in a room where one section of the inmates lived from one nick to the next, while the other, numerically the larger, honestly ransacked the rubbish heaps of Moscow to earn themselves bread, hooch and a bed for the night.

I dozed off. There was no sense in resisting sleep, the matter was in any case already settled. But long before five I was woken by a great racket. The racket was being created by a newcomer, the one Vasya had promised to 'plug' and who was so green that when going to the lavatory for a minute he had left his overcoat and belongings on the bed, returning, of course, to find them no longer in their place. It had all been done so quickly that he was completely mystified and even thought it must be someone's idea of a joke.

'If this is a joke,' he said, pacing the room in his underthings, 'then it's a stupid one. Give me back my things. I'm cold.'

He started looking under the beds and wandering senselessly round the room, but encountered only indifference and curses.

'For God's sake,' he asked all his neighbours, 'didn't you notice who took my things?'

But his neighbours didn't answer. It may well be that they would never have taken his things themselves and were even quietly cursing those who had taken it upon themselves to do so. But none of them actually ventured to speak out openly against the crooks.

'That's how fools are taught a lesson,' said one to the newcomer.

'Go and look for your things tomorrow at the Sukharevka Market,' advised another.

'It's your own fault,' said the warden, brought in by the noise. 'There are warnings up everywhere.'

And he pointed out a notice on the wall, to which the rubbings-out of some humorist had already given a somewhat ambiguous meaning.

'*Beware of   eves*,' read the novice on the wall, then thought for a moment and grew resigned.

Kolya lay there whistling to himself. Vasya wasn't there. He returned a little later, when all was quiet again, and whispered to Kolya: 'Nine of the best. . . .'

And I realised that fate had sent the friends a victim in place of myself and that now that they had money for drawers and a bath they might well be satisfied with this instead of waiting up till five to put a half-nelson on me.

That evening the situation was exactly the same except that there was no jacket; wanting to sleep undisturbed, I had handed it in for safe keeping. In the attire of the two friends no change whatever had taken place: they still had no long togs and were dressed in dirty shirts, which meant that their nine of the best had been blued on something else.

'What fools we were to oversleep this morning,' said Vasya to Kolya when the conference was resumed on Vasya's bed. 'That tenner was ours for the taking.'

'He's handed in his jacket, the bastard,' opined Kolya. 'There's nowhere else the scum could have put it. . . .'

'What good does the skunk think that will do him?' said Vasya angrily. 'He must have the ticket on him. All we need to do is find out which boot he's hidden it in.'

'What about the left one?' Kolya suggested. 'The lace on that one is done up round the top.'

'We'll soon see,' said Vasya, 'We'll check 'em both. Got your razor on you, Kolya?'

'I don't care for tickets,' observed Syenka, who was also present at the meeting. 'You'll never get away with it if they can read. They remember the number.'

'Let him remember it,' grinned Vasya. 'He'll wake up at seven and we'll collect his things at five. . . .'

Listening to them I shivered, for the ticket was indeed in my left boot and I could only be amazed at how little chance I had of outwitting Vasya and Kolya. I waited for the right moment, then went to the office and handed in the ticket for safe keeping as well, then went back and changed my boots deliberately in front of Vasya, so that he could see there was nothing in them. He watched me with a bored expression, showing that he was long since fed up with such jokes.

The night passed without incident but in the morning I decided to sell the jacket so as to be rid of it for good: keeping it brought nothing but trouble.

It was now that the conversation with the dealers took place, the one I spoke of at the beginning. When the dormitory origins of my jacket came into the open its price stuck at six roubles. I should have reconciled myself to this figure and taken the six roubles, but I kept delaying, waiting to see whether someone else wouldn't come along who would give me more. And sure enough a man did come up to me who told me that if the thing was a good fit, he wouldn't grudge a tenner for it. Accompanying him and acting as his consultant was a man who assured me that they wouldn't cheat me over the price, that if I had been a dealer they would have had one kind of conversation with me, but since I wasn't trading for profit, since I was selling the last thing to my name, and was hard up—was I some kind of actor, perhaps, or a student?—then their conversation would be of quite a different character. In this man's voice there was a note that was somehow familiar to me, a note of sympathy, conviction and high principle. . . .

Unfortunately it was only some minutes later that I finally remembered who he was. . . .

That evening I lay down once more near Vasya and Kolya,

smoking a dog-end but saying nothing and just listening. That day the weather had started to thaw a little, granting a respite to people without togs. Kolya had two black eyes, the result of an unsuccessful operation at the Sukharevka Market, where they had tried to do a snatch job. Vasya hadn't suffered in this affair: he had wheedled his way out of it. Now Kolya was taking his revenge on him, loudly telling us how Vasya had snivelled when it came to blows, how he had begged forgiveness, pretending to be dimwitted, and wailed: 'I'll never do it again.'

The story amused everyone in the room: they looked at Vasya and tried to picture him in this situation. And only Vasya himself looked away in boredom and disgust, surprised that people should see anything funny in it.

'I saw someone with that fleecy jacket at the Smolensk Market today', said Kolya to Vasya, when their attention had turned once more to me. 'The bastard went and sold it. . . .'

'Good for him,' grinned Vasya. 'That means he's got the money on him. I know his little secrets. He couldn't have got through a tenner in one day. He's stuffed his gut with white bread and sausage, of course, but he's still got nine roubles fifty on him. Don't go to sleep, Kolya, keep your eyes skinned. . . .'

But at this point I turned to the friends, feeling for the first time that my dependence on them had come to an end and that I could be frank with them. For although it was true that earlier they had indeed known all my secrets in advance, there was one little circumstance that had escaped their notice.

'Don't waste your time on me,' I said to them with gloomy candour. 'I have no money.' And I don't have a ticket either. I'm skint. If you want to know how much my jacket fetched and where the money is, ask the crook who conned me today at the market. It was your friend, Syenka, the man who said that skinning people like me was not really his line of country.'

Victor Rostopchin

Hard Times

It is existence, but by what name
to call it? It is not sleep, not waking—
it is between them—and through it
man's reason borders on lunacy.
>   *E. Baratynsky*

●

They began with the small top drawers of the chest. Not the left-hand but the right-hand: there in a corner at the back, under some napkins, lay the cardboard box with paper lace frills stuck round the edges.

Timidly, distraught somehow, nervelessly and perhaps unthinkingly the hands moved towards the box, hands that were still not old but were dry and white, with slender fingers—on one of which a dulled gold ring still gleamed and on another, like a straw of gold, a signet with a red stone that was as thick as a drop of wine or syrup from cherry jam.

This indecision and distraughtness grew in the obvious hesitation with which the hand touched a little box lined with red velvet. The tiny lock clicked gently and the lid opened to reveal a glistening white silk lining. The light was reflected from the silk and from the golden spoons inside. They must have been loved by someone, for the pale fingers, which at first had stopped, began carefully to touch each spoon as if to caress them, and feel them: as if these golden manmade objects that were always kept locked in the red velvet case, had suffered like a living creature. They were felt for like something kindred, something alive, something especially dear and precious.

Wasn't this the reason for the confusion in the movements of the fingers and hands when they touched the drawer of the chest and slowly, unhurriedly, took from under the precious napkins and handkerchiefs this (as it were) secret hoard of gold in the red box? Wasn't this why the loving touch on each spoon was so careful—as if only to wipe off the dust? Although in fact there was no dust at all and the gold could not possibly tarnish or lose its first, ancient beauty. And in the centre of the lid on a little white silk mount a monogram was worked in gold thread, surmounted by a coronet and accompanied by a delicate and playful inscription in a foreign tongue.

There were two more cases, also lined with velvet, and the sorrowful, troubled eyes looked long at the gold in them: in these the gold was set with rosy amethyst.

Again and again the woman raised the earrings to her ears; again and again she put the slender bracelet on her left wrist; and then once, just once, tears came from her eyes and dropped on to her batiste blouse. Tender regret must have been present in those tears and it must have been difficult for her, if not impossible, to reconcile herself to something.

There were many other things in the top drawers of the chest and in the green cloth-covered desk that stood on heavy, round, turned legs. And on top of it stood photographs in frames and an inkstand with yellow lids to the pots, and pens that were both thick and thin and pencils that were black, red and blue.

In the left-hand drawer of this desk, which usually had a key sticking out of the lock, lay two cigarette-cases: one thin and of gold, its lid plain but for two initials under a coronet in the corner and a tiny Latin inscription on the inside—*Sic transit*. The other cigarette-case, which was thicker and heavier than the first, had decorations on the lid. It was of matt silver and looked worn: two or three fat cigarettes still remained inside with light brown strands of tobacco straggling out of them. One could probably determine the exact tobacco by the aroma: Mesaksudi, Stamboli or, very likely, the special Herzegovina Flor.

But the tobacco that used to be kept in this same drawer, only in another box, had not been there for a long time: a blue plush tobacco pouch had been thrown on to the desk right next to the inkstand— its worn sides bulged; beside it, on the pink blotting paper that was fastened to the table by drawing-pins, was scattered greenish-yellow cheap tobacco—Lirny or Elets shag.

One day some other hands opened this drawer and hurriedly moved towards the cigarette-cases. Their shaking fingers with yellow wrinkled skin and short-clipped nails trembled convulsively. They grasped the cases quickly and tightly and took them from the desk, slamming the drawer back brusquely as if in spite. And the stiff, angular fingers went on trembling and no respect was shown either to the smooth, sad gold of the lid or to the elegantly twined letters, whose heads met under the coronet, or to the soft dullness of the silver or to the graceful pattern of lotuses on it.

●

Of course no one could remember just how and when—whether all at once or gradually—the lower drawers of the chest had been opened; or when those same pale, slender-fingered hands had taken out the carefully folded tablecloths of antique whiteness or some jacket of a delicate and expensive material that was obviously kept in the chest not for everyday wear, for the sleeves and the lace in front and the pelerine evoked quite another period. It was impossible now to find wide cuffs and women did not wear frothing cream lace at their breast any more or pelerines with several rows of delicate open work. Jackets and blouses like this had probably not been taken out of store for a long time now.

One dress was of white, shiny satin, with creased pleats and bows at the shoulders and waist. It was carefully wrapped in white paper and then even in newspaper that had gone yellow and frayed at the edges. The dress was slim, as if made for a girl. All one saw was a mass of pleats and lace—and probably that was why it was treasured; and probably that was why once a year in spring, when all these fragrant, damp and musty treasures were hung out in the garden in the penetrating sun, this dress was carefully unfolded and hung on a slender cord stretched from one of the terrace posts to the old peartree. It was not hung too near the ground, though, where it could be dirtied by the hens always picking about under the gooseberry bushes or the children digging in the earth; it was here they made their sand pies and sometimes held funerals for some chick that had accidentally been crushed by their father, a man with angry eyes and a heavy moustache, who used to come out of a morning onto the back porch, roll himself a fat cigarette of flaky tobacco and puff on it as he hurried everyone to tea, complaining that he couldn't wait and had had to light up without having drunk his glass of tea.

That spring there were many things that did not appear in the garden. There was no satin wedding dress with flounces and bows, many of the blouses and jackets were gone, together with the light, misty wedding-veil and the long towels whose ends, with their embroidered red and black flowers or cocks had also been trimmed with fine handmade lace. Only the man with the eyes that were more than severe—even frightening—used to sit longer on the terrace steps, sighing deeply, wheezing and clutching at his heart; and he smoked heavily, dropping tobacco from his blue pouch. His eyes wandered oddly, as if unseeing, over a yellow page of newspaper used for wrapping, where there was a lot written about the Red Army and White bandits, about speculation, saboteurs, counter-revolution and sentences being carried out, but very little about bread and corn supplies and nothing at all about coupons for sugar and paraffin;

and where there were no more announcements of private dinners and hot suppers, where people no longer wanted tutors in return for board and lodging, where they no longer offered three-course dinners cooked with pure fresh butter for forty-five copecks, and milk from people's own cows was no longer supplied for eight copecks, a jug.

●

True, they could go once more to the red trunk with peeling sides and lift up the lid, with pictures from *Niva* stuck on the inside, and coloured sweet-papers (Barberry, Punch, *Baiser*, King of Siam) and pages of an old illustrated alphabet with pictures—e.g., a porter wearing an apron with a wooden tray on his head and written under him: *Astrakhanski Bely Vinograd.*[1] However, they wouldn't have to rummage much longer in the low pile of pressed linen that smelt of damp canvas and stale moth balls. But once—and not so long ago— there had been a lot of it in this same trunk; and not just in this one, which was bound with shiny tin bands that divided the top into green and the sides into red squares. And not just in trunks either, but also in the chest with the four drawers where the linen always used to lie tidily, and in which one could faintly catch the scorched odour of ironed linen. In the top two small drawers, meanwhile, with their lingering sweet smell of something like sweets or scent, lay a pile of bordered handkerchiefs; some of them had lace, though it was noticeably torn in places. There were also several coloured handkerchiefs: two or three pale yellow ones and two or three dark red. They were seldom washed, since they didn't leave the drawer to go into jacket or trouser pockets, into a handbag or the slanting pockets of brown schoolgirls' uniforms any more, or to be tucked into a pocketless blouse or under a waist elastic, but went instead into the small breast pocket of a batiste blouse or the blue jacket that hung, pressed and carefully covered by a sheet, in the wardrobe.

What could they find now in this half-empty and ancient trunk? Must they really reach to the very bottom for the last three towels with their richly embroidered ends, the cocks and the big roses, the painstaking, intricate pattern of even crosses and squares, once red and black but now faded to pink and brown—towels which in their day had been laid slowly and deliberately on the canvas lining and so still kept a sort of sense of solidity and permanence, and now evoked

[1] Literally 'Astrakhan White Grapes', a mnemonic for the first three letters of the Russian alphabet (A, B, V). Tr.

a feeling of admiration for the old time's leisureliness, sense of definition and purposefulness, which did not go at all with today's hurry, disorder and poverty.

●

Poverty did not come slowly but seemed to strike with one blow. As if the corner-posts of the house had collapsed, the walls had crumbled and the roof and ceiling had fallen in to crush with their weight the people who had always lived in this house and been peaceful, cheerful and kind, but now had become listless and helpless and silent, like the dead.

And it left the whole family broken up, whereas previously they had all been somehow closer together. The older children were no longer at home. One had died even earlier, before the hard times began, and he saw nothing and did not know of the changes; they had missed him and wept for him, although now they all realised that it was better for him to be dead than to have lived to these years of desolation. And they even envied him and prayed to God (perhaps only in a sudden rage and for a moment) for sudden death, for not everyone can take the rope and firmly and resolutely put his head into the rough noose; not everyone can leap into the cold blackness of the river under the mountain; not everyone (even if he is capable of it) can resolve to put the hard steel to his warm temple and press his finger on that piece of soulless metal.

But the deliverance of death did not come. There was something appallingly oppressive in this waiting; waiting not for something better but for inevitable suffering, when people dropped down exhausted one after another: when death already seemed to be standing at the head of the disordered, squalid bed, whose dirty pillow was crawling with fat lice, each with a black spot on the somehow lacy pattern of its belly.

And because once there had never been lice or even bugs in that house, the waiting for death was hard for all, for there was a hopeless feeling of the heavy power of these dirty-bodied, irrepressible, freely roaming creatures. And so there was almost no doubt that they would win when there was neither the habit nor the ability nor even the will to fight them, nor the means of self-preservation. Now there were no piles of pressed linen smelling of the iron—clean, fresh and cool; even those small piles of batiste handkerchiefs with their barely perceptible perfume of pressed flowers and sprinkled scent remained but a painful and hardly necessary—though nevertheless precious—memory.

And it was more than the dirt that ruled the house, more than the memory of the scent and the linen, of the golden spoons and goblets that pained and disturbed their troubled and unhappy hearts. The scent and cigarette-cases were somewhere even now with others; somewhere and by someone all those things were being kept, although not in these now empty drawers. Greatest of all, sweetest, most painful was the memory of something that many did not now have, something that is not always there but is always necessary, something which, although transitory, is most needed and is of most service of all, and so now most dear.

It was in a cold, dry voice, that the stranger spoke, frowning at the yellow faces of the sick and at the stains made by squashed lice on the pillow. The man spoke of broth ('chicken broth would be best'), a piece of meat, of milk and lemon. And the father was the most affected by this, covering his eyes with his hand and whispering: 'I'd like a plate of cabbage, cabbage soup now, with some milk in it. . . . Or fried potatoes with lard. . . . Oh, oh . . . Where has it all gone?'

●

Then the father died, not in the city but in the village where the whole family had moved and taken shelter in the school—the local authority had taken the elder daughter, a seventeen-year-old schoolgirl, to work as the village schoolteacher. His dry body was taken to the village churchyard, not to the place which had been bought earlier, next to the grave of his elder son in the Troitsky cemetery in the city, where white crosses stood around with weeping angels and railings and cast-iron slabs, and where death was a stranger only to the nightingale which, for some reason, loved the solemn hush of the maples, poplars and limes and the solitary, retiring lilac.

The mother was already forgetting her sold dresses and sheets and tablecloths. Only the satin dress with the bows and misty wedding-veil was not forgotten; nor did she forget the Virgin of Kazan, the icon with its two candles wrapped round with gold bands in the case and its wax flowers. She remembered for a particularly long time (she could not forget) the woman at the dairy market who carefully and attentively examined the icon and expressed a sort of sympathy: 'Lord, we are at God's mercy! And when will it all end? And how will we live till the end?'

The mother now only wanted to get her young children out of the house and put them somewhere in charge of the state. And of course those white, slender-fingered hands which had sorrowed for the gilt spoons in the chest of drawers, those mother's hands, would sorrow too at tearing her children, her son and daughter, from her heart and casting them into some unknown place with its gathering of God knows whose children from God knows where, who everyone said went about emaciated and ragged away from a mother's care.

But what could she do? What could set her heart at rest? And should a mother's heart even continue beating now when everything human, everything warm, had been replaced by something unknown? When there was no love, no attachment; when there was no need for a home, no need even to think of tomorrow when one didn't yet know how the night would pass until the morning, when that same sun would rise again. And the sun had no need of bread or sugar for tea; of markets or milk, of beef bones, liver or tripe; no need for illness or lamentations, good or evil, great or small, but was always just the same—alive, joyful, abundant.

One place, a place in the dark lumber-room, retained traces of the past. There, scattered on the floor and thrown into a box, were old books, magazines and letters. The letters told of health, and of university: of how one hadn't quite managed to get round to see Uncle, although Grokholsky Street wasn't far from the Solodovka hostel and one didn't need the tram; that one must give up a lesson since it was too far to go across the river; that they were in ecstasies in Moscow over Nikolay Stavrogin at the Art Theatre and the Korsh production of *Anna Karenina*; that Utochkin flew over the Khodynsky Field so low he almost brushed the hats of the delighted ladies on the stands; that one can win quite well at the races if one bets on a good horse but that one should prefer the theatre to racing, where, during *The Cherry Orchard*, one can almost smell the cherry blossom. But there were even more with brief greetings on postcards (including one with a picture of Fyodor Chaliapin) for feastdays, Easter, birthdays, name-days. Very often the letters began with an acknowledgement of the receipt of money and a thank you.

There were many books. The children when young used to pore over the pictures in the magazines. And now in *The New Illustrated*, in *The Spark*, in *Field* and *Homeland* one could still read Louis Boussenar's novel, *Captain Madcap*, and in *Round the World* about drama in the Andes, with pictures like 'Here died Antelope'; among the books piled in a heap was a Catechism of the Orthodox Catholic Church by Metropolitan Filaret and a dry little book, *The Fruits of the Teaching of Count L. N. Tolstoy*, and a novel with the first page torn off called *Why Did They Kill Her?*, and history stories, *The Conquest of the Caucasus* and *In Defence of Sevastopol*. There were many books one could not understand; they had been read, probably, by someone now absent and unknown, someone far away: these were books and magazines (letters too even, and postcards with non-Russian stamps and postmarks) in other, foreign tongues. The magazines lay in untidy piles, crumpled, frayed and even sticking together from some liquid that left yellow rings on the pages and smelt of mice and cats. The magazines depicted things that were more than strange for our time—for example, promenades in the Bois de Boulogne and the races at Longchamps, Paul Kruger with a beard going right up to his ears but no moustache, a dinner given in honour of the colonel-in-chief of the 73rd Black Sea Regiment by the officers; the English King Edward VII hunting with Wilhelm II, and a reception given by Foreign Minister, Sazonov.

A single, slender little book that had got there by accident evoked something quite different—*Songs of the Proletariat*, with a hammer and sickle on the cover. From this little book anyone who wanted to could sing that 'we have all come from the people', that 'we ourselves will fill the cartridges', that 'the accursed and the branded' must rise and that 'labour will rule the world'. . . . This one little book, alone, shifted all else and crushed it, harbouring the meaning and the answer to all that now existed, that had come to pass as it were, unexpectedly, and then irrevocably shut out all that had once been habitually held dear, which the father, the man with the eyes of helpless rage, had taken with him when he died, about which the mother sighed, having forgotten her once white fingers that now handled offal and potato peelings, and which was as yet unknown to that small living creature convulsively thrashing its blue, skinny little legs in the air—the child, still less than a year old, that was hungering for something and would not be quieted, indeed could not be quieted for a moment, for the black bit of so-called bread with big straws baked into it, which they put into his mouth when he cried, could not replace the mother's milk which the child hardly knew, for the mother's breast was dry, she had come to know hard times and was slowly dying, slowly perishing in the face of this irresistible force, this feverishly blowing wind of ineluctable, insupportable poverty.

Osip Mandelstam

Fourth Prose

Translator's Introduction

A great deal of what Osip Mandelstam (1891-1938) wrote either is, or has the effect of being, a fragment, some part of a larger whole that kept forever coming apart. The whole was his life, the poems and other writings its scattered members.

Like *The Noise of Time* and *The Egyptian Stamp*, his *Fourth Prose* is a blend of fiction and autobiography. It is different from them in that it was never published while he was alive, and it has never been officially published in Russia. It scarcely has a title. Nadezhda Yakovlevna, the poet's widow, told me that *Fourth Prose* was simply a kind of household nickname: if one takes *Noise* as first, *Stamp* as second, and the critical writings together as third, then this is fourth. The numeral appealed to him on other grounds as well. It carried overtones of 'fourth estate', a term that Mandelstam vastly preferred to the despised 'literature' as the focus of his allegiance. I was told that Mandelstam had destroyed the original first chapter. Why, I do not know.

The story behind *Fourth Prose* is that of a sordid defamatory campaign against Mandelstam. The facts are immensely involved, and obscured by the passage of time, but in outline they are as follows. At the end of the 1920s Mandelstam, who had been publishing his poetry and criticism for some two decades, was at the height of his fame. On the grounds of his poetry he was for the moment nearly invulnerable. But he belonged to that camp of free intellectuals and artists whose sympathies, always on the side of the Revolution, had never been with the Bolsheviks' brutal perversion of the dream; and he was thus, with many others, the constant object of attack, usually private, behind the scenes in writers' organisations and editorial offices, but also, as in the present case, public. Since about the middle of the 'twenties, Mandelstam had been driven to support himself and buy time for his real concerns by a backbreaking load of literary hackwork—as publisher's reader, reviewer, interviewer, consultant, translator. Probably no writer of our time, except possibly Ezra Pound, has had a higher conception of the writer's calling, his obligations to his art and to his reader. One can only imagine his exertions, as he ploughed through the general literary muck from which he wrested a living, to keep what he could of his artistic standards or to salvage what could be saved of the work in hand. In one letter of 29 June 1928 we find the poet whose wife was ill and had just undergone an operation, helplessly begging a certain Venediktov to send the money promised him for his work on a volume of Mayne Reid! (The most Satanic fancy can seldom match the mere routine of Soviet literature.) The money was being withheld, another document tells us, pending someone's approval of Mandelstam's Mayne Reid.

But even in this arena he was not really vulnerable, and so the occasion for an attack on him had to be manufactured. It was done as follows. The publishing house ZIF (initials for Russian words meaning 'Land and Factory') had commissioned him in 1927 to revise and edit two existing Russian versions of Charles de Coster's *La legende de Thyl Ulenspiegel*. These were a version by V. Karyakin, made in 1916, and another by the prominent literary critic A. G. Gornfeld, which had come out in 1920. When his edition appeared in 1928, the unsuspecting Mandelstam was horrified to find his own name on the title page as 'translator'. Had certain other things not happened recently, this might have seemed nothing more than the habitual sloppiness of the publishers. But there was the abrupt dismissal, on political grounds, from the same publishing house of his old friend and former Acmeist colleague, Vladimir Narbut. There were the difficulties about assignments and then about being paid for them. It seemed, and it was, part of a pattern. The ground for the attack had been prepared.

Mandelstam demanded at once that the publisher rectify the error by pasting in a slip with the correct information on the title page, but this was refused. He also telegraphed Gornfeld, explaining the circumstances and offering to turn over to him his own fee, thus taking upon himself a moral responsibility, that, in all reason, belonged to the publisher alone. But reason had nothing to do with it. Gornfeld's role is not clear to me. Mandelstam's senior by 24 years, he was not a creature of the new order; his career in literary journalism had been, if not brilliant, honourable; as a translator he evidently followed the drudging ideal of literal correctness, which is at least an amiable imperfection. But, leaving aside the question whether he willingly offered himself as a utensil, he did play a rather supine role by printing, in a newspaper where the publisher's belated and more or less *pro forma* explanation had appeared, an attack on Mandelstam. The poet, struggling to live from day to day, was enraged by the figurative charge that he had stolen Gornfeld's fur coat and fenced it at a rummage shop. If Mandelstam despised 'authors' and 'literature' as he had come to know them in actual fact, he nevertheless cherished a lofty ideal of the writer and of the fellowship of writers: one cannot read his work without a sense of the covenant that he felt to exist between himself and Ovid, Dante, Villon, Goethe, Pushkin, Herzen. Gornfeld's remark about the stolen coat (the charge of plagiarism having not actually been made) seemed to Mandelstam so perfidious and contemptible a thing to have been said by one writer of another that he blazoned it as the epigraph in a letter to the editor where he answered the charges.

In a few months' time the persecution of Mandelstam took an alarming turn—even though it was only 1929, that 'relatively vegetarian' period, in Akhmatova's bitter phrase—with the entry into the matter of David Zaslavsky. In the interval, Mandelstam had written a newspaper article exposing the slapdash treatment of translation and translators in the Soviet press, and Zaslavsky seized upon it as a device for re-opening the charges in the *Ulenspiegel* case. Zaslavsky is one of the most odious figures in the history of Stalinist journalism. A reliable scourge, he took a prominent part in campaigns against his own former associates, the Mensheviks, and his co-religionists—in the notorious persecution of the 'cosmopolites' after the war. One of his last services to the regime (he died in 1965) was the public savaging of Pasternak during the *Zhivago* affair. Mandelstam, feeling perhaps that Zaslavsky was beneath notice in a dispute involving men of letters, does not even mention him. But his participation may help explain why, in Mandelstam's own household, the whole matter went by the name of 'the Dreyfus affair'.

Such, in general contour, was the bloated and at times—had it not been so sinister in intent—almost comic personal and political campaign against one Russian poet. The *odium sovieticum* spread like a stain through the two capitals. Certain Leningrad writers planned a letter in Mandelstam's defence, then lost their nerve, to his enduring disgust. Moscow writers—among them Vsevolod Ivanov, Pilnyak, Fadeev, Pasternak, Kataev, Fedin, Olesha, Zoshchenko, and Leonov—did publish a warm letter in his defence. An arbitration court of FOSP, the federation of writers' organisations, eventually produced an ambiguous decision: Mandelstam had been treated unfairly, but, on the other hand, the moral fault was his that no suitable arrangement had been made with the earlier translators. The matter might not have ended there, however, had not a powerful protector of Mandelstam's, Nikolay Ivanovich Bukharin, intervened. He saw to it that the persecution was stopped, and then he arranged that the poet and his wife be sent on a trip to Armenia.

Armenia was a godsend, but it was *Fourth Prose* that effected, in artistic terms, an even more startling cure. It was a desperate act of self-therapy. By this outburst, Mandelstam seems to have defined himself, and also the 'new reality' that now obtained in his country, in a kind of transport of fury. It was an explosion, a scream, a howl of his injured humanity—and, whatever else it may have accomplished, it cleared his lungs. His breathing freed, an awful five-year period of poetic silence, the 'deaf-mute' time as he called it, came suddenly to an end. The *Fourth Prose* is what preceded and largely made possible the poems dated '1930' and onwards in his collected works.

C. B.

●

Venyamin Fyodorovich Kagan[1] approached this matter with the sage economicalness of a sorcerer or of some Odessa-born Newton. All the conspiratorial activity of Venyamin Fyodorovich rested upon a basis of infinitesimals. Venyamin Fyodorovich saw the law of salvation as a matter of keeping to a turtle's pace. He allowed himself to be shaken out of his professorial box, answered the telephone at all hours, made no promises in advance, would not say no to anything; but the main thing he did was try to retard the dangerous course of the disease.

The fact that a professor, and a mathematician at that, was involved in the improbable affair of saving five lives by means of those cognisable, absolutely weightless integral moves known as pulling wires, was a source of general satisfaction.

Isai Benediktovich[2] behaved himself from the very first as if the illness were infectious, something catching, like scarlet fever, so that he too, Isai Benediktovich, might, for all he knew, be shot. There was not the least sense in the way Isai Benediktovich bustled about. It was as if he were racing from one doctor to another imploring them to disinfect him at once.

If Isai Benediktovich had had his way he would have taken a taxi and raced all over Moscow at random, without a shadow of a plan, for that, as he imagined, was the ritual.

Isai Benediktovich was forever repeating and constantly recalling that he had left behind him, in Petersburg, a wife. He even set himself up with something like a secretary—a small, stern, very commonsensical companion—a relative who had already begun to fuss over him, Isai Benediktovich, as though he were a child. To

---

[1] A professor of mathematics at Moscow University. Because of his skill as a translator of mathematical literature, he was asked to be an arbitrator in the *Ulenspiegel* case. Tr.

[2] Isai Benediktovich Mandelstam. A translator, no relation to Osip Mandelstam. Tr.

make a long story short, Isai Benediktovich, by appealing to various people and at various times, was, so to speak, vaccinating himself against execution.

All the relatives of Isai Benediktovich had died in their Jewish beds of walnut wood. As the Turk travels to the black stone of the Kaaba, so these Petersburg bourgeois, descended from rabbis of patrician blood and, via the translator Isai, brought into touch with Anatole France, made pilgrimages to the most unimaginably Turgenevian and Lermontovian watering places where they prepared themselves, by taking the cure, for the transition to the hereafter.

In Petersburg Isai Benediktovich lived like a pious Frenchman, ate his *potage*, chose for acquaintances people no more offensive than the croutons in his bouillon, and, in his professional capacity, made calls on two traffickers in junk translations.

Isai Benediktovich was good only at the very beginning of the wire-pulling, during the mobilisation and, as it were, the alarm. Afterwards he faded, drooped, stuck out his tongue, and his relatives themselves pooled their money and sent him to Petersburg.

I have always been interested in the question where the bourgeois gets his fastidiousness and his so-called decency. His decency is what makes the bourgeois kin to the animal. Many Party members are at ease in the company of a bourgeois for the very same reason that grown-ups require the society of rosy-cheeked children.

The bourgeois is of course more innocent than the proletarian, closer to the womb world, the baby, the kitten, the angel, the cherub. In Russia there are very few of these innocent bourgeois, and that has a bad effect on the digestion of true revolutionaries. The bourgeoisie must be preserved in its innocent aspect, it must be entertained with amateur theatricals, lulled on the springs of Pullman cars, tucked into envelopes of snow-white railway sleep.

●

A little boy in goatskin boots and velveteen Russian coat, his hair carefully brushed back, is standing in the midst of mammas, grannies and nannies, and beside him stands some cook or coachman's whelp, some urchin from the servants' quarters. And that whole pack of lisping, hooting, spluttering archangels is urging the young master on:

'Hit 'im, Vasenka, hit 'im!'

Vasenka gets in a blow, and the old maids, the disgusting old toads, poke each other and hold on to the mangy coachman's brat:

'Hit 'im, Vasenka, hit 'im, while we hold his curly head, while we dance around him. . . .'

What is this? A genre painting in the style of Venetsianov? An étude by some peasant artist?

No, this is the way they train some shaggy shrimp from the Komsomol under the supervision of the agit-mammas, grannies, and nannies so that he can stomp 'im, Vasenka, hit 'im, Vasenka, while we hold him by his black hide, while we dance around. . . .

'Hit 'im, Vasenka, hit 'im. . . .'

The lame girl came in to us from a street as long as a night with no streetcars. She put her crutch to one side and quickly took her seat so as to look like everyone else. Who is this husbandless girl? The light cavalry. . . .

We cadge cigarettes from each other and correct our Chinese gibberish, enciphering in formulas of animal cowardice the great, powerful and forbidden notion of class. Animal fear taps on the typewriters, animal fear proof-reads the gibberish on sheets of toilet-paper, scribbles denunciations, hits men when they're down, demands execution for prisoners. As urchins drown a kitten in the river Moscow in plain view of everyone, so our grown-up boys playfully put the screws on, at noon recess play back-to-the-wall: 'Hey, pile on, press till you can't see him any more. . . .' Such is the sacred law of lynching.

A shopkeeper on the Ordynka gave a charwoman short weight: kill him!

A cashier came out a nickel short: kill her!

A director foolishly signed some junk or other: kill him!

A peasant hid some rye in a barn: kill him!

The girl comes to see us, dragging along on her crutch. One of her legs is short, and the crude prosthetic boot looks like a wooden hoof.

Who are we? We are school children who do not go to school. We are Komsomol freebooters. We are bully-boys by leave of all the saints.

Filipp Filippich has developed a toothache. Filipp Filippich has not and will not come to class. Our notion of studying has as much to do with science as the hoof with the foot, but that does not embarrass us.

I have come to you, my artiodactylous friends, to stamp my wooden stump in the yellow socialist arcade-combine created by the frantic fantasy of the daredevil business executive, Giber, from elements of the chic hotel on the Tverskoy, from the night telephone or telegraph exchange, from a dream of universal bliss—realised as a permanent foyer with buffet—from an uninterrupted counter with saluting clerks, from the postal-telegraph aridity of air that makes one's throat tickle.

Here there's an unbroken bookkeeper's night beneath the yellow flame of the second-class bulbs of the railway station. Here as in Pushkin's fairy tale, a Yid is betrothed to a frog, that is to say, there's an endless wedding ceremony between a goat-footed fop, spawning theatrically, and a well-matched devil from the same stew, a Moscow editor-cum-coffinmaker turning out silk brocade coffins for Monday, Tuesday, Wednesday and Thursday. He rustles his paper shroud. He opens the veins of the months of the Christian year that still preserve their pastoral Greek names: January, February, March . . . He is the terrifying and illiterate horse-doctor of happenings, deaths and events, and is tickled pink when the black horseblood of the age spurts forth in a gushing fountain.

●

I went to work for the newspaper *Moscow Komsomol Member* straight from the caravanserai of the TSEKUBU.[1] There were twelve pairs of earphones there, almost all of them broken, and a reading-room made over from a church, with no books, where people slept like snails on little curved divans.

The servants at TSEKUBU despised me for my straw baskets and because I was not a professor.

In the afternoon I would go look at the high water and firmly believed that the obscene waters of the river Moscow would flood the learned Kropotkin Embankment and that TSEKUBU would telephone for a boat.

In the mornings I would drink sterilised cream right on the street from the mouth of the bottle.

I would take someone else's soap from the professors' shelves and wash myself at night and was never caught once.

People from Kharkov and Voronezh would come and all of them wanted to go to Alma-Ata. They took me for one of their own and asked my advice as to which republic was the best deal.

Many of them received telegrams from various places in the Soviet Union. One Byzantine little old man was on his way to his son's house in Kovno.

[1] An acronym designating the committee for the relief of scholars, established in 1921. Tr.

At night TSEKUBU was locked up like a fortress and I would rap on the window with my stick.

Every decent man got his telephone calls at TSEKUBU and in the evening the servants would hand him a note as if giving the priest a list of those to be prayed for. The writer Grin, whose clothes the servants used to brush, lived there. I lived at TSEKUBU like everyone else, and no one bothered me until I myself moved out in the middle of the summer.

When I was moving to another apartment, my fur coat lay across the carriage as it does when people leave hospital after a long stay or have just been let out of prison.

Things have come to the point where I value only the proud flesh around the wound in the word trade, only the insane excrescence:

And the whole ravine was cut
To the bone by the falcon's scream

That is what I need.

I divide all the works of world literature into those written with and without permission. The first are trash, the second—stolen air. As for writers who write things with prior permission, I want to spit in their faces, beat them over the head with a stick and set them all at a table in the Herzen House, each with a glass of police tea in front of him and in his hand the analysis of Gornfield's urine.

I would forbid these writers to marry and have children. After all, children must carry on for us, must say to the end for us what is most important to say. But their fathers have sold out to the pockmarked devil for three generations to come.

Now that's a little literary page.

●

I have no manuscripts, no notebooks, no archives. I have no handwriting because I never write. I alone in Russia work from the voice while all around the bitch pack writes. What the hell kind of writer am I!? Get out, you fools!

On the other hand, I have a lot of pencils and they are all stolen and of different colours. You can sharpen them with a Gillette blade.

The blade of the Gillette razor with its faintly notched bevelled edge has always seemed to me one of the noblest products of the steel industry. The good Gillette blade cuts like sedge grass, bends but doesn't break in the hand—something like a calling card from a Martian or a note from a dapper devil with a hole drilled in the middle.

●

I am a Chinaman, no one understands me. Idiot-shmidiot! Let's go to Alma-Ata where the people have raisin eyes, the Persian has eyes like fried eggs, the Sart has sheep's eyes.

Idiot-shmidiot! Let's go to Azerbaijan!

I had a patron—People's Commissar Mravyan-Muravyan,[1] most pissantic People's Commissar of the land of Armenia, that younger sister of the Land of Judah. He sent me a telegram.

Dead is my patron, the People's Commissar Mravyan-Muravyan. Gone from the Erevan anthill is the black People's Commissar. He will no longer come to Moscow in the international car of the train, naïve and curious as a priest from a Turkish village.

Idiot-shmidiot! Let's go to Azerbaijan!

I had a letter for People's Commissar Mravyan. I took it to the secretaries in the Armenian residence in the cleanest, most ambassadorial street in all Moscow. I was just on the point of leaving for Erevan under the auspices of the ancient People's Commissariat of Education to conduct a terrifying seminar for those roundheaded youths in their poor monastery of a university.

If I had gone to Erevan I should have run for three days and three nights to the large buffets in the railway stations to eat buttered bread with black caviare.

Idiot-shmidiot!

On the way I should have read Zoshchenko's[2] very best book and been as happy as a Tartar who'd stolen a hundred roubles.

Idiot-shmidiot! Let's go to Azerbaijan!

I should have taken courage with me in my yellow straw basket with its great heap of linen smelling of alkali soap, and my fur coat would have hung on a golden nail. And I should have got out at the

[1] Askanaz Artem'evich Mravyan was Commissar of Foreign Affairs in Armenia in 1920-21 and from 1923 headed the education ministry and served as Deputy Chairman of the Council of People's Commissars there. Tr.

[2] Mikhail Mikhailovich Zoshchenko (1895-1958), the best and most popular Soviet satirist. Tr.

railway station in Erevan with my winter coat in one hand and my senile cane—my Jewish staff—in the other.

●

There is a splendid line of Russian poetry which I never tire of repeating in the bitch-loud nights of Moscow. Which, like a spell, disperses evil spirits. Guess what line, friends. It writes on the snow like sleigh runners, clicks in the lock like a key, shoots into a room like frost:

. . . didn't shoot the wretches in the dungeons . . .[1]

There is the symbol of faith, there is the genuine canon of the true writer, the mortal enemy of literature.

In the Herzen House there is a milksop vegetarian, a philologist with a Chinese noddle, a Chink of that breed that tiptoes about the blood-stained Soviet land twittering *hao-hao shango-shango* when heads are being lopped off, a certain Mitka Blagoy, a piece of trash from the lycée, authorised by the Bolsheviks for the benefit of learning; in a special museum he guards the length of cord with which Seryozha Esenin hanged himself.

And I say: Blagoy for the Chinese! To Shanghai with him! To the Chinks, where he belongs! To think what Mother Philology was and what she has become. Full-blooded and implacable she was, and now she's become fool-blooded and in everything placable.

●

To the number of murderers of Russian poets, or of aspirants to join these murderers, has been added the murky name of Gornfeld. This paralytic D'Anthès,[2] this Uncle Monya from Basseiny Street, preaching morality and the State, carried out the orders of a regime totally alien to himself, which is, to him, more or less the same as a touch of indigestion.

To die from Gornfeld is as silly as to die from a bicycle or a parrot's beak. But a literary murderer can also be a parrot. I, for instance, was nearly killed by a polly named after His Majesty King

[1] From a poem by Sergey Esenin, whose suicide in 1925 is mentioned later. Tr.

[2] Baron Georges D'Anthès killed Aleksandr Pushkin in a duel in 1837. Tr.

Albert and Vladimir Galaktionovich Korolenko.[1] I am very glad that my murderer is alive and has in a sense survived me. I feed him sugar and take pleasure in hearing him repeat, from *Thyl Ulenspiegel*, 'The ashes are knocking at my heart', a sentence which he alternates with another, no less pretty, 'There is no torment in the world greater than the torment of the word . . .'. A man capable of calling his book *Torments of the Word*[2] was born with the mark of Cain, as the sign of the literary murderer, on his brow.

I met Gornfeld only once, in the dirty editorial office of some unprincipled rag where, as in the buffet of Kvisisan, a crowd of spectral figures had gathered. There was as yet no ideology then, and no one to complain to when you were insulted. When I recall that deprivation—how could we have lived then?!—huge tears well up in my eyes. Someone introduced me to the biped critic, and I shook his hand.

Papa Gornfeld, why did you complain to the *Bourse News*, I mean to the *Evening Red Gazette*, in the year of Our Soviet 1929? You would have done better to weep into the pure literary Jewish waistcoat of Mr Propper. Better to have told your woe to your banker with sciatica, kugel, and tallith . . .

●

Nikolay Ivanovich[3] has a secretary who is, really and truly, an absolute squirrel, a little rodent. She gnaws a nut with every visitor and runs to the telephone like an inexperienced young mother to a sick baby.

A certain scoundrel told me that truth was *mria* in Greek.

So that little squirrel is genuine truth with a capital letter in Greek; and at the same time she is that other truth, that stern card-carrying virgin—Party truth.

The secretary, frightened and compassionate, like a hospital nurse, does not merely work but lives in the antechamber of the office, in the telephone dressing-room. Poor Maria from the connecting room with her telephone and her classical newspaper!

[1] The writer Korolenko was editor of the journal *Russian Wealth*, to which Gornfeld contributed regularly. Tr.

[2] A collection of Gornfeld's critical articles, first published in 1906. Tr.

[3] Bukharin (1888-1938), whom Lenin called 'the most valuable and greatest theoretician of the Party', was editor of *Pravda* ('Truth') and a member of the Politburo. For his opposition to Stalin he was expelled from all his Party positions in 1929 and shot in 1938 after one of the notorious 'show trials' of the Great Purge. Tr.

This secretary differs from others in that she sits like a night nurse on the threshold of power, defending the wielder of that power as if he were gravely ill.

●

No, really, let me be tried! Allow me to enter in evidence! . . . Permit me, as it were, to file myself. Do not, I implore you, deprive me of my trial. . . . The legal proceedings are not yet at an end and, I make so bold as to assure you, will never be at an end. What happened before was only the overture. Bosio[1] herself is going to sing at my trial. Bearded students in checked plaids, mingling with caped policemen and, under the direction of their goat precentor, ecstatically chanting a syncopated version of the Eternal Memory, will carry the police coffin with the remains of my case out of the smoke-blackened hall of the district court.

Papa, Papa, Papochka,
Where, O where's your Mamochka?

The Writers' Union is too close—
She will come back with a dose.

Mama's blind in one eye, right?
And this case is sewn up tight.

Alexander Ivanovich Herzen! . . . Allow me to introduce myself. . . . It was, it seems, in your house . . . As host, you are in some sense responsible. . . .
You were so good as to go abroad, were you? . . . Meanwhile, something disagreeable has happened here. . . . Alexander Ivanovich! Sir! What am I to do? There is absolutely no one to turn to!

●

In a certain year of my life, grown men from that tribe which I despise with all the strength of my soul and to which I neither wish

[1] Angiolina Bosio, an Italian soprano, who sang for several seasons in St Petersburg, where she died in 1859. There is evidence that Mandelstam once wrote or planned to write a novella entitled 'The Death of Bosio'. Whether he did is not known, but a passage of his 'Egyptian Stamp' is devoted to her. Tr.

141

to, nor ever will, belong, conceived the intention of jointly committing against me an ugly and repellent ritual. The name of this ritual is literary pruning or dishonouring, and it is performed in accordance with the customs and the calendrical needs of the writers' tribe, the victim being selected by vote of the elders.

I insist that writerdom, as it has developed in Europe and above all in Russia, is incompatible with the honourable title of Jew, of which I am proud. My blood, burdened with its inheritance from sheep breeders, patriarchs and kings, rebels against the shifty gypsyishness of the writing tribe. A creaking camp of unwashed Romanies kidnapped me as a child and for a certain number of years dawdled along its obscene routes, vainly striving to teach me its one craft, its one art: theft.

Writerdom is a race with a revolting smell to its hide and the filthiest known means of preparing its food. It is a race that wanders and sleeps in its own vomit, one that is expelled from cities and hounded in villages, but it is always and everywhere close to the authorities, who grant its members a place in red-light districts, as prostitutes. For literature always and everywhere carries out one assignment: it helps superiors keep their soldiers obedient and it helps judges execute reprisals against doomed men.

A writer is a mixture of parrot and pope. He's a polly in the very loftiest meaning of that word. He speaks French if his master is French, but, sold into Persia, he will say 'Pol's a fool', or 'Polly wants a cracker' in Persian. A parrot has no age and doesn't know day from night. If he starts to bore his master he's covered with a black cloth and that, for literature, is the surrogate of night.

●

There were two brothers named Chenier. The despicable younger brother belongs entirely to literature; the elder, who was executed, executed literature himself.

Jailors love to read novels and, of all men, have the greatest need of literature.

In a certain year of my life grown men with beards and wearing horned fur caps brandished a flint knife over me, with which they meant to castrate me. Judging by the evidence, they were priests of their tribe: they smelled of onion, novels, and goatmeat.

And it was all as terrifying as in a child's dream. *Nel mezzo del cammin di nostra vita*—midway on the path of life—I was stopped in the dense Soviet forest by bandits who called themselves my judges. They were old men with scrawny necks and little goose heads unfit to bear the burden of years.

For the first and only time in my life, literature had need of me, and it crumpled me, pawed me, squeezed me, and it was all as terrifying as in a child's dream.

●

I am morally responsible for the fact that the ZIF Publishing House did not make a contract with the translators Gornfeld and Karyakin. I—furrier of precious furs, and practically suffocated with literary hides—I am morally responsible for having inspired a Petersburg cad with the desire to allude in a libellous anecdote to that warm Gogolian fur coat, torn by night from the shoulders of that most ancient member of the Komsomol, Akaky Akakievich. I tear off my literary fur coat and trample it under foot. In nothing but my jacket and in a thirty-degree frost I shall run three times round the boulevard rings of Moscow. I shall escape from the yellow hospital of the Komsomol arcade straight into a fatal chill, if only not to see the forty bright Judas holes of that obscene building on Tverskoy Boulevard, if only not to hear the clinking of pieces of silver and the counting of printer's sheets.

●

My dear Romany of the Tverskoy Boulevard, you and I together have written a novel of which you have not even dreamt. I am very fond of coming across my name in official papers, bailiff's subpoenas, and other stern documents. Here the name has an absolutely objective ring to it, a novel sound to the ear and, I must say, most interesting. From time to time I am myself curious to know what it is I am forever doing wrong. What sort of pineapple is this Mandelstam, anyway, who for so and so many years was supposed to have done such and such and, like the scoundrel that he is, keeps dodging it? . . . How much longer is he going to keep on dodging it? That's why the years are wasted on me; others accumulate more respect with every passing day, but for me it's the reverse—time is flowing backwards.

I'm to blame. No two ways about it. I shan't wriggle out of this guilt. I live in insolvency. I save myself by dodging. How much longer am I to go on dodging?

When that tin subpoena arrives or that reminder, Greek in its clarity, from the social organisation; when they demand that I name my accomplices, cease my skulduggery, tell where I get the counterfeit money, and sign an undertaking not to travel beyond certain specific limits, I agree on the spot; but immediately, as if nothing had happened, I start dodging again—and so it goes.

In the first place: I ran away from somewhere and I must be sent back, extradited, found and returned. In the second place, I am being mistaken for someone else. No hope of proving my identity. Pockets full of trash: cryptic jottings from a year ago, telephone numbers of dead relatives and addresses of persons unknown. In the third place, I signed with Beelzebub or with the State Publishing House, a grandiose, unfulfilable contract on Whatman paper smeared with mustard and emery powder pepper in which I undertook to return twice over everything that I acquired, belch back fourfold what I misappropriated and to perform sixteen times running that impossible, unimaginable, that unique thing that might, in part, acquit me.

With every passing year I am more incorrigible. As though by a conductor's steel punch I am riddled with holes and stamped with my own surname. Every time someone calls me by my first name I tremble, I simply cannot get used to it, such an honour! For once in one's life to be called Ivan Moyseich by somebody! Hey, Ivan, go scratch the dogs! Mandelstam, go scratch the dogs! To some Frenchy it's *cher maître*, dear teacher; but me? Mandelstam, go scratch the dogs! To each his own.

An ageing man, I scratch the master's dog with the bitten stump of my heart, and it's not enough for them, it's not enough. The eyes of Russian writers look at me with canine tenderness and implore me: drop dead! Where does this cringing spite, this grovelling contempt for my name come from? The gypsy at least had his horse, but I am horse and gypsy in one person. . . .

Tin subpoenas under the little pillow . . . the forty-sixth contract in place of the wreath of burial ribbon on my forehead, and a hundred thousand lighted cigarettes instead of lighted candles. . . .

●

No matter how much I work, if I carry horses on my back, if I turn millstones, still I shall never become a worker. My work, whatever form it may take, is seen as mischief, as lawlessness, as an accident. But that's how I like it, so I agree. I subscribe to it with both hands.

It is a question of how you look at it. What I prize in the doughnut is the hole. But what about the dough of the doughnut? You can gobble up the doughnut, but the hole will still be there.

Real work is Brussels lace, the main thing in it is what holds the pattern up: air, punctures, truancy.

But in my case, brethren, work's of no benefit; it doesn't go on my record.

We have a bible of work, but we don't appreciate it. It's Zoshchenko's stories. The only man who ever showed us a worker has been trampled in the dirt. But I demand monuments to Zoshchenko in every city and town of the Soviet Union, or at least, as for Papa Krylov, in the Summer Garden.

That's a man whose work breathes truancy, in whose work Brussels lace lives!

At night on the Ilyinka when the department stores and the trusts are asleep and talking in their native Chinese, at night jokes run along the Ilyinka. Lenin and Trotsky walk about with their arms around each other as though nothing had happened. One has a little pail and a fishing-rod from Constantinople in his hand. Two Jews walk about, an inseparable pair—one inquirer and one responder, and the one keeps asking, but the other keeps evading and evading, and there's no way for them to part.

A German organ-grinder walks by with his Schubertian barrel-organ, such a failure, such a sponger. . . . *Ich bin arm*. I am poor.

Sleep, my darling . . . M...S...P...O.[1]

The Viy[2] is reading the telephone directory on Red Square. Lift up my eyelids. . . . Connect me with the Central Committee. . . .

Armenians from Erevan walk by with green-painted herrings. *Ich bin arm*—I am poor.

And in Armavir on the city coat of arms it is written: the dog barks, the wind carries.

[1] Initials of the Moscow Union of Consumers' Societies. Tr.

[2] The monster in Nikolai Gogol's story of the same name. Its eyelids reached to the ground. Mandelstam's heavy eyelids were remarked upon by nearly everyone who left a memoir of him. Tr.

V. Goryushkin

Before Sunrise

Akim awoke, and a few pale watery stars shone in the sky. Beside him was the warm body of his wife, but he couldn't put his arms round her, for they were missing from the elbow. . . . So he lay without stirring. He would have told her how much he loved her, remembering how easily he once made the words come; but he could not. Akim had lost his tongue long since, it had been carried away by a shell in the war.

The windows of his hut were open. Outside it was July and the lime tree was in blossom. From an iron hook by the stove hung a cradle. In it was his son, the son of Akim the Cripple. Akim had no hands and no legs, his tongue was useless, but he possessed a son. His son had hands; and legs; and a voice to be marvelled at.

Akim smiled with quiet joy, remembering his dream. The dream had been of an enormous field, so huge and boundless that it took your breath away to look at it. . . . He was on a tractor, hands over the steering wheel, his foot down on the accelerator, a song bursting from his throat. Then Akim realised he was shouting with the voice of his son, that he had long since forgotten the sound of his own.

Akim closed his eyes again. He would have given anything to see himself in that field with those hands, those legs, that song. He would not ask for anything more, to save his life.

Soon his wife would wake up, slip quietly from under the covers and go to milk the cow in her nightgown. She would leave the outer door open, and he would hear her say a reassuring word to the cow. Then the streams of milk would start banging into the pail, and the chickens would wake up and start clucking. . . .

Akim loved the summer, because in the summer his wife carried him out on to the verandah, where he sat until dinner. And there was a lot to see before dinner. . . .

Their neighbour usually sent his cow out to join the herd, but the herd was already grazing in the ravine for he had overslept. Hastily he greeted Akim in a voice still hoarse from sleep and went frowning on his way, wondering why Akim the cripple should have a wife, while he, the healthy one, had none. Akim felt sorry for his neighbour, he wanted to say a comforting word, but all he could do was wrinkle his left eyebrow; and besides, perhaps it was better that way, because Akim didn't know why his wife loved him.

The peasant women greeted him as they went by with their hay-rakes and the cheekiest winked and whispered a few ardent words in his ear, asking when she could come and see him; she knew that Akim wouldn't tell his wife, of course, because he couldn't. The women burst out laughing and Akim blushed and grinned like a little boy. Because the women were a cheerful crowd, and they made him feel good.

In the yard the cock came to life, ruffling his feathers, and inviting the hens on to the dungheap he had discovered. A succession of roosters' war-cries rolled through the village, now dying away and now flaring up again. Fluffy clouds, like stray ducklings, dawdled over the village; the sky was a deep and peaceful blue. A swallow flew in under the verandah roof and placed a worm in the yellow gape of its young.

Vasya the blacksmith, who had grown up and fought together with Akim, came by on his way to the forge and said:

'Your whiskers are growing, Akim, my old son. When I knock off work, I'll come and shave you. My razor's a beauty—I've still got the one I had in the war.'

He ran his hand upwards over Akim's face. 'What a lovely day it is. . . .' And the blacksmith rubbed the unshaven cheeks, sighed, and went off to the forge where his mate and the blazing hearth awaited him, to earn his and his children's daily bread.

The grass along the road was sickly, just single blades, but there was an abundance of dense green plantains and they were all in flower, covered with little beads of white. The dust on the road was soft and hot and the sparrows fluttered and bathed in it. And Akim knew that if he were to crawl down the path through the garden and down the slope beyond, he would see the spring, with an oak water trough which he and his dad had chiselled out themselves. As a youth he had fought with Vasya the blacksmith by that spring and both had drawn blood. Akim no longer remembered what that fight had been over, but he had won it, and not with tricks or sticks, but honestly.

'But what had honesty to do with it?' thought Akim. 'One was weaker, the other stronger, that was all the honesty about it. And why did this happen to me, especially to me? How is one to take such things? . . .'

The thatched huts flowed on somewhere across the ravine and beyond Akim's horizon. He wanted to see where the village ended, how he longed to see where it ended. But perhaps the village didn't end. Perhaps it stretched over the whole world, round the round earth and back again the other side, like a line round the rubber ball that the kids played with.

Over the village floated the ringing of the forge, dissolving in the greater bell of the deep blue sky, overflowing, echoed by the song of the lark. How he longed to take off and fly over the world, see the whole earth as it really was, but the only trouble was—he had no wings. Once when the dew was still white on the fields, Akim had suddenly felt that the time had come. He breathed in the air of the wide open spaces, shut his eyes and then—and then he was flying and flying; or perhaps he wasn't, who knows? But he wasn't going to open his eyes until he suddenly heard the schoolmaster's voice:

'You're a lucky fellow, Akim,' he said, and Akim knew that the schoolmaster wasn't making mock of him, but really meant it. His face was wreathed in a respectful grimace. Looking at the schoolmaster, Akim was reminded of a mare, emaciated by a long winter and a neglectful master. 'You've time to contemplate. You live on a higher plane, unattainable to us ordinary mortals. It's not as if we lead frantically busy lives, but all the same. . . .' The schoolmaster shook his head. 'Did you say "sanctity of labour"? What does "labour" mean when, because of it, we scurry about all over the place like insects, and before we've time to look around, it's winter, time to die. And why did we rush all over the place—nobody knows. Just the same, I studied, dreamed, thought I would see a better world. But when I sit down to mark my tests, my hands are covered in dung. . . .'

'He's jealous,' thought Akim, 'and who is he jealous of? Me, a limbless torso. What's going on in the world, what's going on?'

'I thought the purpose of life was work, serving other people. . . . But that's just dogma! Terrifying, life-killing dogma. And you're allowed no doubts, and no confirmations either. You're like a horse bitted and bridled, shafts on either side, and as for turning left or right—not a hope, that's what the whip is for.'

'If only I had hands,' Akim was thinking, 'I'd plough up the earth with my fingers.'

'Contemplation,' the schoolmaster went on, 'is the greatest blessing given to man, his highest spiritual state. But here am I talking to you, while my sick wife is expecting me home—the sow is due to farrow, and somebody must see she doesn't eat the litter. Isn't that a joke—my children's future, my wonderful ideals, my relations with my wife, all depend on a sow in-pig. . . .'

The schoolmaster wasn't directing his questions at Akim, but talking to himself, to that winged cripple that lives inside every one of us. But Akim wasn't bored, he was looking along the village, trying to see to the far end.

Then the schoolmaster's wife appeared, bony and perpetually pregnant. Seeing her husband, she called out tenderly, pleadingly:

'Kolya! Kolya, my love!' Even in Akim's presence she contained herself, but at home she gave free rein to her feelings, shouting about her ruined life, weeping, hissing: 'Tramp, good-for-nothing, intellectual!' But now she stood by the mountain ash hedge, with a sickly smile on her face: 'Kolya, my love!' The schoolmaster painfully suppressed a cough, saying as he left: 'I try to feel that my pupils need me—I immerse myself in the life of my children—I try to get by somehow. The most terrible thing of all is—impotence.'

'There goes a man who can read and write, who's got arms and legs, and still tortures himself. Why?' Akim asked himself for the umpteenth time, without finding an answer. Along the road marched a platoon of soldiers, raising swirls of dust behind them as they sang about Sergeant Kolya, who had lost the gift of speech at the sight of dark-browed Masha. Grubby urchins marched alongside, joining in the choruses.

Akim stopped dreaming about the verandah, and turned over like a caterpillar, painfully but very carefully, so as not to wake his wife before time. She must be worn out . . . alone the whole time . . . twenty years as if alone. She slept deeply, breathing heavily, as if weeping. Weeping. He could not weep, could not say to her, 'Stop it, why mess up your life?' He could only grunt and roll his eyes; but if he could have spoken, he would have said: 'They've got special homes where they keep people like us, who've suffered for the motherland. Those that haven't arms can dance, those that haven't legs can play dominoes, those that haven't arms or legs can sing songs, those that can't sing gaze at the sky, those that can't see . . . I'd like it there, it would be nice and peaceful. So what if you loved me when I was a whole man? So what if I was once the breadwinner and built this house for us—I was well then. But all I'm good for is begging in the church porch. Don't ruin your beautiful life, no one obliged you to saddle yourself with a hopeless cripple. . . .'

Marya had brought Akim home across the fields on a little sledge one cold January night, the stars like wolves' eyes blotted out by his wife's back. The squeaky snowy path suddenly gave way under the runners, Akim bellowed, his face in a snowdrift. Marya had lifted him out, murmuring, 'My own Akimushka,' wiped the froth from his lips, replaced him on the sledge, and the brilliant crackle of the snow rose triumphantly again to the stars. But Akim's bellow and his wife's tears remained there, on earth.

Winter was like the torments of hell, unending as the snowy wastes outside, in the half-dark hut with the weeping candle end and the mournful cricket. Marya was busy with her housework, with all her cares, while he was on his back, looking for weeks on end at a little lump of tow which had come loose from under a board. Whichever way you looked at it, it had to be pushed in, the hut would be chilled, firewood would be wasted. It wasn't very high, if you stood up on your leg-stumps and pointed with your arm stumps . . . but then it was right up under the ceiling, perhaps you wouldn't be able to reach.

Akim grunted, pointing with his arm, but Marya didn't understand, she looked at the ceiling and fussed about straightening the pillow and bringing water, and finally she sat down and burst into tears. How was she to spot that tiny piece of caulking? But the cripple could think of only one thing, raging uncontrollably and beating his stump against the log wall. Marya wiped away her tears: 'Akimushka, what is it? The ceiling? The roof? Are you hungry?' Akim shook his head. 'Wrong, wrong. . . .'

Marya planted her beetroot and potatoes, thinking to herself: 'What can he want?' And when the following winter came, the cripple would begin again, and Marya would ask once more: 'Is it the roof? The sky?' Akim felt his head would split. His face was purple, the sweat stood out on his forehead, his lips were drawn. He twitched, then grew still, his breathing became inaudible—was he alive or dead? Marya looked into her husband's open eyes, but saw nothing, only a stale, unfulfilled longing; she asked with a sigh, 'Is it God?' The short sharp word was like a slap in the face. But the cripple remained calm and quietly shook his head.

In the sixth year the caulking that had so long occupied Akim's thoughts worked its way out and fell somewhere behind the bed, and Akim began to think that Marya would understand him at last. He was inexpressibly glad, contented and good tempered; but not for long. . . .

Akim's nostrils widened and turned white, the smell of his sick body tormented him, he felt that he stank worse than pig's dung. Marya bathed him with scented soap, while Akim inspected his sores, comparing himself to some loathsome may-fly grub, twisting and wriggling.

Now and then he would remember his medals. He would start to grunt, thumping his bloated chest with his stump, and Marya would know immediately and reach for the box where the medals were kept, along with her buttons and thread. Akim had a lot of medals and decorations—enough to go right across his chest. On public holidays, Marya would pin them on his old jacket and sit Akim outside on the verandah. Sometimes at night he was unable to restrain himself, and would wake Marya, pointing to his chest as if to say: 'Where are those medals of mine?'

The hut was warm and quiet, and by the light of the guttering candle Akim had been looking at his medals all night, a month, a year, ten years. . . . Marya became fearful when she looked at Akim. Then one day, Akim crawled over to the window, butted his head through the glass and put his neck on the jagged edge. All winter he lay ill and barely conscious. Marya's expression hardened and when the spring thaw came, and the roads turned to mud, the cripple's ears caught a conversation in undertones, carried by chance on the wind.

'Fate's played you a cruel trick, Marya, but we've all been in the war, we could all have been like that. You're a woman, you need someone to lean on, a man's help.' A man's hoarse voice was persuading, pleading. 'What does it matter to him? There are homes for people like that. . . . Don't ruin my life, Marya. . . .'

Akim strained his ears, afraid to miss a word.

'Look at me—hands, feet, a fine smallholding, but what use is that in God's name without you? Special homes. . . . All luck, a trick of fate. . . .'

'What do you know about fate? . . .'

Then Akim heard a scuffling by the hedge, as of geese flapping their wings, and the sound of heavy breathing, and his wife whispering: 'Let me go, do you hear? I love him, do you hear?'

The July nights were short and the breath of the lime trees was sweet.

Akim pressed closer to his wife's flowing hair, let down for the night, and recalled how she had carried him on to the verandah and blushingly told him about the baby. He had thrown himself off the verandah into the puddle in front of the house, tipped his face into the mud, kissed the earth.

From the depths of the ravine the mist rose, drifting and spreading, as if seeking shelter, catching at the bushes and tops of the trees: 'Help me, take me in. . . .' wept the mist, leaving tears on the broad leaves of the indifferent burdocks. But everything was quiet. In a little while the sun would come up. The dew in the meadows would vanish and day would forget that the mist had wept—until it was time for the next sunrise.

Varlam Shalamov

A Good Hand

Late one night Krist was summoned to the 'stables', as the inmates
of the camp called the little house huddled against the knoll on the
edge of the settlement. It was the home of the investigator of
'especially important cases', as the camp jokers put it, for there were
no 'cases' in the camp other than especially important ones—every
misdemeanour, or appearance of misdemeanour, could be punished
by death. Either by death or by complete acquittal. But complete
acquittals were unheard of. Ready for anything and indifferent to
everything, Krist walked along the narrow path, a well trodden path,
leading to the 'stables'. The light went on in the small cookhouse—
the breadcutter must be starting to weigh out the rations for breakfast. For breakfast tomorrow. Would Krist have a tomorrow and a
breakfast tomorrow? He didn't know and was glad not to know. He
felt something under his foot, something not like snow or an icicle.
Krist bent down, picked up a frozen rind and realised at once that it
was a bit of turnip-peel, the iced-over skin of a turnip. The ice had
already melted in Krist's hands and he put the peeling in his mouth.
There was obviously no point in hurrying. He went over the whole
path, beginning where the huts ended, realising that he, Krist, was
the first person to traverse this long, snow-covered road today, that
so far no one else had come this way along the edge of the settlement
to see the investigator. Little bits of turnip were freezing to the
snow all along the path, looking as though wrapped in cellophane.
Krist discovered a good ten bits, some big, some small. It was a long
time now since Krist had seen people who would throw turnip-peel
into the snow. A prisoner couldn't have done it—it must be a free
worker. Maybe the investigator himself. Krist carefully chewed and
swallowed all the peel and his mouth smelt of something he had
long forgotten, his own soil and living vegetables, and in a joyful
mood Krist knocked on the investigator's door.

The investigator was short, lean and unshaven. Here he had only
his office, plus an iron bunk covered with an army blanket and a
crumpled dirty pillow. His desk was homemade, with warped
drawers tightly packed with papers and some sort of files. On the
windowsill was a box full of cards. The book-shelves were also piled
high with bulging folders. The ash-tray was made of half a tin of
preserves. A clock with a pendulum stood on the windowsill. The clock
showed ten-thirty. The investigator was lighting the iron stove with
paper.

The investigator was pale and white-skinned, like all investigators.
He had neither guard nor revolver.

'Sit down, Krist,' he said, using the polite form of address, and offered him an old stool. He himself was sitting on a chair—a homemade chair with a high back.

'I've looked through your case,' he said, 'and I have a proposal to make. I don't know whether it'll suit you.'

Krist stiffened. The investigator paused.

'I've got to know something else about you.'

Krist looked up and could not stop himself belching. It was a pleasant belch, with the irresistible taste of fresh turnips.

'Write an application.'

'An application?'

'Yes. Here's a sheet of paper and a pen.'

'An application? What for? To whom?'

'Anyone you like! All right then, do a poem by Blok instead. It doesn't matter what. Get it? Or write out Pushkin's *Little Bird*—

Yesterday I opened wide the dungeon
Of my feathered aerial prisoner.
I returned the singer to her freedom,
Gave the groves and thickets back to her,

declaimed the investigator.

'That isn't Pushkin,' whispered Krist, straining every nerve of his withered brain.

'Who wrote it then?'

'Tumansky.'

'Tumansky? Never heard of him.'

'A-ah! You're trying to get some sort of proof? You think I might have killed somebody? Or written a letter to someone outside? Or forged a store chit for some of the criminals?'

'Not at all. We don't have any trouble getting proof of that sort of thing.'

The investigator smiled, revealing his swollen gums. No matter how insignificant it was, that fleeting smile somehow lightened the room a bit. And Krist's soul as well. Involuntarily he looked at the investigator's mouth.

'Yes,' the investigator said, catching Krist's glance. 'Scurvy, it's scurvy all right. Even we free people can't get rid of it here. No fresh vegetables.'

Krist thought about the turnip. He, and not the investigator, had got the vitamins in that—there are more in the peel than the pulp. Krist wanted to continue this conversation and tell the investigator how he had sucked the skin of the turnip which the investigator had thrown away, but he couldn't quite pluck up the courage, fearing that officialdom would pounce on him for excessive familiarity.

'Well then, have you got it or not? I want to see your handwriting.'

Krist still couldn't make it out.

'Write,' dictated the investigator.

' "To the Chief of the Mines. Application of prisoner Krist, date of birth, charge, sentence. I request to be transferred to lighter work. . . ." That's enough.'

The investigator took Krist's unfinished application, tore it into bits and threw it into the fire. For a moment the light in the stove grew brighter.

'Sit down at the table. At that end.'

Krist's handwriting was like that of a calligrapher or an old-fashioned clerk; he himself was very fond of it, although all his colleagues had always laughed and said it wasn't much like the handwriting of a professor with a PhD. It wasn't the hand of a scholar, writer and poet, but of a store-keeper. They laughed and said Krist could have made a career as the tsar's clerk in the story by Kuprin.

But Krist wasn't embarrassed by these jokes and had continued to go to the typing pool with neatly written-out manuscripts. The typists had liked him for this, but giggled about it among themselves.

Fingers that had grown used to the pick and the spade simply couldn't get a grip on the pen, but at last they somehow managed it.

'Everything's out of order. It's simply chaos,' said the investigator. 'I know it myself, but you'll be able to help me get things straight.'

'Of course, certainly,' said Krist. The stove was burning properly now, and the room was warm.

'I wouldn't mind a cigarette. . . .'

'I don't smoke,' said the investigator roughly. 'And I've no bread. You won't go to work tomorrow. I'll tell the sergeant.'

And so once a week for several months Krist would go to the unheated, uncomfortable quarters of the camp investigator to copy out papers and file them.

The snowless winter of 1937-38 had already entered the huts with its lethal winds. Every night the sergeant ran through the huts hunting and waking people whose names were on some special lists for 'transport', and now they even stopped thinking about all these nocturnal doings. If there was a transport, that was that—the work was too backbreaking for you to think about anything else.

Hours of work were increased, military escorts for the prisoners were introduced, but when a week had passed Krist, still clinging to life, would make his way to the familiar office of the investigator and file papers for hours on end. Krist stopped washing and shaving, but the investigator seemed not to notice his sunken cheeks and inflamed eyes. And Krist went on writing and filing.

The number of papers and folders grew so large that it was absolutely impossible to get them into order. Krist was copying out some sort of endless lists on which there were only names; the tops of the lists were folded back and he never tried to penetrate the secrets of this room, although it would have been simple enough to straighten out the sheets of paper lying in front of him. Sometimes the investigator would pick up a pile of 'cases', which appeared as from nowhere and which Krist had not seen before, and hastily dictate lists of names to him.

The dictation ended at twelve and Krist went to his hut and slept and slept—the morning parade for work didn't concern him. Week after week went by and Krist got thinner and thinner and wrote and wrote.

And then one day, picking up the latest folder to read out the latest name for the list, the investigator suddenly stopped short. He looked at Krist and asked:

'What's your full name?'

'Robert Ivanovich,' answered Krist with a smile. Perhaps the investigator had decided to call him by his name and patronymic instead of just 'Krist'. Perhaps he always used the polite form of address—it wouldn't have surprised Krist at all. The investigator was young; he could have been Krist's son. Holding the folder in his hands, without reading out the name on the cover, the investigator went white. He blenched until he was whiter than snow. Hastily he fingered through the thin papers filed in the folder—there were about as many as in any other folder in the heap lying on the floor. Then the investigator firmly flung open the door of the stove and the whole room at once brightened, as if a soul had been lit to its very depths and there, at the bottom, something very important and human lay revealed. The investigator tore the folder into pieces and pushed them into the stove. It grew even brighter. Krist understood nothing. And without looking at him the investigator said, 'No imagination! They don't understand what they're doing. They just don't care.' And looked hard at Krist.

'Let's go on writing. Are you ready?'

'I'm ready,' said Krist. And only many years later did he realise that it was his own file.

By that time many of Krist's comrades had been shot. The

investigator had been shot too. But Krist was still alive and sometimes—at least once every few years—he would remember the
burning file and the firm hands of the investigator tearing up Krist's
'case'—a present to the condemned from his executioner.

Krist had a good hand, a redeeming hand, the hand of a
calligrapher.

Varlam Shalamov

Caligula

The note was delivered to the company at dusk, before the hooter went. The commandant lit the wick-lamp, hurriedly read the sheet of paper and went out to issue the order. Nothing struck him as peculiar.

'Has he got something missing?' asked the duty guard, pointing at his forehead.

The commandant glanced coldly at the soldier, who now felt alarmed at his own frivolity. He looked away at the road.

'It's coming,' he said. 'Ardatyev's bringing it himself.'

Two escorts with rifles were just visible through the fog. Behind them came a carter leading a grey, emaciated horse. In the rear, at the side of the road, a big, heavily built man was striding through the snow. His white, knee-length sheepskin coat was unbuttoned and his big fur hat was pushed on to the back of his head. He was mercilessly beating the bony, dirty, sunken flanks of the horse with a stick. The horse was quivering at every blow and continued to plod along, unable to quicken its pace.

The escorts stopped the horse at the gatehouse and Ardatyev staggered ahead. He was panting like a winded horse himself, and the commandant, standing at attention, caught the smell of spirits.

'Ready?' Ardatyev asked hoarsely.

'Yessir!' answered the commandant.

'Drag it in!' roared Ardatyev. 'And put it on your food-roster. I punish people, and I'm certainly not going to let horses off! I'll make the thing work. Three days now it's been skiving,' he muttered, pushing his fist into the commandant's chest. 'I was going to jail the carter. He's ruining the plan. The pla-a-n. . . . Then he swears it's the horse, not him, that's not working. "I g-got it," hiccupped Ardatyev, "I b-believe you. . . . G-give me the reins," I said. I pulled the reins and it wouldn't move. I beat it and still it wouldn't come. You swine, I thought, how can I fiddle your worksheet now? You can go to the punishment cells, damn and blast you, with all the other enemies of humanity. Seventy-two hours as it's your first time. On sheer damn water.'

Ardatyev sat down in the snow and took off his fur hat. His damp, tangled hair fell over his eyes. He tried to get up but suddenly lurched and fell to the ground.

The guard and the commandant dragged him into the guard-room. Ardatyev was asleep.

'Shall we take him home?'

'Shouldn't bother. His wife doesn't care for him.'

'What about the horse?'

'Better put it in. He'll kill us if he wakes up and we haven't jailed it. Put it in number four with the intellectuals.'

Two prisoners who were used as armed watchmen carried some wood for the night into the guardroom and began to stack it round the stove.

'What do you think of that, Pyotr Grigoryevich?' said one of them, looking meaningfully towards the room where Ardatyev was snoring.

'What I think is that it isn't the first time. . . . Caligula . . .'

'Yes, yes, Derzhavin,' went on the other, drawing himself up, and declaimed with feeling:

> Caligula!
> How radiant was your senate horse in gold
> And yet it shed no radiance because
> 'Tis only good works shine. . . .

The old men lit up their handrolled cigarettes and the room slowly filled with clouds of light-blue smoke.

Vladimir Bukovsky

Miniature stories

Stars

When I was little my granny used to take me for walks round the Kremlin. Along the embankment, across Red Square and into the Alexandrovsky Gardens. All the way round. There were always lots of cars on Red Square. They were green and covered with dust. Granny said they were khaki-coloured.

When I walked across Red Square I always stamped my feet. It was nice to stamp on the Square. How I loved those walks round the Kremlin. Granny used to tell me all sorts of tales about it. She told me about the theatre, about Ivan the Terrible, the Royal Bell and the Royal Cannon. It's the biggest cannon in the world. And the oldest. Granny told me such interesting things. She talked about the Tsars, and the Boyars too, and the Kremlin bells. They used to ring every morning. And everybody used to go to the Kremlin. Masses and masses of people. There were always lots of people at the Kremlin. All in their best clothes. And all very gay. I was always asking Granny to tell me stories. She told me such interesting things. And when we passed by the Spassky Tower, she always said:

What proud man could lift the Bell,
Or move the Royal Cannon's weight,
Or be slow to doff his cap
At the Kremlin's holy gate!

I always tried to imagine that proud man. There he was, standing at the Spassky Gate, hands on hips and looking up, with his head flung so far back that his cap almost fell off. And he looked so valiant.

Granny and I used to walk for hours. From morning to evening. In the evening we always sat in the Alexandrovsky Gardens. And when it grew quite dark and the stars on the Kremlin towers began to sparkle, I would shout:

'Oh, Granny, look! The stars have been switched on!'

And she would reply:

'They haven't been switched on. . . . They shine all the time. It's just that you can't see them in the daytime. They're ruby. Stars made of ruby. Great big rubies which came from beyond the Blue Mountains. They were made into stars so that the stars would shine all the time. Ruby shines in the dark, you see.'

And I knew that as soon as the sun went down, the great big ruby stars would begin to shine. I was very glad that they were real ruby and that it shone so beautifully. When we got home and I was put to bed, I always shut my eyes and saw the ruby stars. They shone ever so brightly. And they gave me a warm, restful feeling.

And I used to dream of strong men, good men, coming from beyond the Blue Mountains. They walked for miles and miles. It was terribly hard work dragging the rubies. But they went on and on, fighting their weariness and helping each other. They forded rivers and crossed mountain ranges. They went on and on, despite their weariness, because they knew they had to bring the rubies, they had to make the stars, so that they would shine for people in the evenings when the sun went down. And they came. They brought the rubies and made the stars. That I knew for sure. And no one told me I was mistaken.

Many years passed. Now I didn't go for walks round the Kremlin any more. I went to school. I hadn't time. But I knew that as soon as the sun disappeared those stars would begin to shine. I knew it for sure. I was absolutely convinced of it. Many years passed in this way, it must have been about four, or maybe more. One day it so happened that the whole of our class went on an excursion to the Kremlin. I went too. Nobody took his cap off. They all stood and gazed. And listened to the guide. I moved a bit away from them. I knew about the Kremlin already. The theatre, Ivan the Terrible and the Tsars. The guide was boring. I was standing beside the Royal Cannon. It was big. Of course it was, but I couldn't believe that it was the biggest in the world. But maybe it was, after all. I didn't know for sure. I stood and thought about it.

What proud man could lift the bell,
Or move the Royal Cannon's weight,
Or be slow to doff his cap
At the Kremlin's holy gate!

I stood and thought. And somebody behind me shouted:
'Hey! Careful there! Don't scrape it!'
I looked round. There was a lorry standing behind me. Green and covered with dust. Khaki. Standing on the lorry were some soldiers and they were unloading a huge ruby star on to the ground. It was very big and ugly close up. I went over and took a look inside. The star was made of glass. Red glass, with ordinary light-bulbs inside.
'Hey! Careful! Don't break it!' shouted the soldiers as they dragged it out of the lorry.
'What!' I said. 'Isn't it ruby, then? It *is* ruby, it *is*! And ruby shines in the dark when the sun sets.'

The soldiers laughed. A passer-by said:

'No, it's not ruby, it's just glass. And anyway, ruby doesn't shine in the dark.'

'You're lying!' I said, 'you stinker!'

'I'm not lying,' he said, 'and don't call me names. What can I do? It's the truth.'

I knew he wasn't lying, but something inside me wanted to call him names. I went off home. I didn't want to look at the Royal Cannon any more. Or at the Royal Bell.

Many more years passed. Maybe six or thereabouts. I don't know. For a long time I hadn't been near the Kremlin. I just didn't want to. But then one day I had a terrible longing to go to the Alexandrovsky Gardens. Just to sit on a bench for a while. Nothing more. And I went. I must have sat there and looked at the pathway. It was the path I used to walk along with Granny when she used to tell me about the theatre, and about Ivan the Terrible, and about the Tsars, and about the Kremlin bells.

What proud man could lift the bell,
Or move the Royal Cannon's weight,
Or be slow to doff his cap
At the Kremlin's holy gate!

I smiled. How long ago it had all been. Strange.

'Look, Granny! The stars have been switched on!' I heard a small boy say.

I looked up. Just a small boy with his granny. On a walk. A walk round the Kremlin, most probably.

'They don't switch them on,' I said. 'They're ruby. Ruby stars. Ruby shines in the dark, you see.'

'No fear,' said the little fellow. 'That's not ruby. I know it's not. It's just glass with bulbs inside. They switch them on when it gets dark. I know they do.'

The Village

Hanging layers of smoke, now rising, now falling. In one corner, voices, arguing wearily and insistently: 'No, now take Blok, Blok thaid. . . . Lithen to me, will you!'

In another corner a tape-recorder playing, and a woman's tremulous voice singing, evidently in French.

He was already slightly drunk and for some time wandered about among the chairs, spilling vodka on the way; then he just sat down, with a smile, at the piano. A disconcerted, affectionate smile.

'Don't give a damn, if you can,' sang the woman's voice in a strong vibrato. 'Drink, and be merry, for what else is there to do? It's years since I gave a damn about anything.'

He sat there for a long time, swaying unsteadily, watching the smoke layers rising and falling. Then someone flung open the window. The smoke layers merged and were sucked out and away in a thin stream.

'Give up thinking. Why this folly? It's years since I gave a damn about anything,' sang the woman.

But he still sat there, swaying slightly on his chair, just smiling at the piano. He saw things again. Now he was sure it was the same thing again. Slightly to the left there was a log barn with a thatched roof. Some sort of farm implements were standing by the wall, some sort of wooden wheels and a barrow, but the main thing was the thatched roof, a deep reddish-brown. Beyond it—peasant cottages, grey and built of logs, and then fields and haystacks. Some peasants were standing by the huts and one of them was unharnessing a horse.

'Why think so much?' the woman sang. 'After all, there's no other way out for us. What can we do? Be merry, if you can.'

She was singing in French, but the meaning was perfectly clear.

'Only a poet thuch ath Blok, Blok. . . . Lithen to me, will you, Thasha!'

On the right a peasant sat astride a log, rolling a cigarette.

At home, everything was as before, except that the desk stood a little lower than usual. The window was a large one, with no bars. A single pane. Through the window and to the right—bare boughs. The sky was blank, except for the occasional bird flying past. But that didn't alter anything.

All this time he had the impression that snow had fallen. And he desperately wanted to see a snowflake on the window. Sometimes he thought the light had grown brighter. Then he would go to the window and stand gazing out at the wrinkled earth. There was no snow. Sometimes he saw bright specks hitting the windowpane and settling on the sill.

The huts had gone completely black and the thatched roof of the barn was no longer visible. All around lay snowdrifts, but that peasant was still unharnessing his horse. The yellow field wasn't there either, but on the other hand, someone was chopping firewood.

He could hear it and smell the wood. The harrow still hadn't been cleared away, it was completely buried.

They told him it was necessary and took him away. That was before the snow. Once there they let him out for walks in the yard. The yard had a stone wall with two trees growing beside it. Their leaves were yellow already, and even russet. He gazed at the withered russet leaves. It was damp.

'And in the village they're already bringing in the hay,' he said. But that wasn't true, he hadn't seen it.

The Bell-ringer

. . . You know, it's amazing, how far the madness went!

In the morning you could even say it was pleasant, especially from afar. The peal of the bells was multiplied by the sparkling dewdrops, sank into the mist, and stirred the hearts of believers to compassion.

'It's our new bellringer trying his strength,' people said round about.

As lunchtime approached, when the air filled with the scent of pies and rye-cakes, the bells rang in steady, solemn tones, like a ritual invitation to table, rending many a stomach, and the people began to show signs of a certain puzzlement and annoyance.

'Why ring for so long? It doesn't look as though anyone's died, and no one's been born, and there doesn't seem to be a fire either.'

None the less they ate a hearty meal.

In the evening, when they awoke from their afternoon sleep, the peal of the bells still streamed from the bell-tower down into the lake like molten gold, and they grew somehow sad, they remembered the deceased and many shed tears.

But still the bells did not cease.

At sunset you could even say it was beautiful. You know the sort of thing: water, the setting sun, bells pealing. Melodic, measured, melancholy.

That night no one slept. And no wonder! How could you possibly get to sleep with the bells pealing like that? But more to the point, their sleep was chased away by an inexplicable sense of apprehension, even fear. They barred the shutters. They were afraid of theft and arson.

And so it went on for several days and nights. You can imagine what it was like! The district began to be overtaken by madness.

Frenzied dancing and praying, weeping and fighting alternated by turns. The people tried fasting, penances and flagellation. There were cases of self-immolation.

And only on the fifth day did the pealing suddenly cease.

The people who went up into the belfry had great difficulty in unclenching his hands and freeing the bell-ropes. His swollen face was quite black, and there was blood on his lips. To my mind, there was no sense by that time in dragging him down from the belfry.

An Incoherent Question for the Doctor

But don't think I've come for nothing, Doctor, without a reason. I wouldn't dream of troubling you. It's just that I can't stand it any more. I tried to ignore it at first, but that didn't work. If it was just on and off . . . but it's all the time. And don't think it's nothing serious. I mean, if only I had a breather once in a while. I'd never have come and troubled you then. But there's nothing actually wrong with me. I've got no complaints. I can work. And I can breathe on the whole, well, I mean inhale. No trouble there. It's just that I can't sort of take in a proper lungful, I can't get relaxed, somehow its never a complete breath; it's just as if there's something in the way, or no air left. I've got no complaints on the whole. I can work and help the wife with the kids. No trouble there. And I'm breathing, like, I mean, I'm inhaling air. Maybe I'm just no good at describing what it's like when it comes on. Maybe that's why even the doctors can't help me, because I'm so incoherent. They ask me what illnesses I had as a child. They've taken samples. But maybe it's something completely different. But don't go thinking it's all so simple. I wouldn't dream of bothering you, if only I could stand it. If it would just let up now and then. It's simply agonising sometimes, the way I want to breathe in a proper lungful. Specially when spring comes. The man next door is always telling me: 'Stop running around doctors. It's all a farce. Let's have a drink instead.' Says it helps. Maybe he's right, Doctor? Maybe, it does sometimes? Now don't go thinking that I'm complaining. I can work, even, and I can breathe on the whole, I mean, I inhale oxygen, no trouble there. It's just that I can't sort of take in a proper lungful, I can't get relaxed, somehow it's never a complete breath, it's just as if there's something in the way, or there's no air left. How can I explain it to you so that you will understand?

The Aquarium

The snails went on crawling up and down, up and down, leaving their trails on the glass.

And there was glass on all sides, but it reflected those same water-weeds and same stones, so it was hard to distinguish them from real ones. And the fish kept bumping their noses against the walls. They just wanted to have a look at some new water-weeds. After all, one does need a change of scene once in a while.

They knew every grain of sand in the place, every single leaf. Even the darkest corner of the aquarium, where there was a big fish which stirred occasionally, and with which they were not on familiar terms. This fish wasn't like them. It was bigger, it was a shimmering blue, whereas they had a bright red stripe on their tails.

And the snails went on crawling up and down, up and down. Sometimes they left a trail, and patches of smudgy grey appeared on the glass.

No one could understand why they were attracted to a place where there were strange plants and no snails. For they were young, they swam after each other. And who could see them, anyway? Except for the big fish that lived in the dark corner and didn't have a red stripe on its tail. But that fish was ill and wasn't eating the crayfish that swam on the surface.

Only the snails went on crawling up and down, up and down.

But on the other hand, how interesting it was on the other side of the glass! So many water-weeds, pebbles and unfamiliar fish with red stripes on their tails. Sometimes they swam right up close, but even so they never actually managed to make their acquaintance.

They swam together and kept their eyes fixed on each other the whole time, so as not to lose their way. After all, anything could happen, and what's more the big fish had grown very restless and swum out of its corner. It was dark blue, and breathed heavily, as though under a strain. The next morning it was back skulking in its corner and was quiet again.

And they went on swimming after each other and trying to get through the glass, to where they could see identical fish with red-striped tails swimming up to meet them.

On the third day after the big fish had quietened down in its corner, one of the fish grew restless and his mate just couldn't understand why he wasn't swimming after her and why his breathing was so heavy. She was there next to him and wanted to cheer him up, but he kept trying to get away from her.

He didn't know himself what was the matter with him. It was just that he felt drawn to swim over to the big fish in its dark corner. So he did.

It's very awkward swimming belly upwards and he kept trying to right himself. But he couldn't. It was very embarrassing. But then he realised that he would soon be going beyond the glass and he calmed down.

Only the snails went on crawling up and down, up and down.

Little Man

I can't appreciate beauty by ear. It may all be very beautiful, but I can't appreciate it. And in front of me there's a little man with a lost gaze. He may babble on about Céline, Joyce or Freud, but all the same I know he's lost his bearings.

Maybe it's because he's devoured by hell-fires. Not enough fluid, the fluid that fortifies.

This little man has large flapping ears. He can't appreciate beauty by ear.

Look at me, little man! Tell me all about God and Truth. You know everything, after all! But none the less you have lost your bearings somewhere back there, in the hustle and bustle of the journey. And even if you were to split in two, there would still be one flapping ear left on each half of you. You're no good, little man. You'll disappear, I shall remain.

I went out into the street and suddenly felt the weight of my own body. My feet were sticking to the pavement. Have you ever felt the stickiness of gravity?

Alla Ktorova

My Sister's Applegarth

> Do you remember, Granny,
> how you used to tell us stories
> about that applegarth?
> *Zlatovratski*

In fifty years' time, Granny will say:
  'I do remember, indeed I do. . . .' And she will squeak:

Oh, my sister's applegarth,
Applegarth secluded,
Mountain brooks of clearest hue
Do not chuckle through it.[1]

But today, being no grandmother as yet, she'll only toss her head in curlers and sigh:
  'It was such a lark that you couldn't help but cry.'

I ponder what it might have been like, this 'My Sister's Applegarth', and watch a man stretched out on the grass in the Central Park Zoo. This is New York. The man is lying on the grass with his head screened by the four sides of a cardboard box, while I sit alone on a bench by the dolphin pool and blissfully melt into daydream. A thin thread of memory slowly spins out of the past.
  'Pavel Sergeich—oh, Pavel Sergeich!' Fyodor Gurevich, the old usher, is talking mournfully to someone on a bench outside the Provincial Theatre. 'It's disgusting, Pavel Sergeich, it makes you sick. . . . Look, I even knew Chaliapin, he used to talk to me, and now. . . . No, no, it's all disgusting, quite disgusting, it's time to die. . . .'
  'What are you saying, Fyodor Gurevich! You still have . . .'
  'No, no, don't try to talk me round. . . .'
  Then, a few days later, there is a soft tap at the door.
  The gentle old eyes are shining after a tiny drink, no more than a thimbleful.
  'Pavel Sergeich. Oh, Pavel Sergeich!'
  'Well, what's happened, Fyodor Gurevich?'
  'Just that we'll stay alive a little longer, Pavel Sergeich. To spite them! Alive-oh! . . .'

And so, the actors in this hundrum masquerade will be, in order of appearance:

[1] The first four lines of a poem by Pushkin. Tr.

VADIM PONARIN—a young man.

MORIZCHEN AND SONINKA—two turtle doves.

AUNT GRUSHA—a tiresome, semi-incidental character.

The action takes place on the revolving stage of 'My Sister's Applegarth', in contemporary Moscow.

An antique little Fabergé egg marked 'XB' (Christ is Risen) swinging over the ten-foot-long day ottoman. A glued together antique porcelain cup from the Kuznetsov Factory standing on the first shelf of the dresser. On the second shelf—photographs of Grandfather and Grandmother. Tucked into the frames were some of the white crane feathers with which Russian ladies used to embellish their aigrettes long ago. And the aigrette itself still survived. Kept in a basket.

The room contained: baskets, a picture and cardboard boxes.

BASKETS, stuffed with 'priceless objects'.

Beaver jackets and an overcoat. 'Organdy' Brussels lace of 1856—money could not buy it in our atomic age. Three or four sable pelts (now worth seventy new roubles each at GUM Department Stores). Ladies' yellowish night-dresses of fine lawn and skeins of thick bay wool.

A PICTURE without a speck of dust on it.

A copy of a still life by Kiselev: two red-muzzled apples and a white pear. Also a priceless object.

CARDBOARD BOXES containing age-old capes of genuine silk satin. Kept in case they came back into fashion. A frequent occurrence nowadays.

In short, all these fetching baubles were to be found in the twenty-two-square-metre room in Maly Komsomolski (formerly Maly Zlatoustovski) lane, the domicile of:

SONINKA AND MORIZCHEN

I shall refer to them by these names, even though they are neither kith nor kin of mine.

The rumour that the couple were descended from foreigners who used to trade at the Kuznetsky Bridge was substantiated by their full names: Sofia Franzevna and Moriz Yulianovich. They had settled in the Maly Zlatoustovski during the early years of the Revolution and were distinguished from the other citizens residing there solely by the fact that they almost invariably spoke German to each other.

Soninka looked like a good natured, but dilapidated and suddenly shrunken toad.

Morizchen resembled a hungry little hare.

Returning from work in the evening, wrapped like a child in a muffler tied by a band at the neck, with a boat-shaped Persian lamb hat on his head and enormous mittens—presented to him by some cabby during the cold revolutionary years—on his hands, he would gently push open the door, so as not to disturb anyone by making it squeak, and shyly coo:

'So-o-ninka, *Puppele* . . .'

'Mo-orr-i-zchen . . . *mein Leben* . . .' came the reply chirping back to him.

They would melt into a tender embrace, and then proceed to dine. On Polish silver plate made by Norblin, with napkins tucked under the chin and pigeon-bone tooth-picks. . . . Morizchen would peer at the saucer of fried potatoes, stretch out his neck like a cock-bird focusing on a distant grain of corn and ask timidly:

'Soninka, *Puppele*, could I possibly help myself to another morsel?'

Sofia Franzevna and Moriz Yulianovich were a pair of turtle doves. They never quarrelled. They kissed and cooed at each other all the day long. Actually, Moriz sometimes threatened that he would surely be getting jealous of *Puppele* and the young *Leutnants* to whom she taught German at the *Akademie* on Pokrovski Boulevard. But these ominous threats were as far as it went. On Sundays they would betake themselves to little Ilinski square for a walk and sit a long time by the historic monument to the heroes of Plevna. . . .

They lived their modest little lives. They munched their daily bread. They did not reach for the stars. They did not burden the earth.

VADIM PONARIN was a splendid young man. You won't find many such young men around nowadays. He was a little like Lyala, the doll which long, long ago used to be in the window of the vast *Torgsin*[1] department store.

Lyalya had a round face, kind jet black eyes and a dimple on her chin.

'Mummy, Mummy darling, please buy that doll for me, please buy me Lyalya. . . .'

'Don't even ask, there's no money. . . .'

[1] The name of the special department store established in Moscow for foreigners to be able to purchase quality consumer goods for foreign currency. Tr.

'There is, there is—you had a penny today, I saw it. . . .'

Such timid subterfuges used to bring tears to my mother's eyes.

Vadim was nineteen.

'He has fulfilled his Young Communist tasks. He is an activist. He is morally stable.'

This was the character reference that stood in all the reports issued to him by the youth organisations which had brought light into his life as a Pioneer and Komsomol member. But that was only outside, in organisations. At home he would greet his neighbour in the corridor no matter how often he met her.

One day he happened to tug a little forcefully at the door of a certain unmentionable place and . . .

'Oh . . . how do you do, Larissa Mikhailovna!'

'How do you do, Vadyusik.'

He practically addressed dogs, never mind people, in a courteous way. Like Taneyev, the composer. He never had a cross word for his parents, nor even the neighbours across the yard. To be quite honest, he couldn't even if he had wanted to: he stammered. But for the rest, he was a model young man.

Vadim Ponarin had finished school a few years earlier. First he entered for the Chemical Technology College, but failed by two marks and was refused. Then he worked like a beaver right through winter, crammed his subjects, paid an Englishwoman three roubles per lesson twice a week—private lessons!—and the following autumn achieved a pass into the Printing Institute, where the competitive entrance examination was not too difficult. He got full marks in all subjects.

To celebrate his successful entry into the College, his parents presented him with a *Vyatka* motor scooter—one more recruit to the ranks of potential suicides.

Victor Alexandrovich, his father, still very young and handsome, worked as a Technical Control engineer in the Ministry of Chemical Industry, and was doing well. His mother, Valentina Nikolayevna, book-kept in Foreign Trade. Everything in their home was all one might wish it to be. Their cup was brimming over. And the room itself was splendid—eighteen square metres on the Zubovsky Boulevard, south side. Every morning the sun danced in the Ponarins' room. And everybody in the family was happy, particularly Vadim after his success in entering the Institute. He was in first heaven. Only the first so far—the seventh had still to be reached. But not too quickly. And without making too much of a racket.

Young people have gone to the dogs nowadays, don't you agree? Completely to the dogs. No sooner has a chap got out of school and gone to college than he ups and falls in love. But how can one fall in love, I ask you, things being what they are?

You push open the door to the lobby on your way home from the latest hooly. You fumble for the stairs with your foot. There's no light. Why on earth not? By what dispensation? Has the bulb burnt out or what? You scuffle the torn and ragged lino, you feel for the stairs while holding on to the wall and then:

'Stop it, stop it. . . .' Hands are withdrawn swiftly on both sides.

It was they who put out the light. Oh, the wretches. In any case they've got nothing to fear from me. I won't tell anyone. If it was Uncle Vlas now, the caretaker, or the house manager. . . . That would be different. . . .

Vadim and Kira are sitting on the peeling windowsill of the lobby. They kiss (being in love). Kira is studying at the Faculty of Russian Language and Literature of the Potemkin Pedagogical Institute and wears a dress of the latest Bulgarian shrunk cotton. Her hair is tied with a ribbon into a pony tail. In Moscow they call this hairdo 'I'm Mummy's little silly'.

All right, sit there, go on, don't be scared. I won't tell anyone that you polish the windowsill every night, that it was *you* who deliberately removed the bulb, and that by your grace and favour poor old Manya broke her leg in the dark, spent three months in hospital and now. . . . Go on, sit there, sit, and go on kissing. . . . I'm good-natured, I'd ask you in if I had a room of my own, my own personal four walls, even if they were only made of cardboard, or hanging blankets. . . . Yes, I'd ask you in and damage my reputation—and spite the neighbours. Let them protest, let them hiss ('procuress!'). I hope you wouldn't permit yourselves anything 'of that sort'. But I have no chance to be kind. I have nothing of my own. No walls, no secluded applegarth, no sister. . . . I too live in the public eye. Often I have a dreadful dream—I am in the street in my birthday suit. I am scared that somebody will see me. . . . I look around—and everyone else in the street is 'dressed' exactly like me. And nobody is ashamed. . . . They've got used to it. . . .

To put it in a nutshell: where is one to find a room? Separate accommodation? So that Mother can't peep, so that Father can't eavesdrop, so that the neighbours can't titter all over you in the corridors?

Do you want a room?

You can have one.

There are three ways.

The first is to rent one privately from somebody.

Take a couple of old-age pensioners, a man and his wife. They have two rooms. What do they need two for, twenty-two metres for the pair of them? Isn't that a bit lush? The housing standards specify nine square metres per living soul. And two for a dead one. And now this ageing couple want to speculate a bit, to line their pockets on the side. They want to become idlers and parasites on society. They want TO LET THEIR SECOND ROOM.

Rent: thirty to fifty roubles a month.

'Your scholarship, Kira darling, comes to twenty-five roubles a month, mine's the same. That's fifty roubles. Then your parents and mine will give us fifteen each—another thirty. In other words, eighty all told, forty for the room, forty to live on. No—that's very little. As for me, Father won't go above that. . . .'

The second way is to make an exchange.

But you have to make a deal, as the saying goes.

'Your room, Kira sweetie, is fifteen metres, ours is eighteen. We'll put an advertisement on the board outside *Children's World*[1]: 'Exchange two rooms, all conveniences, different parts of town, for three, smaller area considered, one can be in old house without conveniences.' So, we exchange two very good ones for three not so good. Our parents get the best two, and we take the worst one, without conveniences, somewhere in the basement. But we have to make absolutely sure we pick a house scheduled for demolition. Then we'll sit tight for five or six years, until they bulldoze the old ruin and give us the equivalent metres in some new house in Cheremushki, Tekstilshchiki or, best of all, near Serebryanny Bor in Khoroshevo-Mnevniki. . . .'

But no. . . . What's the use. . . . Who's going to exchange three for two? Except for a big (illegal) premium. A hundred and fifty for every extra square metre? You'd have to be very careful about a thing like that. The neighbours might find out about it, God forbid. . . . No, we'd be too scared. . . .

Yes, but you said that there was still a th-th-third. . . .

A third way? What might that be?

[1] A department store in Moscow. Tr.

Yes, Vadik and Kirochka, there is a third way. You can, you can indeed obtain a room! Without too much trouble, without dishonesty, without cheating the government, without sharp practice. Without spe-cu-la-tion! Legally. Yes, le-ga-lly!

Practically nobody even knows of this law. It's probably just as well. The more you know, the sooner you grow old.

LYRICAL DIGRESSION: the laws, oh the laws! They are sacred, but there is no obligation to know them. We Muscovites try to act 'according to circumstances' rather than according to the laws. People have always been quick on the uptake in Moscow. It is no coincidence that way back in the prehistoric days of tsars Peter I, Nicholas II and Alexander III there was the saying: 'Moscow kicks straight from the toe'.

As it happened, Moriz Yulianovich died unexpectedly in June. He came home from work, opened the door a fraction as usual, thrust his lean little snout into the gap, eyes closing with tender feeling, and bleated sweetly:

'So-o-ninka, *Puppele*. . . .' And then all of a sudden. . . .

People die all over the place nowadays, particularly men, mostly young ones just over forty, and more often than not of a heart attack or a stroke. One minute you're talking to him, laughing, promising to go to a newsreel on the Sretenka with him—provided absolutely nobody at work finds out about it and telephones his wife—and then a few hours later you hear that that man has given up the ghost. . . .

'Why is it, Leopold Ilich,' I asked my favourite centenarian, Professor Minor, 'that so many comparatively young people are dying nowadays?'

'Because, child, one doesn't live on one's nerves for almost fifty years without paying for it. Nature takes its revenge. . . .'

And so *Puppele* remained alone. With the baskets, the picture and the cardboard boxes. At her age she should have been able to claim a pension but, tragically, she fell short of the qualifying period. She had been employed at her *Akademie* for only fifteen years. . . . In order to achieve the qualifying period—twenty years—would she really have to work another ten? What a terrible prospect! Her legs were already getting rocky as it was. Would she really have to settle for the fifteen-rouble minimum to which she was entitled? But why settle for the minimum? How about Morizchen? Wasn't she entitled to something for him too? Was our *Puppele* getting stingy? Turning Scrooge? Skinflinting?

'She's not entitled to anything for the head of the family,' rasped a female bass-baritone in the kitchen with spiteful glee.

'She and her Moriz were just living together unregistered. They were too scared to register, because he had a foreign surname and she a sort of Russian one. She told me so herself, yesterday!'

Well, how do you like that little titbit? There's a pair of turtle doves for you!

Thesis: Soninka can't work, her legs won't carry her. That's for one. And for another, she simply can't summon the strength. She wants to sit among her priceless possessions, sipping coffee from the china cup once upon a time manufactured at the Kuznetsov factory, and read Spielhagen's *On the March* in German Gothic print. One might, of course, sell the copy of Kiselev and the odd knick-knack from the baskets and cardboard boxes. But that would only be a short-term solution, while she requires something lasting. Besides, what's all this suddenly about selling 'priceless objects'? Money is an unreliable commodity, while priceless objects should be saved, not sold off. . . .

Antithesis: we have a law according to which a room may be obtained with almost no special trouble worth mentioning.

Neither the Ponarins, nor *Puppele* knew about this law or had even ever heard of it. They had never run across such matters and hadn't the slightest inkling of their existence.

Only one personage in our masquerade was in the know about the whole business, namely:

THE TIRESOME SEMI-INCIDENTAL CHARACTER.

Every day this personage went to work in a yellowish three-storey building on the erstwhile Pokrovka, now Chernyshevsky Street, on which there was a plate: 'Legal Advice and Notary's Office'.

What did this personage do there, what function fulfil?

'Hey, Grush, that's enough sitting around with your arms folded,' shouted Marusia, the cleaner, who tidied the office every morning before the staff arrived. 'Get hold of a duster, will you, and . . .'

'I'm no cleaner, I'm a missanger,' Aunt Grusha (none other than the tiresome semi-incidental character) would proudly snap back.

'Missanger, cleaner—it's all the same,' would come Marusia's crushing retort. 'Putting on airs. . . .'

Aunt Grusha worked as a 'missanger'.

Her looks were a matter for argument. Some might wholeheartedly approve, others wouldn't have had her for free. Make a present of her to a devil you know and even he might hand her back. There used to be a cheery old man in a grey apron at the corner of Krivokolenny Lane and Pokrovka, with a basket of fried rice pasties made in a café and then sold for five copecks apiece. People used to come crowding round, not so much queueing as elbowing each other. Aunt Grusha also thrust her right side into the ruck grabbed hold of something soft and warm and began to extricate herself from the press, bearing down with her well-squared shoulders on the small fry such as a diminutive little man with an attaché case. But the old man spotted her and roared all over the street:

'Oi, whiskers! Where are you off to? Three pasties you snitched, so how about some cash then?'

Aunt Grusha was amply bewhiskered, well benosed and a trifle thievish.

She lived in the same house as *Puppele* and often used to hang around her neighbours' kitchens.

One day the enchantress of young *Leutnants* shuffled forth from her room in soft carpet slippers:

'Are you going out, Grusha? Would you be so kind, if it's not too much trouble, to post my letter?'

Posting other people's letters? Why, that was no trouble at all.

Grusha unstuck the envelope over the steam of her own personal kettle and got stuck into the letter (she had once done two years in a church school).

'For my years, Emmie, I still feel pretty hale,' Soninka had penned to her friend Emma Yurevna, in one of the Baltic States. 'After all, don't forget that I am only sixty according to my passport, but seventy in actual fact. It's not something one should deliberately close one's eyes to!'

Deliberately close one's eyes?

And the tiresome semi-incidental character's eyes bulged with sheer astonishment. And not in the least deliberately.

And so, 'Missanger, cleaner—it's all one.' Particularly in so far as the Ponarin family was concerned. Aunt Grusha had been invited to the Zubovsky Boulevard on 'strictly confidential' business and for half an hour already had been twisting and turning on her chair and lapping tea.

'Oh, I do love to cheer myself up with a cup of tea,' she often used to say.

But the present beverage didn't meet with her approval, because it wasn't good Indian tea at forty copecks a packet, which she loved and always served herself loose out of the chest, but our own Soviet Krasnodar tea at twenty copecks, and so watery 'you could see Moscow through it'.

'Well, there you are, Valentina Nikolayevna, it's just as I was saying—whoever deserves such luck, if not your young Vadim?' droned Aunt Grusha. 'Eh? And it isn't as though she was forced to it or anything. It's she herself, she herself who's in favour! I only hinted. As soon as I found out how old she was and how hard up she was I just suggested it, there and then. And she said to me, she said: "Aunt Grusha, just find me a girl or a young man from a respectable family. . . . Somebody who doesn't bring people in and who's nice and quiet. Of course, she said, I shall have my conditions too—let him bring me various commodities when there's a shortage. . . . Or look after me if I fall ill. And on top of that—fifteen roubles a month." '

'Well,' Victor Alexandrovich, Vadim's father, resolutely cut into the conversation, 'fifteen roubles a month isn't much of a sum. We can manage that. Fix it, Aunt Grusha, fix it and we'll see that you're well rewarded. Yes, yes, this arrangement suits us very, very well. Thank you, my dear, thank you very much indeed! Only, the whole business must be tied up pretty quickly—with a single thrust, as you might say. . . . Yes, thank you very much indeed. . . . I owe you a present.'

Aunt Grusha gave a business-like grunt.

'Once I've promised, that's the end of it. You can rely on me. I'll give satisfaction. 'Course, they have to write out the agreement and certify it in a notary's office. You can use ours if you want. I've already fixed up plenty that way,' she boasted. 'Put down, say: "I register Ponarin, Vadim Victorovich, at my domicile, I accept his guardianship, and if anything should happen to me my square metres shall pass to him . . .".'

'And if anything should happen to me . . .'

WHICH BEING INTERPRETED MEANS: if, by ill luck, I should die, decease, kick the bucket, pass on, snuff it, join my ancestors, get measured for the box or go to a far better world than this one, then '. . . my room passes to him'.

Sofia Franzevna was happy. In the evenings, sitting in her twenty-two-square-metre applegarth beneath the copy of Kiselev's still-life (two red-muzzled apples plus a white pear), she would murmur:

'Fifteen from my pension and fifteen from him—thirty net. . . . On top of that, he pays for the electricity, heating, telephone, gas and cleaning. Other unforeseen payments for communal services also go on his bill. No, it's all right, I'll get by. . . .'

And so our young Vadim became a G-U-A-R-D-I-A-N. How he throve! How he blossomed! How much more handsome he grew! Actually, Kira snorted to begin with: 'Whatever next! Registering with a woman. . . .'

Yes, but what s-s-sort of a w-w-woman . . .,' stammered Vadim. 'Didn't Aunt Grusha m-m-make it clear, for which many thanks, that she's over seventy?'

Apart from that, it was also agreed that the young guardian would not take up residence, but merely register there. For the rest, he would pay his fee: a regular supply of scarce commodities, payment for communal services and fifteen roubles a month net. Sometimes, as time and opportunity allowed, he would also have to provide service in kind, that is—pay a couple of visits a week, carry out minor repairs about the place—mend the radio, patch up a window, oil a lock—and if the old lady should fall ill, call a doctor, shake up the bed and run to the chemist for medicine. True this was hardly man's work, but 'Mummy and you, Kira darling, will lend a hand . . .'.

Very well. . . . It will do for the time being. . . .

How splendidly, brilliantly, velvety-smoothly everything worked! Every day the telephone wires between Maly Komsomolsky Lane and Zubovsky Boulevard hummed with mutual helloes from early morning on.

'Hel-l-l-o! Sofia Franzevna?' purred and stuttered Vadim on the telephone. 'Am I d-d-d-disturbing you?'

'Hell-oee, hell-oee, dear Vadim Victorovich,' warbled *Puppele*. 'Not at all, not at all. . . . I am always happy to hear you. . . . How are things with you? Have you handed in your Latin test? I kept my fingers crossed for you all last night and was hoping against hope you wouldn't get that dreadful first speech of Caesar's against Catherine.'

'Everything is absolutely tiptop!' answered Vadim with a manly rasp in his voice. 'Evdokimov collected the speech against Catiline. I got an easy one. Don't worry, Sofia Franzevna, don't worry—everything is on the level, everything is in the clear.'

Until, one day, tireless Comrade Grusha took a sideways look at *Puppele* in the kitchen and quoth:

'Well, Sofia Franzevna, does he behave properly to you? Did I fix you up with a fine, upstanding young man?'

Soninka pleasurably fluttered her half-closed lids, like a hen. Oh, to find such a young man—nowadays . . .! Real money, fifteen roubles of it, on the eleventh of every month without fail, the same day that all the other pensioners collect. . . . Three visits a week, and never empty handed, always apples or biscuits. . . .

'But they had oranges in the Steklyanny shop on Pokrovka yesterday,' intervened somebody with malicious innocence from the other end of the kitchen.

The roses on *Puppele*'s cheeks turned from tender peach to a thick mud colour.

'Apples?' hissed Aunt Grusha. 'For that sort of space? Trying to get away with biscuits and apples for twenty-two square metres? Look at Vera—I set her up with a guardianship for Akulina on Chetvertaya Meshchanskaya Street in the Riga, what used to be the Shcherbakovksi, district—she brings her old lady potatoes—clean ones from the market! From the *mar*-ket! Now there are oranges all over the place, and he gets away with biscuits? Fancy letting him off with bits and pieces like that. . . .

'Well, of course, Grusha, of course I'd rather have oranges,' remarked Soninka pensively.

You push open the door to the lobby on your way home from the latest hooly. You fumble for the stairs with your foot. There's no light. Why on earth not? Sh-sh. . . . It's them. They've either switched off the light, or else taken out the bulb and broken it. No, they didn't do it themselves—they put Vova Zalivkin up to it, for five copecks. Oh, wretches, wretches. . . . You've got nothing to fear from me. I won't tell anyone. If it was Uncle Vlas, the caretaker, now, or the house manager. . . . That would be different. . . .

Kira looks away and pouts irritably:

'No, how long is this business going to go on for? Are we going to sit on these stairs for ever? A year and a half gone, and no end in sight! Soon you'll be through at your technical school and I at the institute. You know yourself that if we haven't registered we'll be directed where to work. . . . No, Vadim dear, I'm telling you for the last time, make up your mind. . . .'

'But how am I to blame, Kira sweetie?' answers Vadim with a whine, stuttering and biting his fingers to the quick. 'Who could have guessed she wasn't even thinking of . . . You can't take somebody by the throat, can you? Just another year or two. . . . Be patient. . . .'

It's easy enough to say 'a year or two', easy enough to say 'be patient'. A year went by, then another. The end of the course was already in sight. Instructions on where to work were already round the corner. You had to hurry down to the marriage registry, declare your address, start a baby—or at least plan one—and then (oh, bliss), then you could stay in Moscow and be put down for 'independent job selection'.

'Well, what about it then, Aunt Grusha?' said Victor Alexandrovich, Vadim's father, getting straight down to brass tacks. 'What is your enlightened opinion on this problem? We wish no harm personally to Sofia Franzevna, but is time passing or is it not? And what are we to do about time?'

'As to time,' boomed Aunt Grusha, who had arrived for a clarification of the situation, 'time is time, of course, and who knows how long she intends to . . . We're a bit out in our reckoning here. But then I can't see to everything, can I? After all, I've only got my two hands and two feet, haven't I?' The beauteous Agrippina placed the side of her hand at right angles to the edge of the table and punctuated her incisive thoughts by thumping the one on the other. 'And you're a fine lot, aren't you? Vadik, or you, Valentina Nikolayevna, should have gone to the *Polychronic* beforehand and found out the way things were. What is she? And how is she?' These last two rhetorical questions were uttered by citizeness Agrafena with special emphasis. 'Is she on her last legs or what? Age is all very well, but if she's healthy she might last to a hundred. . . . In thirty-nine now, I remember, they found she had a growth. She was treated at Klifasovsky's. There might be consequences, mightn't there? But no, now it's Aunt Grusha's fault all round, I suppose!'

'But the main thing is time,' cried Valentina Nikolayevna, bursting into tears, 'that's what it's all about, Aunt Grusha, time, time's passing. They're young, you know, they want to live, and when do you expect to live, after all, if not when you're young. . . .'

'Ah well—li-i-vi-ng, is it?' Aunt Grusha skilfully slipped a *Goldfish* sweet into her pocket for her grandson, Seryozha. 'Never mind, they'll live it up yet. . . .'

Something scraped, banged and rustled in the corridor. Vadim stumbled into the room. From his uncommonly heavy breathing and more lustrous than usual Lyalya-doll's eyes, it was easy to conclude that he was, as you might say, 'under the influence'. To get his courage up.

'Grr-eetings to the assembled com-company,' he began, unbuttoning his jacket with a vent down the back (miserable hipster!) and tossing it across the heads of those present on to his divan. 'Ss-o. In the existing circ-circum-circumstances we can speak out. Would you please inform me, Aunt Grusha, at long last, when your baize carpet slippers are going to kick the bucket? As interpreted into the great and powerful Russian tongue: when will this aged ruin exp-p-pire?'

'Now, now!' clucked Aunt Grusha threateningly, 'don't you go nervousing us! You really frightened me, you did. . . . What do you think you're up to. . . . All trick-cycling or something! And what an argification, I ask you! She isn't doing it on purpose, is she? You're the one who's to blame and you're complaining.'

'Me? The one? To blame?' The guardian's features suddenly assumed a porcine look. 'Do I pay the agreed amount of cash or don't I? Do I bring her scarce victuals or don't I? Indeed I do. Including saus-sa-ges,' he hissed, emphasising every syllable. 'Yesterday I got hold of three hundred grammes of lightly s-s-smoked s-s-summer s-s-sausage for her, and not in one piece either, but s-s-sliced! Did I get her a ticket for the première of the Moscow Art Theatre's *Road Through Sokolniki*? Indeed I d-d-did!' he wailed with anguish. 'And n-n-now, if you please, after all that she informs me she's thinking of going to a friend in Riga this summer for a cure. What *is* this? M-m-mockery? D-d-d-discrimination? I-i-ignoration?'

'The crematorium's waiting for her—and she's off to Riga?' A groan of astonishment escaped Aunt Grusha's breast. 'Is that really so, ducky?' And then the 'missanger' of the Legal Advice Office began to chortle with a sly, clucking titter.

'Does she think I intend to roast in the lobby for the next ten years? That I'll pop in to the Special Armenian Delicatessen for fresh flans every time? Flan for the harridan? No, it's too much, much too much! No, she can go and whistle for them! "Sofochka, Sofka Franzevna, Sofka-a-a *Crap*orna, where are thou now-ow-ow?" ' he brayed, adapting a not altogether unknown and not exactly drawing-room ditty, and attempted to shake his narrow shoulders, spattering an untold amount of spittle in all directions.

'Now don't you go calling names, don't you dare, you've no right,' said Aunt Grusha, whistling angrily down her nose.

'Vadyusik, who do you think you're talking to? Don't be so cheeky!' yelped Valentina Nikolayevna.

With a groan of despair the father rushed out into the corridor.

Madame Grusha then graciously put an end to this piece of lively French farce.

'Well, all right,' once more she struck the edge of the imported oilcloth with the side of her hand, 'I'll do you a special favour. Good people like yourselves deserve a favour. Don't cry, ducky, I'll tell you something now that will make you thankful to Aunty Grusha for the rest of your life.'

Vadim's ears pricked up with excitement and pleasurable antici-pation. A tender glow suffused his apple cheeks. His great, black Lyalya-doll's eyes suddenly narrowed to flat, yellowish, copper farthings.

'Away with Sofia. We'll annul the agreement. I'll have a word with her. It can be done. I've seen hundreds of cases like that in our Legal Advice Department. Of course you're a good guardian, mild-tempered. That's hard to find. Maybe she won't want to at first. But I'll fix it. Sofia Franzevna, I'll say, what are we to do if they need it in a hurry now? And what's the good of crying over him? It isn't as though he was the whole world, is it? And supposing I find you somebody better off, for twenty a month plus rates, what about it then? Of course she'll agree. . . . And even be glad to.'

Aunt Grusha drew breath. Then, after a moment's pause for recollection, the sweetest smile lit up her stern, benosed and bewhiskered visage.

'I've got another combination in mind for you: Alexandra Stepanovna on Vadkovsky Lane. Cancer. Eight months gone already. Another six months is the most she can hold out for. There's just a pale shadow left of the woman.' Madam Grusha gave a sorrowful sigh. 'Only don't be daft,' she turned to young Vadim, who by now had perked up again, 'as soon as you sign for the guardianship and register, move in for keeps and get the housing sheet made out to you as head of the household. And the main thing—hold on to your floor-space! Don't let the square metres go—they're there for the taking.'

She nodded thoughtfully.

'To tell the truth, I was saving this woman up for a post-graddit I know, or rather I promised her, I did—she kept on asking and begging. Agrafena, she said, Matveyevna, she said . . .'

'Oh dear, a postgraduate. . . . Well, what about her? Won't she hold us responsible for cutting in?'

'Oh no. Such a little lady! We'll find someone else for her too.'

Agrafena Matveyevna, alias Grusha, eyed another sweet. And as she did so she verbally introduced on to the revolving stage a wholly (rather than semi) incidental character.

'I just haven't found time to visit Lyubov Vasilevna. I haven't found the time. . . . I just haven't. . . . She's bound to have a few more.'

'Lyubov? What Lyubov? And what's she got?'

'She's a deacon's wife in one of the churches here,' replied the Ministry of Justice employee somewhat reluctantly. 'We got to know each other at our Legal Advice Office. It's a bit awkward for her, so now she operates through Aunt Grusha. She always informs me.'

'Good Lord, and what does she inform you about? And about who?' Valentina Nikolayevna's eyes bulged with horror.

'About who? Why, about old women, of course. Who else?'

Aunt Grusha wiped the corners of her mouth with her fingers in ecstasy. 'Lonely old women, they see 'em all up there. Some are still pretty lively, others have one foot in the grave. . . . They've got nought to do in their old age all day long, so they go to the church in droves. . . . The deacon tells his wife and she informs me. . . . Not for free, of course, but in return for recognition. . . .'

Aunt Grusha suddenly twitched her small moustaches with envy.

'Doesn't matter how much you give some people, it's never enough, never enough. . . . They've really made hay in this deacon's job, all she does is buy gold the whole time, you can't see her for watches and rings and brooches, and it's still not enough, still not enough. . . .'

'All right, Aunt Grusha, all right—it's nothing to do with us. You just get moving with the business you were talking about! Solve this problem for us once and for all! A quick thrust, as only you know how. If everything is all right by the time young Vadim finishes his technical school, you'll get the sort of recognition from me that your deaconess wouldn't even think about in her wildest dreams.'

Agrafena Matveyevna gulped down the last of her Krasnodar tea and up-ended the glass.

There is also an epilogue to this story. If such it can be called:

1. Alexandra Stepanovna, the old lady that the semi-incidental character fixed up for Vadim, died three months after he had assumed guardianship over her. Our young hero finally settled down in his twenty-two-square-metre domicile, married Kira and now works for the *Moskovski Komsomolets* newspaper. Kira is a postgraduate and is defending a thesis on 'How N. G. Chernyshevsky's ideas on the man of the future have been modified in the light of Soviet reality'. They are doing very nicely, long for a couple of kids and have purchased a Hungarian cupboard, a Rumanian sideboard and a Czech dressing-table, all highly lacquered. Last summer the young newly-weds holidayed in the Crimea at their own expense and this year they are off to Italy on a package tour. They live, they live, and they are living very nicely, thank you.

RHETORICAL QUESTION: And when can one live, after all, if not when one is young?

May God grant this young couple . . . whatever they wish for themselves.

2. Aunt Grusha goes on working in the Legal Advice Office, where lawyers draft guardianship agreements for students, lecturers, postgraduates and smaller fry. As a reward for her invaluable assistance in successfully solving the 'square-metre' problem of the Ponarin family, Grusha received a dress length of the most fashionable drip-dry material, a pair of extra-thin soled shoes and thirty Government Gold Loan bonds at ten roubles apiece. If you don't trust the government, or don't wish to wait for the draw, you can go to the Savings Bank and cash them at any time. Aunt Grusha personally doesn't trust the government. She cashed the certificates at their face value, thirty certificates for three hundred roubles. She spent half the proceeds on an *Avangard* TV set and drinks tea on official holidays with Lyubov Vasilevna, the deacon's wife, who:

3. Says that the best thing nowadays is to put your money into gold, which has made its appearance in the State Jewellery Shops, while all kinds of TV sets and refrigerators are not worth bothering about—if they are of domestic manufacture, that is, because all you can do with them is paint them and throw them out. Foreign ones are another matter, but where can you lay your hands on one? Her soliloquies are accompanied by the gentle and melodious tinkling of gold earrings, each the size of your thumb.

4. That adorable widow, the irreproachable turtle dove, Sofka Perestranzevna, is still alive.

TO THE PRESENT DAY!

'Oh, my sister's applegarth, applegarth secluded. . . .'

Nothing makes sense, yet the heart melts. . . . What is it like, this applegarth? Is it like a peargarden? Is it juicy, without pips? I swoon, I faint with pleasure. And there is so much that is pleasurable here. . . .

Applegarth SE-CLU-DED!

I take out a large handkerchief, lie down on the sofa behind the cupboard and cover my face with the handkerchief. What bliss it is to be alone, at long last. . . .

'Are you asleep?'

Not a word from me.

'Are you asleep, yes or no?'

'Shsh—I am not at home. . . .'

In New York Central Park a man is lying on the grass. He has fenced off his face from the world at large with a cardboard box.

Fifty years will pass and you will exclaim:

'Was she soft in the head or something, that cuckoo who wrote the story?'

But now, in a minute, you will re-read and suddenly understand the title and you'll tweak the author's nose and hiss spitefully:

'Don't laugh at someone else's sister, my friend—yours is still an old maid.'

Victor Velsky

My Apologia

What I have written here is both my apologia and my confession. I have described how I came or was led to that fatal decision that it is my purpose here to explain. I have hidden nothing, but maybe in my haste I have not been as explicit as I would have liked. I have told everything that had to be told, not concerning myself with style, but just with the truth of my own soul. It is indeed of little concern to me who gets hold of my notebook and when, and who reads it. I had to have it out with myself and that is what I have done.

Where shall I begin? I'll begin in the classical manner, with my uncle.

'My uncle has most honest principles. . . .'[1]

And I'm not joking. My uncle did a lot for me, he was like a second father to me.

My uncle was a professor, an art-historian specialising in medieval art, and a solitary old man. In his declining years he wanted to share his learning with some youthful being, i.e. me. I was 14 at the time, my mother had just remarried after my father's death—he was a journalist—at the front. My mother soon consoled herself with her new family and found a modicum of happiness in its bosom. As far as I can remember, she did not get on with her first husband, my father, and they were virtually separated.

I began to hate her new family, her new children, and was glad when one day a dry, stiff, almost Dickensian gentleman appeared at the door and said that under the circumstances it was his duty to his late brother to see to the education of the boy, i.e. me. My mother and stepfather talked it over and decided that I could live with my uncle—he was a professor, and professors had lots of money. It took a load off their minds. Soon after I had settled at my uncle's, my stepfather retired, sold our Moscow flat and moved to the Crimea, where he bought a cottage with a vineyard in some small holiday resort. They're not too badly off, in fact they have a pretty cushy life, my stepfather gets his pension, sells home-made wine and lets out rooms to visitors. They have two children and hardly ever think of me and vice-versa, though sometimes, when I feel like seeing my mother, I pay them a visit. They receive me well but are even happier to see me go. . . .

So, a solitary child, virtually cast out by his family, I settled in the old bachelor's flat, never having known (and never to know) the joys of family life.

[1] The first line of Pushkin's novel in verse, *Eugeny Onegin*. Tr.

My life was unlike that of any other children of my age. The dark, dusty little flat was crammed with bookshelves, casts of statues from the portals of Gothic cathedrals, crucifixes, madonnas, stained-glass panels in the windows—even the sunlight could not get in to us. And silence, silence, silence. . . . Uncle was silent when he got back from his lectures. The old woman, Khristina Nikonovna, who cooked and cleaned for us, was silent. The books, relics, walls—everything was silent. Uncle had neither radio nor telephone. No one visited us, it was horribly dreary. So much for my 'sentimental education'. It had a traumatic effect on my spiritual development.

My uncle had no intention of educating me, nor could he. I was able to do as I liked, provided I did not disturb the established order of things in the flat. I did not become a madcap—I was always too calm and collected for that—instead I turned into a little mole, searching for a way out to the light. I had no friends at school or in the street, and no wonder—the other children instinctively sensed something different about me and victimised and tormented me. I read a lot, even too much—so much superfluous, heavy stuff indeed that it gives me a headache now just to think of it all. I was average at school, not because I didn't want to do my homework, but because I didn't like saying much and always answered in monosyllables. In the upper forms I was called 'the silent one', 'the hermit', 'the anchorite', but they admired me for my silence—reserved, close-lipped people always are admired. And that's how it was till my seventeenth year.

At seventeen I read the whole of Nietzsche and the whole of Anatole France. France taught me how to use words, how to express myself freely and ironically. Nietzsche made me more conscious of my own personality, my human dignity. New, paradoxical, daring ideas turned my head. 'Tra-la-la! Let's dance our own dance!' Long live 'the gay science'. We're not just mindless frogs, we'll be stronger, wickeder, profounder, lovelier! Spiritual convalescence was what I needed. Like Zarathustra I left my hated cave and returned to the people I had never loved.

In the Lenin Library, where I started going to pursue my studies, I found company for myself. They were people older than me, some of them a lot older, who accepted me as an equal. They all wrote a bit, and dreamt of some extraordinary future. They understood everything and were clever and well-read, so their conversation was not just idle chatter, yet at the same time they used to have parties with girls and drink and fool around.

By this time I was already studying in the philosophy department of Moscow University. It was terribly hard for me to get a place and I managed it in 1948, thanks partly to my uncle's reputation and to the influence of his friend, Professor A. I entered full of dreams about making a systematic study of the science of sciences (at that time I could still dream), but soon regretted my decision. Philosophy never came into it, we studied Marxism. It was a terrible period. Zhdanov's[1] draconian decrees on ideology had just recently been issued and though Zhdanov himself died, his ferocious culture-hating spirit lived on. The words 'toadying to the west' flashed across the pages of newspapers and magazines, the rabble-rousing slogan, 'cosmopolitan', became increasingly current. The Museum of Modern Western Art was dismantled, jazz was banned, books of contemporary western authors were called seditious. The 'Kremlin Hermit' was silent, merely deigning from time to time to answer questions put to him by *Pravda*'s correspondent. Large-scale arrests took place.

Intellectuals were arrested, professors were removed from their chairs. There were departmental meetings, at which students fulminated against cosmopolitan professors. The professors confessed their sins and heaped muck on one another. Each mounted the stand, expressed his gratitude for the principled criticism levelled at him, thoroughly depreciated his achievements, and then started abusing one of his friends. Back-stabbing flourished. In our department they removed Professor A. They said the old man never went out and since 1937 had kept a small suitcase with underclothes in it under his bed. His wife sold their belongings and his daughter left the parental home.

Naturally my uncle was removed too. He was, in any case, an obvious westerniser and 'toady', though as a matter of fact, all he recognised was the Middle Ages—in his view the most highly integrated period of cultural development. Some students jumped up and asked him what he thought about Soviet art! Uncle answered candidly that he didn't know there was such a thing. This imprudent remark lost him his job. Some young post-graduate took over uncle's course on medieval art. Strangely enough, the students thought a lot of uncle, and when he had been suspended they sometimes called on us with flowers and thanked him for his lectures. Uncle did not like displays of superfluous emotion and soon sent them packing. He started writing a book.

But it was not only adults and prominent personalities who were

[1] Andrei Zhdanov (1888-1948) was a member of the Soviet Politbureau from 1939 until his death and immediately after the war was the Party's chief spokesman on cultural policy. Tr.

arrested, the terror also affected youth. Several students disappeared from our course. We tried to forget about them. At this time I felt that the black cloud might envelop me too. As soon as Uncle was removed, I noticed how the attitude of several of the lads, especially those involved in social work, changed towards me; people started avoiding me. But this was not the real danger. The real danger lay in our circle of friends. Although we tried to keep off risky subjects, it was impossible not to talk about what was going on. There was, besides, a certain intangible spirit of disapproval about our crowd. I had the sense to stop seeing them.

But it was already too late. One day N, who was in the philosophy department and worked on the next floor, approached me in between lectures and told me that they had taken T. T was not one of our crowd, but he knew us all well. The circle was closing in on us. What did it matter if the hares caught in that circle were harmless—who cared? The hunt was on, and it was late in the day to start arguing one's innocence. The main pieces of 'evidence' that could be used against us were as follows: firstly, there was this group of friends, and a stable group at that; secondly, the purpose of this group was obscure; thirdly, all its members were near relatives of people who had been repressed or had fallen into disgrace. The inference was clear—our group was up to no good.

This sense of being accused without there being any cause for it was a terrible, desolate feeling. It seemed we were internally guilty! Although we did not give expression to our sentiments, we were against what was going on, or rather we were not 'for' it, and also we stuck together to some extent. Someone already had his eye on us, that was clear. Maybe there was already a traitor in our midst. This was a constant nightmare. There was, in fact, something essentially dream-like about it. I had had a dream like that when I was a child: a German officer points his pistol at me, I fall to my knees, implore him, scream, then there's a shot, but I can't wake up. . . . This strange, elemental feeling of horror now had substance to it. There was no escape. There was just the fear. In vain I tried to reassure myself that nothing had happened, that this was a lot of nonsense, that I was scaring myself. I was literally quaking with fear all the time. The fear that was hanging over all of us achieved its quintessence in me. I couldn't stand it. I lost my nerve.

One episode, which could hardly have been a coincidence, made a particular impression on me. The teacher who took the seminar on dialectical materialism called me out. As it happened, for some reason the Party organiser of the course was present, though he was not in our group. I answered satisfactorily. But the point lay not in my answer, but in me. This was no new ploy for them. The same tactics had been used with an Uzbek student. This youth, who was rather frail, got carried away by Gandhi (whom he read about in Romain Rolland) and started preaching his ideas to all and sundry. He was cunningly provoked at the seminar, spoke his mind and a few days later, early one morning, was taken straight out of his warm bed in the hostel. It seems he was a 'bourgeois nationalist'. There was no doubt about it. Probably they wanted to catch me out in the same way. The instructor asked me some crafty questions on the relation between theory and practice, on dogmatism, on the correct interpretation of the Party resolutions with regard to ideology, but behind it all there was this feeling that I would slip up at some point. I gave all the right answers, but even so, this character felt he had to expatiate at length on the evils of dogmatism, on the fact that a mere verbal knowledge of Marxism did not mean much, one had to be devoted to it body and soul, etc. The finger was pointing at me and I had to do something about it—there was no time to be lost. There was nothing for it but to stake everything on one last desperate throw. This was my knight's move. Desperation cleared my mind and lent me strength.

When the instructor had finished what he had to say and just as he was about to set the work for the next seminar, I got up and asked for permission to speak. It seemed to me as though his eyes and the Party organiser's gleamed with malicious joy. The room grew tense. I began speaking in a deliberately quiet, calm voice. I said that you (i.e. the instructor) have spoken today of the relationship between theory and practice, of dogmatism and bigotry, with someone clearly in mind. As no one besides myself has spoken today, this person is obviously me. I don't know what fault I am supposed to have committed to deserve your criticism. I have only just started on my studies and you've got nothing against me. The only thing you have is that my uncle, Professor Velsky, has been called a cosmopolitan in the wall newspaper. But why should a nephew have to answer for his uncle? (At these words the audience began to laugh, though everyone realised it was a nasty situation.) I've nothing in common with my uncle. (So much for Uncle!) You are purposely singling me out from the collective. (I turned his own weapons against him—used demagogy against a demagogue.) You are creating impossible conditions for me to study in. I feel obliged, therefore, to leave your seminar and to ask the dean's office to transfer me to another instructor. With these words, I left the lecture room.

They took fright. I had chosen the right tactics—I didn't defend myself or confess, I did my own attacking and exposing. Also I brought things out into the open, called a spade a spade, and anyway it was a recognised fact that children were not responsible for their parents. In the interval between classes the Party organiser sought me out, and putting on a friendly voice (what scum they were!) said that I'd lost my temper over nothing, that no one had me in mind and it was pointless my going to the dean's office, that everything would be fine, that, of course, my uncle was irrelevant, that my comrades thought a lot of me, etc. It was obvious he didn't want me to make the quarrel public. I answered that I didn't bear anyone a grudge but I was transferring to another group. It was impossible for me to retreat, they would have tried to finish me off (which they succeeded in doing later anyway). The other lads congratulated me, criticised the instructor for his tactlessness (was that all it was?) and indeed began to see me in a different light and even to respect me.

But there was nothing to respect in me. Now I have to come to the hardest part of my confession, in comparison with which the escapades of that unhappy sexual psychopath, Jean-Jacques Rousseau, seem like so many childish pranks. I shall not try to glorify or belittle myself. The shame of it will stay with me all my life. I became a traitor.

I had in my possession some manuscripts belonging to R, one of our group. Not long before he had brought them to me and asked me to keep them; he himself then disappeared. R wanted to be a writer. He had stacks of poems and stories. Apparently he was talented. He let me read his work and I read it. There was nothing particularly inflammatory about it, but there was something 'not right' there, as they say. Now I wondered in alarm what would happen to me if they decided to carry out a surprise search in my home. And this was bound to happen now they had taken T. Even if T kept silent, my name was in his notebook. They would ransack the homes of everyone, participants and non-participants alike. What could I do? How could I save myself? There was direct evidence against me. Keeping seditious writings, concealing them, failing to report them, this in itself made me an accessory. And anyway I was a participant in the group. There was no way out. I had to commit myself.

My reasoning was as follows (for my eighteen and a half years I reasoned pretty well): I ought to seek out R and give him back the manuscripts, but . . . (1) R had vanished somewhere, (2) he had evidently suspected something and brought me the manuscripts to hide, (3) the manuscripts ought to be destroyed, (4) it was useless destroying them, since R might reveal their existence to the MGB[1] and then I'd be done for. Even worse, if I burnt the papers I would simply be compromising myself still further—it would be clear that by destroying the evidence I was behaving like a criminal. Finally, (5) R might be a provocateur, palming off papers on me he was frightened to keep himself, or (6) at best R was just an idiot who was involving others in his own downfall.

Yes, I was older and wiser than my years (wiser!) and realised only too well where the danger in all this lay for me. Once, before the war, when I was about ten, I had overheard a conversation between my mother and father about 1937[2] and I could still remember how people had been ruined because of a Trotskyist book by someone else.

There was no other way out. I had to commit myself. I had to take the manuscripts to the MGB and tell them the whole story. Thus I would betray everyone and save myself. The alternative was to sit and wait patiently for the inevitable to happen.

I walked along the street and, despite the gloomy autumn weather, the world seemed a lovely place to me. People were walking about, laughing, leading their normal lives, and even if something awful was happening close by, life carried on. And I was going to be cut off from this life and why—because of someone else's stupidity! Besides, what were these people to me, did I care for them? No! It made no difference to me if they existed or not. All I had to do was commit myself and my life would be secure. Nothing could save them now anyway, whereas I still had a chance to extricate myself.

Walking the streets in this manner, I managed to convince myself that I had no alternative. So I'd be a scoundrel, but wasn't R a scoundrel for dumping those crazy bits of writing on me? In any case, one way or another all of them were doomed and one would escape. So let that one escape at least. They had brought it all on themselves. That was true, but then what about me? I had done the same, by being so careless. But less than the others, so why should I have to suffer the same as them? No, I wouldn't! They were them, but I was something different, a living being apprehending a world that would cease to exist without me. So my youthful solipsism came to my aid, saving me and ruining me at a single stroke.

The most awful part of it was making up my mind. Far worse than simply waiting. Because making up my mind was something positive, a harder thing than waiting passively. And how I wanted

[1] Ministry of State Security, predecessor of the KGB and likewise responsible for administering the secret police. Tr.

[2] 1937 was the year in which Stalin's 'Great Purge' reached its height. Tr.

191

to avoid making a decision! How the soothing thoughts came flooding in—that my fears were uncalled for, that I was imagining it all, that I was in no danger. But finally I convinced myself. I knew that thousands of people as guiltless as me had been taken away. Nothing had saved them. There was no miracle. It was no use my waiting. I had to save myself.

In a panic, I grabbed the papers and rushed to the MGB. I knew that the Reception Centre was at Kuznetsky Bridge and went there. Even today, ten years later, it disgusts me to remember what I did and what I said. I was referred to an ordinary-looking, rather uninterested individual in plain clothes. I said that I wanted to make a special statement. I said that by mischance I had found myself in possession of an acquaintance's papers . . . (Like a flash came the question: 'His name?' 'R'. He wrote it down. 'All right, carry on!') I hadn't read them for some time, but now I was convinced that their content was suspicious and I had come to find out what I should do. Questions followed: 'Who is this R? How do you know him?' etc. I told him about our circle, I gave everyone away. He asked me to sit at a free desk and to put it all down in writing. I wrote down everything I had told him. He skimmed through the sheet and said casually: 'All right, we'll look into this.' 'Are you going to keep the papers here?' 'Yes. You can go. If you're needed, you'll be sent for.'

I went out into the street with a strange, incongruous feeling of relief. Life was going on around me and I could start living again. Strangely enough there was no consciousness of having done anything shameful. That came later. But for the time being I strolled about carelessly, feeling free. Inside, perhaps, in my innermost self, I had shrivelled up and hardened and my youthful greenness and naïvety had vanished for ever. I was half-damned already. But now that I'd actually committed myself everything was allowed. Yes, it was exhilarating to feel no fear of heights—to look down and not be afraid.

To test myself, I visited a girl I knew, who always made me feel shy. I was worked up, animated and bold. I caught her looking at me in astonishment. I could feel that she liked me. But I no longer needed her. I no longer needed anyone.

That evening, at home, I felt afraid again. But the day had tired me out so much that I slept well enough. The next day I was tormented by fear. I didn't go to the university. I was totally incapable of doing anything those days. All I did was wander about and pass the time in bars. I felt better amidst the noise and hubbub of anonymous, drunken people. And I could hide in the cinema, too, in the darkness.

But after two days, returning home late one night I found a search in progress and some men waiting for me. They took nothing at the time, even apologised to Uncle, but they asked me to accompany them. However, no warrant for my arrest was produced and this was a hopeful sign. Uncle completely lost his presence of mind and gazed after me in a state of shock.

I was taken to the MGB. (We went by car—it was parked on the same side as our building.) I was led along deathly silent passages— a long corridor, a straight carpeted path, a line of ceiling lights stretching into the distance, identical numbered oak doors leading off and nothing else, not even ashtrays.

I was interviewed by three men in plain clothes. One of the senior men, I realised, was in charge, though he sat apart from the others. They questioned me, tried to catch me off guard, to trip me up. 'You'd better get it into your head that you've got to tell the truth here,' they said. 'It'll be better for you if you do.' They were civil enough and didn't threaten me. I answered all their questions briefly and clearly, without saying anything defamatory. But this gave them little joy. They kept on hoping for something more, something out of the ordinary—they were dreaming of an underground, terrorist organisation, and decorations and bonuses for themselves for uncovering it. I couldn't oblige them, I was a traitor, but not a slanderer. . . . However, once a scoundrel, why try to excuse myself? I said that there were some unhealthy tendencies in our group, as R's papers had shown me, but nothing worse than that. 'Are you sure?' asked the most junior member of the trio with an ironical smile. He was sitting at a table and writing everything down. 'That's my opinion, yes.' 'Ah, your opinion. . . .' 'And where, in your opinion,' said the second one, 'where might these unhealthy tendencies lead?' 'I realised they couldn't lead to anything good, that's why I came to you.' 'You're being frank with us, are you, Velsky?' said the main in charge. 'How did you fall into these ways? How is it that you are involved with enemies of the people?'

I realised that things might go badly for me and the only way I could save myself was by advancing even further into the mire. I writhed and squirmed and said that it had taken me a long time to realise it, but that I had realised it finally and had come to them myself. (I stressed this.) 'I'll tell you all I know and answer any question you like.' They wanted me to describe each member of our circle, and this I did. They wanted me to remember what one or another of them had said, and I did. I spilled everything. I was so mesmerised by the whole situation that I really believed all my former friends were enemies. 'Go on, go on,' they urged. 'We know everything about you, don't worry.' When I'd nothing more to say and they were tired, two of them, apparently satisfied, went out and the one at the table sat for a long time writing the examination record. There were 32 pages of it. He handed it to me to read through. The record was drawn up so cleverly and convincingly that my comrades really did look like enemies from it. I signed each of the 32 pages without hesitation. It didn't make any difference to me now, I would have signed anything. 'You have nothing to add?' asked the MGB man. 'I should like it to be noted that this is a frank confession!' 'That's unnecessary', he smiled. 'We've your statement—that's enough.' He stacked up the sheets neatly and laid them in a drawer which he locked. Then he started smoking contentedly, looking at me with a smile. He was silent, the swine, enjoying his power over me and my nervous apprehension.

He smoked his cigarette half-way through and extinguished it, then took a form and scribbled something on it. What was this? My heart missed a beat. But why, I'd told them everything. . . . 'Let's go. Put your things on.' He led me out of the office, closed the door, went into the adjacent office, quickly reappeared and led me through corridors and down staircases. Finally, we emerged into the side entrance lobby where there was a man on duty. My companion handed him the form and I realised it was a pass—a pass back to life. 'You can go,' he said drily by way of farewell, turned on his heel and disappeared. The duty man checked the pass and my passport, glanced at the photograph and at my face, returned the passport and silently nodded towards the door.

I had never been so thirsty for the cold autumn air. It was already morning, the sky over the houses was blue, crows were flying and cawing above the town, the yard-keeper's broom was rustling over the asphalt. I was free. Behind me the windows of the MGB building blazed like ever watchful eyes.

At home my uncle, who of course had not slept all night, was waiting for me with a pale, frightened face, and I realised how much he loved me! Me, a scoundrel and a traitor! But was I alone guilty? Who had driven me to it, who had turned me into a traitor? Was I the only one? It was going on all round me! And who still had a clean conscience, who could tell me that? We were all traitors, to a greater or lesser extent, in one way or another, traitors by virtue of our passiveness, our fear, our hypocrisy, our lying! So what had I, a frightened eighteen-year-old child, to be ashamed of! There were worse cases than me. Shame on us all!

I gave Uncle a shortened version of what had happened, begged him not to worry. I told no one of my treachery, and anyway there was no one to tell, as I'd never had any close friends. In any case what close friend could you tell such a thing to! Not even the friends I'd betrayed found out about it, and indeed some of them, I gather, shielded me, testifying that I was not involved. Even those who survived don't know. Let whoever reads this account, whether he be friend or enemy, know the truth and learn what it means to be a traitor!

It is agonising to recall all this, and even more agonising to realise that I ruined innocent people and that if it had not been for my cowardice, nothing would have happened. It seems to me now that any prison sentence would be easier than to bear such a stigma, but I've no illusions about myself; these positive feelings are just superficial and I shall always be a scoundrel and a traitor.

If only it had not happened, if only it had not happened!

As they say in novels, 'time went by'. They called me twice to the department again, asked for more evidence and clarified my earlier deposition. At my last meeting with the interrogator, he had a few parting words for me: I should think about all that had happened, it would be a good lesson for me. I wasn't going to be put on trial, but I should remember that they would not forget me. He hinted that from now on they would keep an eye on me and they might use me again. I remembered this conversation two years later, but at the time I rejoiced that the nightmare was over. Wounds heal quickly when you are young. (Am I so old now?)

I began to live, as they say in novels again, 'for sensual pleasures'. I did not get close to anyone, did not make any intimate friends. My acquaintances were just companions in pleasure. Naturally, no one at the university knew anything of my private life. The prevailing atmosphere was one of asceticism and bigotry and any diversion—drinking or intimacy with a woman—was regarded as a sin for future workers on the ideological front. (In those blissful years you were expelled from the Komsomol for fornication. Thank God I wasn't a member, and our activists always avoided me, sensing something strange about me, and did not try to draw me into the organisation.)

Meanwhile, public hysteria was growing. If, before, it had affected only the upper strata, leaving the masses more or less untouched, now everyone was in the grip of its evil spirit, everyone wanted to destroy the cosmopolitans—they'd smelt blood. The glorification of

Stalin became wildly fanatical. Banshees of both sexes thrashed about frenziedly on platforms. When his health was proposed, everyone rose simultaneously and drummed their bony knuckles on the table, these skeleton people. As the cult developed, it became increasingly necessary to seek out new enemies. Saturn was devouring his children. The gods were hungry.

Something was up with Uncle. He spent every day reading Latin books, muttering to himself the whole time. One day I was coming home from my mistress—one could call her that. She was a real woman, proud and beautiful, who knew what she was worth. My liaison with her flattered me inordinately. She lived in a narrow street, near a Catholic church, and just as I was leaving her, feeling very self-satisfied, some people were coming out of church. I stopped to look at these eccentrics who still believed in God, when suddenly, in the crowd of comely old men and women, I caught sight of my uncle. He must have noticed me, but gave no sign—nor did I. My uncle had become a practising Catholic. The Middle Ages had finally devoured him.

I did not discuss the matter with Uncle, at that time we hardly ever conversed. There was nothing to talk about, we hid from each other. We led a strange life. Uncle had some savings and we lived on these. In spite of our straitened circumstances, we never made use of my grant and I did what I liked with it. I had a tremendous intoxicating thirst for life. That which had always been foreign to my nature now practically obsessed me. I frequented parks and dance halls, cafés and restaurants and the sports stadium, and loafed about Gorky Street. I even learn to dance. I must taste everything life has to offer, I thought. At the university I was an average kind of student, doing what was asked of me. It wasn't very hard. The main thing was to enjoy life to the full.

Two years after that episode—it was summer—my friends from the secret police came to life again. One morning, when I was alone in the flat, the bell rang. A young man entered whose appearance spoke for itself. I understood at once. He showed me his identification card and glancing about him, started saying something like: 'It's a real museum here. . . .' Then he asked me politely if I had time to accompany him. I went, wondering what was up and what else they wanted from me.

This time I was taken to a different office. There were two men there, one of whom was that same senior officer. 'So, you see, we haven't forgotten you,' he said, laughing softly. They were silent for a while and then asked: 'Comrade Velsky, do you know why you've been called?' 'No.' 'Tell us what you've been doing since last time.' I said that nothing very interesting had happened to me. They asked me about my studies. Then something else. When they learnt that I wasn't a member of the Komsomol they shook their heads. And so they felt their way for a time, talking of this and that. They were interested in the frame of mind of my fellow-students: 'Have you noticed nothing out of the way?' I realised what all this was leading up to and steeled myself. Now I was not frightened, but furious. So that's what they wanted me for! I had been a scoundrel once, I would have to go on being one for ever! No! I wouldn't—never again!

Finally, they came to the point: 'Comrade Velsky, can't you help us? 'How?' 'I'm not telling you how yet, I'm asking you to agree to help us.' 'I can't agree if I don't know what it's all about.' Then the second one patiently started explaining things to me, hinting more and more broadly that the job of a doctor is not only to cure illness but to prevent it too. The same went for public doctors—the security organs. Of course, this was a thankless task, but a necessary one—what do you think? I agreed that it was necessary (to hell with them!). They were interested in what people were thinking, what they were talking about, what their state of mind was, and so on. I mixed with students and so might be able to give them information of this kind. They would go into the details later. 'I see, you want me to be an informer?' I asked straight out. I was no longer frightened of them. They nodded. 'I'm afraid I won't be able to live a double life. It's not my style, I'm a nervous type and I'll make a mess of it.' Then one of them said: 'You're a clever fellow, Velsky, so don't make out you're some kind of innocent. We let you off the hook once, now you've got to make it up to the country for your lapse.' The second one said more softly: 'You can take your time, we won't hurry you. We'll give you a week, say, to think it over. Come back in a week's time and tell us what you've decided. A pass will be made out to you.'

Leaving the MGB building, I found I hated them all in a way that it is impossible to hate any single individual. If only one could blow up this Bastille and put up a notice on the site saying 'Dancing here!' Yes, but who could be sure that the people wouldn't build a new Bastille, even worse than the old one?

All I wanted to do was to find some hole in some God-forsaken place and crawl into it. But where? Where could you hide from them? The only thing was to face the music. So, I'd be punished for my treachery after all. I deserved it and now I'd take what was coming to me. I even began to feel grateful for this opportunity to redeem myself by doing something honourable.

What saved me? Was it God or the chance intervention of circumstances? (And indeed, what is it that protects me in this life? What force? Who is my master and who preserved me from the abyss? God or the devil, good or evil?) I received a telegram from the Crimea to the effect that my mother was dangerously ill. I put the telegram in an envelope with an accompanying note and handed it in at the little window of the booth, like a public call-box, in the M.G.B. reception office.

Fortunately my mother recovered and everything turned out all right. I swanned it at the seaside, returned after a month, towards the beginning of term, and wasn't called to the department again. Whether they had forgotten about me or whether they were having one of their periodic upheavals, I don't know. Anyway, matters of great moment were being settled and there was no time to bother with small fry. Shortly afterwards, the 'doctor-poisoners'[1] were arrested. It smacked of anti-Semitism, which was receiving official encouragement at this time.

At the university things went badly for me. Either I was being mistaken for a Jew, or else they were looking for new 'enemies' to rout; at all events the storm was gathering over me.

Yes, those were terrible, bloodthirsty times and I still cannot understand how we managed to live through them. Something sinister, perhaps even apocalyptic, was in the air. Public hysteria was mounting by leaps and bounds and it seemed that everyone around, including oneself, was about to be overwhelmed by a fit of monstrous convulsions. Enemies were supposedly everywhere: one had to war against them outside and now it seemed they were inside too and had to be exposed. Speeches were made about the need for vigilance. People no longer just saved their skins by informing, as before, but also were given medals in place of those ancient pieces of silver (e.g. the celebrated 'unmasker' of the doctors, MGB agent Lidia Timashuk). It seemed that what lay ahead would be so terrible that the years 1937 and 1949 would pale in comparison. There was no escaping the nightmare, a giant hush descended before the gathering storm.

The glorification of Stalin reached such stupendous, outrageous heights that the whole thing began to look like a joke of the devil.

[1] A reference to the so-called 'Doctors' Plot', according to which a group of doctors was arrested in 1952-3 and accused of conspiring to eliminate state leaders. A majority of the doctors was Jewish. The charges were officially repudiated after Stalin's death.

There was certainly something diabolical about it, showing the hand of the prince of darkness. A new work (at that time no one guessed it was to be the last one) by the 'supreme genius of our age, the oracle of science . . .' appeared—and our teachers went into transports over it. The wretched, primitive, puny thoughts of this senile oracle were slavered over everywhere in specialist seminars that were held on 'this work of genius'. This cud, chewed by so many mouths, sickened even the most loyal Stalinists (and nearly all those in our department were loyal).

The clouds gathering over me were bound to burst at any moment. The department, the activists on our course, desperately needed something sensational to happen—the vigilance campaign was then in full swing. Progress with us always means that there has to be someone against. That's how it was at the beginning and that's how it has remained. It is inevitable. A villain was needed, our latterday idolators needed a human sacrifice. The masses already had it in their blood, they had been raised on trials and sensational exposures. 'Force is the midwife of history'—our Marxist Aztecs have assimilated this idea better than anyone.

(Men! You are more idolatrous than peaceful heathens, you sacrifice a million times more human beings than all the bloodthirsty cults of the past, yes, you, you men of the twentieth century! Underneath this mask of civilisation lurks a beast that has no equal among the natural world of beasts. This beast is capable of destroying everything—and will destroy it.)

Eventually I too slipped up—at a time when everyone around was shouting about vigilance, I relaxed my own vigilance and one day was caught out. I failed to prepare myself adequately for a seminar on production relations and burbled some sort of nonsense, or rather, forgetting what the 'oracle' had said, I simply gave Marx's interpretation. There was a subtle discrepancy on this point in the oracle's work and every effort was being made to gloss it over. My mistake was regarded as nothing less than a 'hostile attack'. Soon afterwards a denunciatory article appeared on me in the departmental newspaper. It said that apart from his 'attack', Velsky did not take part in the life of the collective, avoided the collective, showed himself to be a man of alien views and a peddler of bourgeois ideology, as witness his third year essay in which he defended a bourgeois, voluntaristic view of economics. It is absurd and ridiculous in retrospect, but at the time it was grim. A special meeting was called for the purpose of unmasking me. Again I was caught in a trap.

The answer was brutally simple. To go to the MGB, remind them of the conversation we had had and tell them I was ready to become an informer. The whole thing would stop immediately, I would be able to carry on with my studies and even do myself some good. But not only could I not bring myself to do this, the whole idea was so absolutely repugnant to me that anything else—death or prison—seemed preferable. I developed such a loathing for my surroundings that not only could I not stand classes and seeing the faces of my lovable colleagues, but I could not even bear the sight of the university building, built, as the inscription tells you, by the architect Kazakov and rebuilt by Gilliardi. I would go a mile out of the way to avoid it, just as I did with the MGB building. These two establishments merged into one in my mind. The MGB was everywhere.

I became apathetic, lost my desire to do anything or to achieve anything. I finally lost all belief in human values. Perhaps it would have been easier for me if I had been shut up. I was already under self-arrest, more or less prostrate and inert. Shigalev's[1] system embraced me too. 'We shall stifle every genius in the cradle,' he would say. And it was even easier to reduce non-geniuses to this infantilely imbecilic condition. I even stopped hating the system and the organs of oppression. I lived a life of fantasy. I could not bear the daily round as such, with its people, newspapers, radio. My mornings began at dusk. Either I sought out the company of ordinary, uncomplicated youth, or else I hung around libraries and clubs, or dropped in on evenings at the institute, where there were young people and at least some sort of semblance of life. In the 'afternoon', if there was no sequel to all this, I lay on my couch smoking a pipe, making up imaginary works in my mind or reading some light piece of entertainment. I dropped off in the morning and slept long. This routine had such a shattering effect on me that even Uncle was astonished. However, he also led a hermit's existence: he sat writing day and night and went out only to go to church—I don't know when he ate and slept. I told him that I had stopped going to the university and he didn't even ask me why. His savings ran out and he sold his lovely stained-glass panel. The money had to last a year. We went underground like two moles and waited there for whatever the unknown future held in store for us. Actually, we didn't even wait, we placed ourselves under house arrest and fell into a kind of nerveless silence, without hoping, thinking or feeling anything at all. And that's how everyone lived. Others only pretended to be living—in fact, they too had stopped hoping, their thoughts had been put there by others, while their very feelings were borrowed. At the time we didn't

[1] The hero of *The Devils* by Dostoyevsky. Tr.

realise and didn't expect what to day seems so obvious, that it all had to end some time. We had reached a state of blank indifference. But the end was near, unless, that is, it was not merely the beginning of the real end.

Stalin's death was a shock to us all, it was even a shock to me. Even if many intelligent people hated the Stalinist regime, we were all, in one way or another, his offspring, we had got used to him and his horrors, we were his slaves. The slave had grown conditioned to his terrible master and did not know what it would be like without him. Up till now everything had been controlled or justified in the name of this divinity. And suddenly the 'god' was no longer there. People felt terrified without him, as though their 'collective father' (as Freud would put it) had died. They had been conditioned to love him and this made them grieve and mourn his passing, while mass hypnosis still paralysed all critical activity. And I too felt the full force of this historic event. But I saw a bit deeper than others, I realised that, though nothing would alter basically, times were changing all the same. Of course, one couldn't hope for an improvement—we had stopped expecting anything like that—but apparently things were not going to get worse.

The changes soon became apparent. Stalin's praises were sung, he was mourned, and suddenly, as though at a word of command, all the voices fell silent simultaneously. No new Mayakovsky was allowed to go through his paces. No mourning Bolshevik was put on show in the museum. A month after Stalin's death, to everyone's surprise, the survivors of the 'doctors' plot' were released. This was more than just astonishing: for the first time the organs of repression were going back on their word. People waiting their turn began to hope again. And then, after the oppressive days of mourning, the heart-rending speeches, the music, the darkness and the gloom of it, we saw that spring had arrived. (Ehrenburg later called this period 'The Thaw'—a very apt description.) The sun shone and I felt I was seventeen again, the past was just a nightmare and the future was bright. It was as though I was seeing the sun for the first time. It was easier to breathe, a heavy load had been lifted off our shoulders. One day I met a colleague of mine in the street, a Jew, quite a decent chap, one of those who had stood aside from it all. Without hiding his joy, he told me that the Central Committee had passed some resolution with regard to historical names and the cult of personality, that now there wasn't going to be a 'Stalin constitution' or 'Stalin hawks', but 'Soviet hawks' and a 'Soviet constitution'. Also, there were not going to be any historico-biographical films.

o

Thus the notorious expression 'cult of personality', soon to become current (though for the time being it was used cautiously without it being made clear who the personality was), came to our ears as early as March 1953, before people had even had time to take off the shoes in which they had followed the coffin of their 'teacher and leader'. And soon after, two other extraordinary things happened: Beria was arrested and farm taxes were reduced. The first affected the intelligentsia, the second the peasants. Beria's arrest inevitably meant changes in the security apparatus and now I could forget my past (that is, if I could forget it!).

I came to life again. I had been dropped from the university long ago for failing to turn up at classes or for exams. If I appealed, I might be able to get myself reinstated, but everything there so revolted me, I was so sick of going round and round in the closed circle of Marxism and parroting its hoary axioms as though they were revelations from on high. . . . Anyway, the department that went under the high-sounding title of philosophical faculty didn't qualify you for anything. Who wanted to specialise in dialectical materialism and dispense that indisputable truth that you did not believe in yourself? As I was not an activist, not a member of the Komsomol bureau, there could be no question of my doing research. I had already had enough experience of life to have lost my rose-coloured spectacles and I knew that in our age a man could only be sure of his bread and butter if he were a technician. I had to get into technical college. Once again I was to go against my natural bent. By inclination and character I am an arts man, designs and formulae have always scared me. But I had to overcome this in myself. And I did. An acquaintance of mine, a final-year student in a technological institute, introduced me to a spinster who worked as secretary to the selection committee. This spinster (who was already getting on) pulled wires for her favourites. I managed to gain her favour and not having done so badly in the entrance exams, became a technical student.

But my heart wasn't in my technical studies, I stuck it somehow or other, trying to get as much time off as possible. My life had changed. Lately my uncle and I had grown closer and, for the first time, really got to know one another. Uncle's condition had deteriorated visibly, he became talkative after the manner of old men, something that hadn't been a characteristic of his before. But his mind was as sharp as ever. His public standing improved, some colleagues who did not hold official positions started visiting him, they prophesied that he would soon have his chair back. If only they had come earlier! Five years of isolation had taken their toll of the old man. . . .

Only now did I realise what an unusual, pure-hearted, righteous man was my uncle—or truer to say, my spiritual father. He told me a lot about his life and he had plenty worth remembering. In his youth art had been his religion. He described how the first time he went to Paris and saw Notre Dame, he had wept for joy. Life made him outwardly hard, but he was always an astonishingly unselfish and good man. There was in him something of the good old Russian saint, something pure and holy that one didn't see straightaway, but that was suddenly blindingly clear (you can't find that quality in people of my generation).

Most of all we talked about God. Uncle explained with great sincerity and conviction that he had found supreme happiness only in God, that all his life he had striven to serve God, only before he had thought about Him less, taken up as he was with the bustle of everyday life, and had neglected the ceremonial side of things. I asked him why he had chosen an alien faith, as we Velskys were a clerical family descended from Orthodox Russian priests. He said that God was the same for everyone, but he had dedicated his whole life to the art that had developed within the bosom of the Catholic Church; its spirit, its images were close to him, he could not be unfaithful to it. Possibly Orthodox religious people would not have understood Uncle, I did completely. Uncle did not preach to me, did not try to win me over like other believers, but after these talks I started pondering questions of faith on my own.

Uncle was convinced that ours was an age of unprecedented, secret, religious searching, that no other age had stood so in need of religion as ours. An unprecedented reappraisal of values was taking place in the world, humanism was going by the board. Man cannot live without faith in higher values. These values are given him not by science, art, politics, but by religion. But ideology cannot resolve the ultimate questions of life and death, man's place in the world. Whether mankind accepts God or rejects Him, it continues to live in Him. To the question as to whether he believed in an after-life, Uncle replied with some lack of assurance that he did, but that this was a matter of the utmost mystery and complexity, that a mere man could not hope to grasp it and must believe like Tertullian—'*credo qui absurdum*', i.e. what from the human point of view is absurd is the truth from the divine point of view, and for that reason Divine Revelation is within the reach of man's earthly vision. We do not need more. I objected to this. I accepted man's need of God, but could not believe in an after-life. Uncle could give me no proof here, nor did he try to, but simply said that one must approach God with an open heart and believe, and then everything would follow of its own accord. Happiness lay in faith and man's best work is dedicated to God.

At the time all this was just so much puzzling sophistry for me. I did not myself experience the need for God. (I am only just approaching that now, though I haven't yet arrived.) I was in the full flood of youth and how I regret now that I frittered those years away. Youth is a time of untapped possibilities.

Again I wasted time in the pursuit of knowledge I didn't need. True, I didn't overburden myself. There were several lads at our college who were so-called 'teddy-boys', and I used to have a good time with them. And again my fellow students started regarding me suspiciously—I didn't belong anywhere. At this time I started to earn a bit of money on the side. I needed it to enjoy myself, I'd long known that without it you couldn't get anywhere. I asked a journalist I knew (I had first met him at the 'Cocktail-Hall' and afterwards often used to stand him a drink) to find me some hackwork. He recommended me to a friend of his on the radio. I started knocking out pieces on all kinds of trivial subjects. Things continued like that for a bit. Soon it gave a new turn to my life.

Conditions were changing visibly. A sort of spiritual emancipation was taking place. First it affected youth. 1956 came, the 20th Party Congress, Khrushchev's speech on the cult of Stalin and Stalinist repressions. Even if it was all only words, people dared to think now. In 1955 one could already talk to one's friends openly and freely about anything. In 1956 there was a further advance, people started asking—true, only cautiously and tentatively—for spiritual freedom. Literature got a bit more lively, Dudintsev's novel on the top Soviet bureaucracy, *Not by Bread Alone*, appeared and caused a sensation. There was a definite intellectual crisis. The whole thing ended with Hungary and retreat. A few hotheads set off on the old, remembered route, some were intimidated and everything returned to the old familiar ways.

I kept out of all this, remembering the recent past, and in any case something much more important happened to me, knocking me off balance for quite a while—in 1956 Uncle died. It was the most tragic experience of my life. I loved him more than anyone else in the world, even more than my mother. The days preceding his death, his last hours, his death itself shook me so much, made such a profound impression on me and are so painful to recall that I shan't say anything about them. Anyway, whom does it concern, apart from me? This episode I am leaving out of my confession. I am writing about myself to explain my own actions and I shan't touch on the memory of this beloved man. Suffice it to say that from then on I started visiting the Catholic church from time to time and each year I had a mass said in his memory.

Now I was completely alone and had to see to my own future. My hatred of the system grew, I wouldn't and couldn't be its submissive slave. I was fairly clear about how ideological oppression worked. In bureaucratic socialism, status depends not on wealth and distinction, but on the post occupied. The post confers both wealth and distinction. Official demagogy and the doubts of the public as regards the ethics of wealth create an illusion of equality. The ignorant—one is completely justified in calling them the herd—continue to wallow in obscurity. Those who understand and who hate the system can achieve something, cynicism enables them to use their initiative. No one nowadays believes in Marxism, except those who find it convenient to, and apart from them, the stupid and depraved. Neither is extreme subjection valued. Nowadays you have to be unshakeable as regards the whole and critical with regard to particulars. This was the wisdom with which I now had to enter adult life. Already at that time I began to glimpse a distant goal. . . .

I realised that it would be considerably easier for me to gain my ends than for others. I was materially secure and had no moral obligations. On my own, with no family, I had a home and means. This was through the sale of Uncle's library to the Architectural Institute. It contained some unique items: albums, folios, old books, even an incunabulum of Aldo Manuzzio. Thus I performed this good deed and carried out Uncle's wishes not to sell the library privately. All I kept for myself were the books on philosophy and Uncle's Latin prayer-book. So, if need be, I could withdraw and sit in out.

It was pointless continuing my course at the technical college. What for? I would never make an engineer anyway. To get one's miserable ration, to go to work everyday and to live without a glimmer of hope was ridiculous. Ridiculous for anyone who understood the basic truth about our society: namely, that everyone exploits everyone, everyone works for nothing except for those few who profit by it. It would have been ridiculous to become an engineer when some lousy journalist could make more than a good engineer, without even mentioning Party, Komsomol and trade union parasites. And the importance of money was steadily growing in our society, it gave you more freedom than ever before during the previous 40 years. In Moscow there were 600 people with over a million roubles, one and a half thousand with close on a million. Parasitical millionaires springing from the upper levels of an intelligentsia that had sold out—'servants of the beloved Party'—began to appear on the scene. It was stupid to be an honest worker in a society based on fraud. You had to fix things so that you could get the most out of the world, giving as little as possible in return. The decisive factor again was not the quality of your work but the position you occupied.

The position of journalist might do the trick for me. The conditions were right—editorial staffs were being expanded, new papers and magazines were coming into being. I mustn't miss my opportunity. With an easy mind I left the technical college and became a freelance journalist. I took on any work I could find. I wasn't concerned about how much I earned, the main thing was to be noticed, for my stock of pulp literature to grow. I turned out hack work for three years. Meanwhile my resolution matured and took on concrete shape. I was not prepared to go short of money—that was certain. However much I loathed the philosophy department, I returned to it. I had only the state exams and degree still to take. Thanks to the help of Professor A, who had returned to the department again, I managed to get permission to sit these exams and present my thesis. Finally, after a year, by God's grace I got my degree. My salvation was now assured. I had a degree, an indifferent one maybe, but a degree all the same, a piece of paper which people would trust. Now I was fully entitled to look for the position I required.

The job came fairly dear—about three thousand—i.e. I spent that much on drinks for my journalist friends, they got in touch with their acquaintances, made inquiries, and finally, after drawing a number of blanks, a job in broadcasting on the German service was found for me. It fitted the bill. I knew the language, had a degree, had some journalistic experience and was already working on the radio. I managed to hold off two competitors and became a staff literary contributor. I was nearing my goal, but it was still to take me two years to reach it—I was too scared the first year. However, it was no use hurrying, everything had to be calculated precisely and prepared for in advance.

At work I tried not to stand out in any way from my colleagues. I was so successful in this that sometimes I caught myself swelling like a turkey-cock and beginning to look all too smug and vulgar. Like everyone else I tried not to show too much keenness, but when necessary I worked like hell and even stayed on late. It was terribly

206

difficult living this kind of double life, and I could feel my nerve going more and more to pieces.

I was growing extremely tense and everything that happened in the outside world touched me on the raw. The globe became a ball of sheer nightmare for me. Over the last few years there had been repeated threats of war. The West retreated, our foreign policy achieved more than even Stalin had dreamt of. The struggle over spheres of influence grew sharper, and we were victorious. But these victories are worse than defeats. And the climax of this is unavoidable unless a miracle intervenes.

A general fatigue settled on society. Ideology had been put to flight and now the country was suffering from a hang-over. Ideas became a mere screen behind which inevitable historical processes took their course. Khrushchev skilfully dealt with his opponents, mounted Stalin's throne and played the fool, like Old King Cole. Gradually he strengthened his hold over the people and moved towards establishing his own cult or mini-cult. It was exactly like Krylov's fable about the snake: 'Even when your skin has changed your heart is just the same.' In spite of Khrushchev's assurances that there were no political prisoners, the KGB secretly went on arresting people, though for the time being there was no full-scale terror. Apparently, that was for the future.

Under Stalin we had lived for the spirit (even if in a distorted way). The main thing was ideological values, communist ideas, enthusiasm —material considerations were insignificant in comparison. What of it if there was a shortage of accommodation, clothes, food—the main thing was our glorious ideas and the future in store for us, the main thing was that we had Stalin the Omniscient to lead us. Khrushchev's historical importance lay in the fact that he played down ideological values and substituted economic, material ones. Under him people did begin to live better, to live materialistically, i.e. for themselves and not for the sake of unrealistic goals. This again has another side to it. The concentration on material objectives led to a spiritual decline. If, under Stalin, this spiritual life had been monstrously distorted, now it ceased to exist altogether. Spiritually people had nothing to live for. No one was attracted by the official ideology and there was nothing new to put in its place. There was a certain revival of interest in religion and, to counter this, anti-religious propaganda was stepped up. But the main thing was that people wanted to enjoy life and get the most out of it, especially the young. Young people changed, became perhaps more egotistical, but also more courageous. An irreversible process of disintegration set in.

Despite some superficial improvements in people's lives, there was something menacing about the internal situation. There was a shortage of money in the country, it was going into an arms race, into feeding the allies. The state liquidated loans, rather than publicly acknowledge its bankruptcy. This caused little surprise, as no one had believed in them before, they were regarded as just another form of taxation, and there was even some satisfaction that they had been abolished for the time being. Labour productivity did not improve. The feudal system of the collective farms was retained. There was no freedom and no hope, just social apathy and general political indifference. 'It's all the same, it makes no difference, it's always been this way.' My task was to break out of this diabolical, diminishing circle and escape to freedom.

No, I've never lived well or peacefully (except at intervals, perhaps, but then only relatively). I'm astonished that people can smile, laugh, enjoy themselves in our time. One has to be too much of an egotist (such as I too have been in the past). Sometimes I wonder how my nerves stood the constant strain, but they did, they got used to it. A man can get used to anything.

I am horribly alone, I have never had any real friends, nor have I now. I've no one I can bare my soul to. At best, a part of it perhaps. I kept on switching friends and I felt that none of them really knew what I was like. With some of them I could talk about women, with others about literature or politics. With some perhaps even about myself. But not frankly, not really exhaustively. And there was no one I could really unburden myself to. I've no one friend who could be all things to me. And I needed this so badly! In due course, these casual acquaintances simply got in my way, and their place was always being taken by others. But after a while, these relationships too became irksome, I found them strangely oppressive and realised that the time had come again for me to withdraw and be on my own, until, at last, I realised that I was a true solitary and was destined to be on my own. It was the same thing with women, though something different occurred recently—but more of that later. . . . For the time being I shall speak about my journalist brethren, about the people I was brought together with every day.

I feel like venting 'all my spleen and frustration on them'. How hopelessly, miserably impoverished they are! How little has remained sacred to them! They know this and even boast about it. When I started, my immediate superior, quite a decent young chap on the whole, said to me: 'Do you know what journalism is? Do you know about the "second oldest profession"? That's a pretty accurate description. . . .' The oldest profession is, of course, prostitution, and we members of the second oldest were cheap, vagrant, intellectual whores. People who knew nothing, read nothing, either naïve youths or out and out cynics (this is the case with the majority), self-seekers, money-grubbers. I was the only one among them who had ever heard of Cima di Conegliano, but, of course, I kept it to myself. The main thing was to be known as 'a good chap', not to refuse to drink with the others, to join in conversations about women. In actual fact, this life, real and sober enough on the surface, was just as dreamlike as the fantastic life I had been living prior to 1953. For instance, some character would come into the room and joyfully announce that Moscow Dynamo had 'taken a dive', and everyone would start excitedly discussing the game, points for and against, the championship position, and so on. And when women got together they started gossiping about clothes, examining a nylon slip, going into ectasies over it, etc. It was a kind of dead land. Most of the people were young, but how dead!

One of them, for instance, a fat, thirty-year-old, balding philanderer with a wife, not averse to a drink (he usually drank at someone else's expense), was the reviewer L. He would greedily grasp at any filthy job asked of him, which others, worse than him, avoided. As a result, he was allowed to go on a mission abroad once a year. He loved everything there (even the urinals). He hated everything here, and especially the people he was deceiving—for the very reason that he had to deceive them. There was F—such a squirt—an insignificant looking chap with a mouth full of porridge. This young fellow, my superior, was very successful and lived with the most arresting of our female colleagues, much to everyone's astonishment. Then there was C, an extremely nice kindly fellow, the boon campanion of a revolting, prominent writer, and a womaniser who'd drifted weakly into marriage but wasn't living with his wife. . . . I won't go on, there were countless numbers of them and I've no desire to describe this low life, it's time I had done with them even in memory. It has given me a headache again just to think of them, so we'll leave them as they are. The two years' hard-labour I spent among such worthless people, 'godless, un-inspired, feelingless, loveless, inert', were enough for me.

The task of writing all this down has tired me out, but there is not much further to go. All that remains is to talk about love (that can't, after all, be missed out) and then to append my indictment.

With women it's best either to speak approvingly or to say nothing at all. I shall do the first. I am a sensual creature and love women.

Several times I have fallen seriously in love, sometimes my feelings have been reciprocated, but always the affair has been short-lived. Sooner or later we'd have our fill of each other and part, and I never felt inclined to attach myself to one woman and settle down. It was the same as with friends. I asked too much of life, my ideal remained unrealised. But very recently, only this spring, something rather different happened. . . .

I met her at an art exhibition—everything was so simple, so unforced. She was cultured and completely unspoilt, and knew something about painting—and we talked. I was with another chap and she was with a girl friend. We walked round the exhibition, chatted, laughed. They decided to leave and we did likewise. She had been looking at me furtively all the while, right up to the moment we approached them, and now, when I helped her on with her coat, her eyes lit up happily. We failed to get into the cinema, her friend wanted to go home, my friend went with her, and we went to a café, had some ice-cream and drank champagne. Then I accompanied her through the light frost, with my arm round her shoulder. In the doorway I kissed her, she at once recoiled and grew embarrassed, but then let me do it again.

I walked home happily excited, feeling the warmth of her fresh, still childlike, unkissed lips on my own. A light, gentle breeze caressed my face, bringing a breath of still-distant spring with it— April in February. I walked and thought: 'To the devil with you, Victor Velsky, what on earth do you think that you, a man who invented himself, are worth in comparison with the freshness of this unspoilt girl, this first fugitive breath of a spring breeze—how little you still understand the world and value it!' I had been thrown completely off balance. It was the same banal old story, only different this time, for I was now a grown man and she but a child; I was ten years older than her and our intimacy meant more to me than just a casual affair. And she was also dangerous for me: my own youth had passed, so that the love of a young, good and trusting soul was all the more precious to me. Yes, set against her I was an old man. In ten years I'd learnt things that God forbid she should learn about in a whole lifetime.

Our meetings filled me with joy. And she, pure child, fell in love with me, creating in me her ideal of an extraordinary man. I probably started loving her—it's not too hard for a lonely heart. . . . But what could I give her? Make her my mistress? One could sense the sensuality in her, her curiosity had been aroused. But it would have been a scandalous defilement of her virginal desires. And besides, I'd be really tied to her then. She would make someone a good wife, but not me. When I realised that I too was beginning to fall for her, to lose my head, I paused and thought the whole thing over. It was unnecessary and harmful to both of us to carry on. I felt sorry for her as a child. Also I had to punish myself for my faint-heartedness and for letting myself get diverted from my goal. Now at last I was conscious that I didn't need anyone. But there were moments, of course, when I wanted to forget this, to live with this single love. She was capable of love and worthy of it. But what about afterwards? Love would pass, become habit, mere affection, and then you'd be back with that same oppressive system you had forgotten about in the flush of it all. There was only one answer—not to be deflected, and to give up everything to achieve my object.

In any case, quite apart from that, it would be better to give up everything. Ordinary human happiness was not for me. Besides, I was close to my goal. I must hang on. One day, still in this childish, playful stage, she asked me to send her a letter poste restante—she wanted to get a letter from me. It was a joke and we timed it for April 1. I wrote her seven vulgar words: 'Do not trust the first of April,' and did not go to our rendezvous. The whole thing was over for me. It was harder than I had thought. I also got a letter poste restante (that's what we'd agreed), and it was filled with such heartfelt emotion that I was reduced to tears and in a frenzy of despair murmured 'Oh my love, my love . . .!' and my heart was broken. . . .

She had understood me better than I thought. In her simple straightforward way she sensed that I was hiding something from her, realised that we were to part and begged me to tell her this wasn't so, that she was just a foolish little girl (as I'd once affectionately called her)—she wanted to see me so badly. I felt like rushing straight over to her, begging her to forgive me, saying it was just a bad joke, telling her everything about myself, everything, and becoming worthy of her love. But I overcame these impulses, the voice of reason had always prevailed over the emotions with me and it did so now. But I am still conscious of the fact that I committed a new act of treachery. . . . Damn these wretched times in which we live! And damn me too!

Farewell, my youth, farewell, my darling girl! No, Ophelia was not to save doomed Hamlet. 'I am alone, all is sinking into pharisaism. . . .'

Probably that's enough about love, probably it would be better to say that I don't know what love is. And who does know, who knows how to love nowadays, who is willing to sacrifice all for it? The age of great lovers has long since passed. Men, warriors and poets are no more—all that is left are sensible, egotistical creatures. Woman has sunk even lower and cheapened herself as never before, losing her dignity and pride. There is no longer an aristocracy or an élite. There are too many people. In this savage, kaleidoscopic ant-hill the value of the individual human being and the significance of his experiences have been lost. Everything has become commonplace, vulgar, available. What else is there to say? Everything is clear. And yet, it seems to me that *she* was special. . . . But— enough. . . .

Now it is night, I am sitting at Uncle's desk, before a crucifix, writing this, I have been writing continuously for three days. I am close to my goal. In another three days I am going to East Germany as a tourist, I shall be in East Berlin and then I shall step over the line. That is my goal, that is what I have been striving for all these years. The plan first came to me four years ago, over the intervening period I have been working at it continually, and now it is nearing fruition. My heart is beating in trepidation. Maybe it won't work? It must. Up till now everything has worked for me, I have managed to survive the last two unbearable years. And yet I feel uneasy. I picture all the difficulties that lie ahead.

I had intended writing my apologia with the object of establishing the reasons that led up to my decision. It seems to me I have not really done this yet. I must put it more clearly.

I cannot live in my own country. The existing order conflicts with my convictions and my dignity as a human being. I have been too often abused. In my youth, the most sacred period of a man's life, I was corrupted, turned into a traitor and a cynic. Like every normal human being, I was born with a capacity for good. As in the fairy-tale, a splinter of ice was thrust into my heart, and it froze. I might have loved people, but instead I hated them. I wanted to follow my own vocation, wanted to think and write, but I had to hide my thoughts and do hack-work. Marxism was always alien to me, I was always interested in more profound, more enduring spiritual questions—I used to have some insight in respect to these, but I wasn't allowed to impart it, I had to become a grovelling nonentity. Even by the nature of my mind, I am unfit for our (no, not my!) society. I cannot live under a dictatorship, in a slave society, where all the rights of a thinking man are flouted. I am a Russian European and my place is in the free world. Where a man does not have to hide what he is thinking and doing, where there is not this constant feeling of fear and humiliation. Man's home is the whole world and happiness exists where life is happy.

I must hurry now, hurry. . . . I shall take my place in the Moscow-Berlin express, and then it's 'Goodbye, great unwashed Russia!' Nothing has changed you, you're still the same evil step-mother to your sons, bureaucratic and cruel. I damn you! Damn you for all the humiliations you have inflicted! Damn you for all those innocent, ruined lives! Damn your tyrants and your servants!

For the first time I damn you to your face, without concealment, heaping my hatred and fury upon you. I damn the Soviet system that has defiled Russia. How have I damned it! It is built on deception and self-delusion, it is in its very essence inimical to the best human impulses. Having been born and having lived under this regime, having seen through it and endured it, I have become its enemy. To tell the truth, I did not want to and no one encouraged me. It was the system itself that brought me to it.

I know that an unjust, oppressive system must vanish one day. The horrible thing is that it will bury the whole world under its rubble. We are all witnesses to the collapse of a mighty social experiment. People wanted to live better and ended up with a police state. What was supposed to be the greatest freedom turned into the greatest oppression. The highest justice dissolved into torrents of blood. It is worth while for people to ponder in the future how all extreme, intolerant but grandiloquent ideas lead to this. The French Revolution degenerated into terror. The same thing has happened with us.

History is indifferent to the individual and his sufferings. I cannot wait any longer for things to work themselves out. There is only one answer—to escape. Holding the views I do, I cannot go on living here. It's not even honest to do so.

Oh, how glad I will be not to have to read your newspapers any more, to listen to your lying radio, lying speeches and eulogies, to lie and pretend to myself. All I must do is take this one step to rid myself of this whole monstrous apocalyptic contraption. And I shall take it.

Even if they find my manuscript, it will be too late. I hope they find it and read all the right bits. I spit in your faces, monsters! Read this and learn how our—no, your—society nurtures its enemies in its bosom. And I know quite a few of these silent, passive enemies. You have done this with your words, your cults, your terrors and prisons. Think it over, again I advise you to give some thought to how ideas of the greatest justice have led to the greatest violence ever done to man. Sooner or later these still-born ideas will vanish or evolve into something else. But I won't take part in the struggle against them. I am too tired and worn out. There is only one thing I want, to forget it all and live in a different society, to be reborn. I have chosen that society. I shall leave and not return.

This is the end of my apologia. There is a lot more to tell, but I lack the strength. It is now five to twelve. Midnight. A long time to go till morning. Dark night over my country. When will morning come?

That's all. Goodbye, step-mother country!

The clock has struck twelve. My new day is dawning.

Victor Velsky

6 August, 1960

I have returned.

How ridiculous and embarrassing it is now to read what I have written in this pitiful exercise book! What a storm in a teacup! How a man shows off and gives himself airs, even when alone with himself! And how weak and pitiful he is!

Yes, I have returned.

I couldn't do it, I lost my nerve, I lacked the will that gives a man the right to cross frontiers. My only consolation is that no one has that will. Not even in the West. The West is barren of ideas, except, as Herzen saw, for that of vulgar materialism. But that's not what I need. I did not go there for scraps and titbits, but for salvation. I went there looking for the ideal. But where could I find it, if it didn't exist in myself? All I had was negation and bitterness, but no ideal that was worth living or dying for.

I could have accomplished all and I accomplished nothing. I could have become 'a citizen of the free world' and I did not. There is no 'free world' for us, there is a foreign world, a world of foreigners, of people who are more fortunate and yet, in their own way, also unfree.

Yes, I could have taken that step, I was in West Berlin. I spent a few hours in that other world, walking among that other, foreign, people. And that is the crux of it—they were foreign to me.

In the beginning I thought I would go up to the first policeman and ask him to take me to the police-station. My heart was beating wildly. Everything was about to be decided. . . . But it all took place in my imagination, I could not act it out in reality. I kept on putting it off. I had thoroughly thought about 'before', but had failed to ask myself about 'after'. To become a citizen of 'the free world' it was not enough merely to be in 'the free world'! If they took me to the station, they would start interrogating me, checking up on me, and then probably send me to a camp for displaced persons, after which they might make use of me as a journalist on the staff of some foreign language radio station. And 'make use of' is the *mot juste*, for I myself wouldn't mean a thing. I would be just an insignificant cog in a vast political machine, the same as at home. I was not needed there, I was alien and there was no other work for me apart from a filthy mirror-image of what I had been doing before. I would not be able to become an honest exile, I would have to become a hired traitor. A traitor again?'

No, I couldn't resolve to commit myself as quickly as that. I had to go on walking a bit more, to think it over. For some reason nobody took any notice of me, nobody was concerned about me. But I was concerned about everything—I looked into people's faces, into shop windows, through the windows of houses—I had to understand it all.

I inspected palaces, went into parks, walked along the river Spree; time was passing inexorably and I found it impossible to make up my mind. A new betrayal, more self abuse? I did not want this, although I tried to convince myself that I ought to go through with it this last time. But would it be the last time? Wouldn't this set off an endless chain of events? And the thought flashed across my mind more and more frequently that I was a foreigner here and that I'd never be 'at home'. On the surface the life around me was peaceful, calm and sedate, but I sensed something wrong about it. This feeling that there was 'something wrong' grew stronger and stronger, while my saving reason remained passive, and then this feeling grew into a protest against the decision I had made.

And—I don't know why—the image of my Homeland impressed itself more and more insistently on my imagination, the image not of a step-mother, but of a meek, good, attentive, but humiliated mother. Could this feeling really be so strong in me? I never knew I even had it, I had regarded myself as a 'European Russian', a 'citizen of the world'. It seems a Russian cannot exist without his country. And I am a Russian! Not a European, not a citizen of the world, but a Russian! A Russian in my dissatisfaction, a Russian in my thirsting after the ideal! A miserable, eternal, Russian nomad!

This awareness that I was inseparably linked with my country came to me as a revelation. No, my forefathers, honest Russian priests, had not worshipped and prayed so that their descendant should go seeking the truth in foreign lands and faiths! If it wasn't to be found at home, then I would find it nowhere! Their prayers must have helped me. My eyes misted over with tears at this sudden, moving perception. This clear insight into something ideal and holy, that could not be ignored, stayed with me for a while. I knew that if I didn't carry out my plan, I was doomed to a moral death, but I couldn't take that final step.

I returned to the eastern sector, went to the hotel and collapsed on the bed completely worn out. The others had not yet returned from their excursion to some factory. Probably no one knew of my trip. They got back late, came trooping into the room and started to tell me about their experiences, but I was totally apathetic. They were concerned about me—I probably looked feverish. They thought I had caught a cold—that being the reason why I hadn't gone on the excursion. One of them brought me a bottle of Stolichnaya that was being saved for a different occasion, and the vodka, that bitter liquid of my homeland, burnt my throat. I finished the whole bottle practically on my own, though without getting drunk, and then fell asleep immediately, sinking into a dark, bottomless pit. . . .

And now it's time I brought this account to an end, if only provisional. This self-analysis, this self-torture, has exhausted me. I can't read over these pages any more, bragging and gibbering! I have had enough. I'm a broken man. I am tired, tired, tired. This is a sad and pitiful story. I cannot stand on my own. I cannot live in this insane world. The only way out is to commit suicide. But even that I won't do—I am a coward, the instinct for life is too strong in me. I can no longer go on working and living like everyone around me—there is a pressure inside my head. I am writing all this through a thick mist of tiredness, using up my last resources of energy—I must finish off this chapter of my life. Here ends the apology, beyond is pathology. I know what lies ahead of me. Terror. Madness has long been dogging my footsteps. I have neither the strength nor capacity to go on living in the real world. I am finished. My idea is finished and, with it, me too, like a spasm of anger. I did not master it and could not commit myself. This feeling for my homeland is not enough to live for, it flared up just once in me. What is there to live for? I have neither negative nor positive convictions, just an enormous, oppressive feeling of fatigue. What can save me now? I am dead. I need nothing. I do not need even myself. I am the victim of deception. We are all being deceived by something or someone. I no longer have the energy to write. The horror of loneliness is upon me, the prison of the soul. They have finished me off. I am suffocating, no air, no light, no people, no laughter. . . . God, if you exist, help me!

I am dead! dead! dead!